'An Irish Empire'?

ASPECTS OF IRELAND
AND THE BRITISH EMPIRE

edited by Keith Jeffery

MANCHESTER UNIVERSITY PRESS

Manchester and New York

Distributed exclusively in the USA and Canada
by ST. MARTIN'S PRESS

Copyright © Manchester University Press 1996

While copyright in the volume as a whole is vested in Manchester University Press, copyright in individual chapters belongs to their respective authors, and no chapter may be reproduced wholly or in part without the express permission in writing of both author and publishers.

Published by **MANCHESTER UNIVERSITY PRESS**
OXFORD ROAD, MANCHESTER M13 9NR
and ROOM 400, 175 FIFTH AVENUE, NEW YORK, NY 10010, USA

Distributed exclusively in the USA and Canada
by **ST. MARTIN'S PRESS, INC.**
175 FIFTH AVENUE, NEW YORK, NY 10010, USA

British Library Cataloguing-in-Publication Data

A catalogue record for this book is available from the British Library

Library of Congress Cataloguing-in-Publication Data
'An Irish empire'? : aspects of Ireland and the British Empire / edited
by Keith Jeffery.
        p. cm. — (Studies in imperialism)
    ISBN 0-7190-3873-1
        1. Ireland—Politics and government—1837–1901.   2. Ireland—
    Politics and government—20th century.   3. Ireland—Relations—
    Great Britain.   4. Great Britain—Relations—Ireland.
    5. Imperialism.   6. Irish question.   I. Jeffery, Keith.
    II. Series: Studies in imperialism (Manchester, England)
    DA950.I686   1996
    941.5081—dc20   95-41312
                                                 CIP

ISBN 0 7190 3873 1 hardback

First published in 1996

00 99 98 97 96   10 9 8 7 6 5 4 3 2 1

Typeset in Trump Medieval
by Koinonia, Manchester
Printed in Great Britain
by Biddles Limited, Guildford and King's Lynn

CONTENTS

[v]

Dedicated to the memory
of Jack Gallagher
and Nicholas Mansergh

GENERAL INTRODUCTION

Imperial historians have long appreciated the interactive character of the culture and politics of the British Empire with those of the congeries of nations that make up the United Kingdom. In his book *Welsh and Scottish Nationalism* published in 1954, Sir Reginald Coupland,. the Beit Professor at Oxford who had been heavily involved in the constitutional discussions leading to Indian independence, recognised that decolonisation in the Empire would test the bonds of the metropolitan state. He attempted to make a clear distinction between the Irish experience, in which the English had been economically exploitative and politically arrogant, with that of the Welsh and the Scots. 'The unity of Britain', he wrote, represented 'a great political and psychological achievement', transforming a Balkans into a multinational state, the triumph of a liberal and humane English tradition.

Writing soon after the Irish Republic had left the Commonwealth, Coupland's book represented a plea for Union, powerful advocacy for the notion that neither the Welsh nor the Scots shared the grievances of the Irish and therefore had no need to continue the break-up of Britain. Nevertheless, in modern times, the inter-relationship of events in Ireland and the search for devolution or independence in Wales and Scotland has continued to be apparent. Proposals for constitutional development in Northern Ireland inevitably raise questions about comparability elsewhere. Such connections have been made for more than a hundred years. From at least the 1880s, Scottish nationalists watched the development of federalism and dominion status in the Empire with some interest and argued for 'Home Rule All Round', the application of imperial placebos to the metropolitan body politic.

But the relationship between the component parts of the United Kingdom and the imperial experience is even more complex than that suggested by these constitutional and political issues. A tangled skein of economic, social and cultural threads, many of them connected to the rich experience of emigration, with its powerful emotional resonances of despair and hope, joined different parts of the imperial core to the so-called periphery. Other linkages were set up through aristocratic and bourgeois expatriate activity in land ownership, administration, industrial and trading relations, military service and policing, together with the attendant cultural baggage which travelled with such people.

It is significant that there is a developing interest in this disaggregation of the role of white nation, ethnicity and culture in the British Empire at this time. When the stresses and strains upon the British state, and the complexity of its relationship with Europe, are becoming more apparent, when the language of 'core' and 'periphery' has come once more to be applied to the metropolis, historians are increasingly fascinated by the manner in which the various cultures of the British Isles have expanded and sustained themselves, at times complicit with British imperialism, at others resistant to it, through the experience of Empire.

These concerns, and more, are well represented in this volume, ranging as it does from sport to economic relationships, representations in the cinema to the activities of imperial associations like the Empire Day Movement, the role of business communities to the influence of the military, Unionism and ultra-loyal politics to the role of the Irish in India, New Zealand and other territories of the Empire. Wide-ranging and stimulating as it is, this book probably raises as many questions as it answers. There can be no doubt that more research waits to be done in this field and that similar studies are needed for other parts of the United Kingdom. This series will continue to provide a publishing vehicle for such path-finding and interactive work.

John M. MacKenzie

LIST OF CONTRIBUTORS

ALAN BAIRNER is Lecturer in Politics at the University of Ulster at Jordanstown. He is co-author of *Sport, Sectarianism and Society in a Divided Ireland* (with John Sugden) and author of numerous articles on sport in Northern Ireland, Scotland and Sweden. He is currently doing research on the relationship between sport and national identity.

T. G. FRASER is Professor and Head of the School of History, Philosophy and Politics at the University of Ulster, and was Fulbright Scholar-in-Residence at Indiana University South Bend. He has written *Partition in Ireland, India and Palestine: Theory and Practice; The USA and the Middle East since World War 2;* and *The Arab–Israeli Conflict.* His edited books are *The Middle East 1914–1979; Conflict and Amity in East Asia* (with Peter Lowe); and *Men, Women and War* (with Keith Jeffery).

DAVID H. HUME graduated BA at the Open University as a mature student in 1986, and MA at the University of Ulster in 1990. His essay 'An historical review of the origins and aims of the Empire Day movement, with a case study of its impact on Ireland and Northern Ireland' was awarded *proxime accessit* for the Royal Commonwealth Society Walter Frewen Lord Prize in 1990.

ALVIN JACKSON is Lecturer in Modern History at the Queen's University, Belfast. He is the author of *The Ulster Party: Irish Unionists in the House of Commons, 1884–1911; Sir Edward Carson* (for the Historical Association of Ireland 'Life and Times' series); and *Colonel Edward Saunderson: Land and Loyalty in Victorian Ireland.* He has held a post-doctoral British Academy Fellowship and was formerly a Lecturer in Modern Irish History at University College, Dublin.

KEITH JEFFERY is Reader in History at the University of Ulster at Jordanstown. Among his books are *The British Army and the Crisis of Empire, 1918–22; States of Emergency: British Governments and Strikebreaking since 1919* (with Peter Hennessy); and *Northern Ireland since 1968* (with Paul Arthur). He has been joint editor of the journal *Irish Historical Studies* since 1988.

DONAL LOWRY is Senior Lecturer in History at Oxford Brookes University. He has previously taught at Rhodes University, Chester College and the University of York. He has published a number of articles on aspects of imperial history and is currently working on the life of General Sir William Butler. In 1990 he won the Royal Commonwealth Society Walter Frewen Lord Prize.

[ix]

PHILIP OLLERENSHAW is Principal Lecturer in Economic and Business History at the University of the West of England, Bristol. Among his publications are *An Economic History of Ulster, 1820–1939* (edited with Liam Kennedy); *Banking in Nineteenth-Century Ireland*; and 'Textiles and regional economic decline: Northern Ireland 1914–70', in Colin Holmes and Alan Booth (eds), *Economy and Society: European Industrialisation and its Social Consequences. Essays Presented to Sidney Pollard*.

JEFFREY RICHARDS is Professor of Cultural History at Lancaster University. He is the author of *Age of the Dream Palace*; *Happiest Days*; and *Sex, Dissidence and Damnation*. He edited the volume *Imperialism and Juvenile Literature* for the Manchester 'Studies in Imperialism' series.

PREFACE

During the preparation of this volume the editor and contributors have in-curred many debts for the generous assistance of fellow-scholars, archivists, librarians and others. I would like particularly to acknowledge the support and encouragement I have received from my own colleagues, especially Alan Bairner and Tom Fraser. Part of the editing was completed during a period of study-leave which was spent as a visiting scholar at St John's College, Cambridge. The Master and Fellows of the college were unfailingly generous and hospitable, and I especially treasure the collegiality of Saturday and Sunday evenings which helped make my stay in Cambridge so pleasant and rewarding. I am grateful to both the University of Ulster (particularly the Faculty of Humanities Research Committee) and the British Academy for granting funds towards my research and living expenses while away from home. From the start John Mackenzie, who first suggested the volume, has been a great support, as have Jane Thorniley-Walker, Michelle O'Connell and Vanessa Graham of Manchester University Press. This volume is dedicated to the memory of two Cambridge historians of the British Empire and Commonwealth, both with Irish roots, from whom I learned more than I can say. It was a very great privilege as an undergraduate and graduate to know these two men who together must be counted among the very greatest Irish historians of the twentieth century.

Keith Jeffery
Belfast, April 1995

INTRODUCTION

The notion that the British Empire was in any way an 'Irish Empire' is not one that will cut very much ice on the contemporary island of Ireland, north or south. Nationalists will assert that the only important relevant point about Ireland's relationship with the Empire is the progressive (and unfinished) breaking of the bonds of British imperial domination, particularly over the past seventy-five years or so. For Unionists the Empire's fate has been, if anything, more pathetic; for them it has become an irrelevance. Once among the more enthusiastic champions of the British Empire, seeing it as a powerful association within which Northern Ireland might flourish, Ulster Unionists now even have doubts about the continued 'loyalty' of what used to be called the 'imperial government' at Westminster.

Despite these attitudes, much academic writing about Ireland, its history and culture, is dominated by the vocabulary of imperialism. Contemporary observers frequently characterise independent Ireland as being 'post-colonial' (implicitly, perhaps, dismissing Northern Ireland for not even having reached that level of political and cultural sophistication). But the Empire as a vital and viable system was not always irrelevant to Irish people or Irish concerns, nationalist or Unionist. Ireland, as part of the metropolitan core of the Empire, supplied many of its soldiers, settlers and administrators. In modern times, Irish people have both sustained and undermined the British imperial system. While (as is noted below) some Irish nationalists came to see the Empire as a liberating framework within which Irish autonomy might successfully be secured, more separatist colleagues made powerful common cause with other subject peoples and provided role models for militant nationalists throughout the British Empire. The paradox that Ireland was both 'imperial' *and* 'colonial' animates much of this book, which includes studies of Irish service in (and for) the Empire as well as the impact in Ireland of imperial concerns and opportunities.

Settling on a title which was both lively and accurate, ideally suggesting the ambiguities of Ireland's relationship with the Empire, presented some difficulties. Phrases of the 'head and/or harp' variety are already well-used, and in any case tend to carry an exclusively Anglo-Irish connotation.[1] 'England's first and last colony' was rejected on the grounds of inaccuracy. Engels's over-quoted assertion that Ireland 'may be regarded as the first English colony'[2] passes silently over the experience of the Welsh, not to mention the Cornish. Ironically the

[1]

Engels view draws on that very British connotation of empire in which the oppression of neighbouring peoples on the same land mass is not considered to be 'imperialism', while the domination of people across the sea is.[3] The suggestion that Northern Ireland might constitute England's 'last colony' will be seductive to some, but it would represent a triumph of hope over any foreseeable experience. Among other possible titles, 'a great empire and the little people', though happily containing an allusion to Edmund Burke, was rejected as too flippant.

The phrase which was eventually chosen – 'an Irish Empire' – is taken from an address given in 1917 by Charles Frederick D'Arcy, then Church of Ireland Bishop of Down and Connor and Dromore.[4] D'Arcy, like his contemporaries Sir Edward Carson and Field Marshal Sir Henry Wilson, was a southern Irish Protestant who increasingly found common cause with Ulster Unionism. But in the autumn of 1917, he still clearly thought in all-Ireland terms and, moreover, viewed the Irish situation in an imperial context. Referring to the Irish Convention, which had been sitting since the summer in what turned out to be a vain attempt to 'solve' the Irish constitutional problem, he observed that it had been 'entrusted with something of far vaster importance than the settlement of Ireland. It has to consider the Irish question in the light of the security of the British Empire, and, indeed, of human civilisation.'[5] D'Arcy's subsequent remarks are worth quoting at some length, since they reflect a belief in the enhanced importance of the Empire to Irish affairs which was characteristic of both Unionists and at least moderate nationalists during that period of political, cultural and intellectual crisis which lies at the heart of this volume – from the late nineteenth century to the 1920s. Here we find a Unionist calling in the Empire apparently to redress the balance of power in Ireland which, especially since Easter 1916, had begun to slip markedly in favour of nationalist separatism.

> We cannot realise the best that is in us as a people except through association with England. The British Empire is an Irish Empire as well as an English Empire... We share in all the wealth of that grand inheritance which they, with our help, have created. And so I say that Ireland has need of England and England has need of Ireland in order to carry on that glorious work which Englishmen, Irishmen, Scotchmen, and Welshmen working together have so wonderfully accomplished.[6]

In what ways, then, was the British Empire also 'an Irish Empire'? In so far as the term 'British' might be held to encompass 'Irish' (as well as English, Scottish and Welsh) – which was clearly Bishop D'Arcy's understanding – it could be argued that the Empire was a multinational enterprise, drawing together the separate national groups of the United

Kingdom (as it was), in the same way as the 'British Championship' in association football or the 'British Lions' in rugby drew together the 'home' nations of England, Ireland, Scotland and Wales.[7] But while Irish Unionists could unproblematically hold themselves to be 'British' and 'Irish' simultaneously, such an identification was never easy for Irish nationalists, and became intolerable following the emergence of an independent Irish state. Thus, while a team officially called 'Ireland' played in the British Association Football Championships right up to the abolition of the event following the 1983–84 season,[8] from 1950 the players in that team were drawn exclusively from Northern Ireland.[9] In rugby the 'British Lions' (officially the 'British Isles') have come to be described, in Irish publications at least, as the 'British and Irish Lions', or, eschewing even the apparently imperial designation 'lion', merely as 'Great Britain and Ireland'. Similarly the term 'British Isles', a geographical description with a clear political sub-text, is often replaced in Ireland with the more neutral though less precise 'these islands'.

Naturally enough the compatibility of 'British' with 'Irish' was easiest for Anglo-Irish Unionists to maintain.[10] J. C. Beckett has explained this by asserting that after the Union, the 'Irishness' of this group 'though still deeply felt, had lost all political content. They were citizens of the United Kingdom; and it was to the larger entity that their allegiance was now due.'[11] It might further be argued that allegiance to, and service within, a yet wider entity – the British Empire – enabled Irish people (and not just the Anglo-Irish) in some senses to be both British and Irish. Perhaps the Anglo-Irish could feel more fully Irish outside the country than within it.[12] As a group they encountered the difficulty of being Irish but not wanting to identify with the Irish majority, who in the nineteenth century asserted an increasingly Gaelic and Catholic Irish conception of nationality. Away from home, where the growing challenge of Irish nationalism was less strident and immediate, they could celebrate their Irish identity without worrying overmuch about the political implications.[13]

As with national designations, the term 'empire' itself presents problems of definition. There are, moreover, clear dangers accompanying 'the use of words with high emotional content and vague meaning'.[14] Richard Koebner and Helmut Dan Schmidt maintain that the term 'imperialism' changed its meaning some twelve times between the 1840s and the 1960s. Mid-nineteenth-century meanings of 'empire' included the British Isles and even just England.[15] Indeed, a similar usage survived in Northern Ireland during the twentieth century, where the 'imperial contribution' made by the province was simply Northern Ireland's portion of tax revenues payable towards central United Kingdom services. Similarly, a distinction was for many years made between the Northern Ireland civil service and the 'imperial' civil service, which did not have any particular colonial responsibility, but was merely the bureaucracy based in London. Some care, therefore, should be exercised when the pronouncements of nineteenth-century statesmen appear to confirm a wide imperial relevance for Irish concerns. During the preparation of the first Irish Land Act in 1870, for example, Gladstone asserted that 'the end of our measure is to give peace and security to Ireland, and through Ireland to the Empire'.[16] But this was at a time when the connotation of 'empire' as the totality of British-ruled territories throughout the world was only just coming into general use. Gladstone's vision in any case was for 'a liberal, free, co-operative, and decentralized Empire', and also a *British* Empire, within which conception he felt Ireland and the Irish could flourish. 'We do not', he wrote, 'want any Bosnian submissions.'[17]

The extent to which inhabitants of Ireland could actually regard themselves simultaneously as 'Irish' and 'British',[18] is difficult (or even impossible) fully to comprehend at the end of the twentieth century when the whole thrust of nationalism and national identity in the modern period – and not just in Ireland – has been towards the increasing particularity of specific national allegiances. The emergence of the sovereign nation state as the most widely accepted form of human political organisation has been accompanied by the assumption that national (and ethnic) homogeneity would be ideal in any polity. Ironically, for most people in the twentieth century, increasing numbers of movements across political frontiers have served to enhance, rather than erode, national identities. For individuals, the most important practical manifestation of national identity is a passport – the international political equivalent of what automobile manufacturers call 'badge engineering'. The possession of a passport provides documentary proof of citizenship, and in many cases also of nationality – though not in that of the United Kingdom, or arguably Ireland.

The passport question, which briefly excited relations between the new Irish Free State and the United Kingdom in the 1920s, illustrates both the difficulty in the Irish context of satisfactorily distinguishing nationality and citizenship, and also the particular importance of titles and symbols in the changing Anglo-Irish relationship. Since the 1921 Treaty provided for the 'common citizenship of Ireland with Great Britain', in terms of international law citizens of the Free State technically remained 'British subjects'. But this wording was clearly unacceptable to the new government in Dublin. When Desmond FitzGerald, the Minister for External Affairs, raised the question of issuing separate Irish passports in January 1923, he proposed using the words 'imperial British citizenship' rather than 'British subject'. London's insistence on

'British subject' merely antagonised the Irish government, who in April 1924 unilaterally began to issue passports stating that the holder was 'citizen of the Irish Free State and the British Commonwealth of Nations' – ironically a less imperial designation than had originally been proposed.[19]

Much of the constitutional debate within the twentieth-century British Empire concerning the increasingly autonomous position of the dominions turned around bringing the legal and constitutional formalities of Anglo-dominion relations into line with the practical assumption of autonomy, especially by the more independent-minded dominions of Canada and South Africa. David Harkness has argued that the Irish Free State during its first decade of life played a significant role as a catalyst in the shift from 'Empire' to 'Commonwealth', at least so far as the dominions were concerned.[20] For some the critical point came at the time of the Anglo-Irish Treaty of December 1921. Writing thirty years after the agreement, Patrick O'Hegarty, who had been a leading member of the Irish Republican Brotherhood and a close associate of Michael Collins, bluntly asserted that the treaty 'broke up the British Empire, killed England's will to Empire ... If to-day India, and Burma, and Egypt are free Nations, they owe it primarily to our example and our softening effectiveness, and secondarily to Japan. We changed not only the nature of the British Empire but its name [to Commonwealth].'[21] Nicholas Mansergh noted the paradox that the question posed in 1921 – 'How may national, republican aspirations best be reconciled with a monarchical, imperial or commonwealth status system?' – was answered satisfactorily in 1949 for India more or less along the lines suggested by Eamon de Valera in 1921 when he proposed the 'external association' of independent Ireland with the Commonwealth. But by the 1940s, when a formula had been worked out allowing India to become a republic while acknowledging the British monarch as Head of the Commonwealth, the matter had become irrelevant for Ireland which had formally withdrawn from the association in 1947.[22] 'By the time the Commonwealth had found the answer the Irish had lost interest in the question.'[23]

The argument that the Irish experience played a crucial role in the disintegration of the British Empire can be applied further. The parallels between Ireland and the white colonies of settlement which progressively achieved autonomy from the 1860s onwards were certainly drawn by Irish nationalist MPs quick to contrast the freedoms being granted to Australians or South Africans with the denial of similar liberties for Ireland. In 1900 Tim Healy, MP for North Louth (and later the first Governor-General of the Irish Free State), had the bad taste to suggest that an Irishman was not to 'be trusted with Home Rule unless he has first been transported'.[24] Irish interest in imperial constitutional developments was to a certain extent reciprocated in the already self-governing dominions, where there was some sympathy for the Irish cause, some identification of common interests and aspirations. In 1882, 1886, 1887 and 1903 the Canadian House of Commons passed addresses to the monarch for a 'just measure of Home Rule for Ireland', and, similarly, in 1906 the Australian legislature urged Home Rule for Ireland – 'for never was a request more clear, consistent or continuous as theirs'.[25] Before he became a republican separatist, Erskine Childers strongly favoured an 'imperial' answer to the Irish dilemma, since the Empire appeared to provide a framework within which both autonomy and allegiance might be accommodated. In proposing 'dominion home rule' for Ireland in 1911 he drew specific parallels with the existing dominions of Canada, Australia and South Africa. It was, he argued, unnecessary to travel beyond the British Empire in the search for an answer to the Irish problem. 'In one degree or another', he wrote, 'every one of the vexed questions which make up the Irish problem has arisen again and again within the circle of the English-speaking races.' 'What is best for Ireland', he added, 'will be best for the Empire.'[26]

The South African politician Jan Christian Smuts was the most out-standing dominion leader concerned with Ireland. Smuts saw great similarities between Ireland and his own country, which following a bitter conflict with the British had apparently become reconciled within the Empire. The common perceived experience which Boers and Irish nationalists had as oppressed communities within the British Empire provided Smuts with a particular understanding (as he thought) of Anglo-Irish relations. A shrewd political calculator, following the Boer defeat in the South African War of 1899–1902 he believed that the benefits of co-operating with the British far outweighed the costs. But the relationship had to be reciprocal. 'Do you want friends or enemies?', he asked Campbell-Bannerman in 1906, 'You can have the Boers for friends, and they have proved what quality their friendship may mean. I pledge the friendship of my colleagues and myself if you wish it. You can choose to make them enemies, and possibly have another Ireland on your hands.'[27]

Smuts believed passionately in the constructive potential of the British Empire, not as an imperial system, but as a commonwealth of equal nations. Throughout the First World War and immediately after-wards he played an important role in the transformation of the Empire (or the 'white' Empire at any rate) into the Commonwealth. Repeatedly he included Ireland in his analysis of imperial developments. In July 1919 he asserted that 'the Irish wound' was poisoning the whole British system and that unless national freedom were granted to Ireland the

British Empire 'must cease to exist'.[28] Reflecting on the constitutional position of the dominions in 1921, he argued that

> unless Dominion status is settled soon in a way which will satisfy the legitimate aspirations of these young nations, we must look for separatist movements in the Commonwealth ... The warning against always being too late in coming to a proper settlement, which the example of Ireland gives to the whole Commonwealth, is one which we can only neglect at our own peril.[29]

While he was in Europe in the summer of 1921 for an imperial conference, Smuts urged the British to make constitutional concessions in the painful progress towards an Irish settlement.[30] He successfully persuaded both King George V and Lloyd George that the King's visit to Belfast for the opening of the new Northern Ireland Parliament should be used to call for conciliation in Ireland and a new departure in British policy. 'I need not enlarge to you', he wrote to Lloyd George, 'the importance of the Irish question for the Empire as a whole.'[31] Smuts drafted a statement for the King to make in Belfast which embodied the South African's optimistic faith in the Empire.

> My world-wide Empire is a system of human government which rests on certain principles and ideals of freedom and co-operation, which must find their application in Ireland no less than in the other parts. And it is my desire that the full and fair application of these principles to Ireland may lead her out of the miseries of the present to the happiness and contentment which characterise all my other self-governing Dominions.[32]

A. J. Balfour, fondly remembered in Ireland as 'Bloody Balfour' from his time as Chief Secretary (1887–91), disliked both the 'gush' of Smuts's draft and its underlying 'innuendo of oppression'. He prepared a version of his own which still embodied a clearly conciliatory tone. In the end Lloyd George's private secretary, Sir Edward Grigg, drafted a speech which drew on both Smuts's and Balfour's proposals, and which met with the King's approval. The imperial context of the Irish situation, which both Smuts and Balfour had stressed, was fully retained by Grigg, himself a powerful apologist for the British Empire.[33] In Belfast the King spoke as 'the Head of the Empire'. It was, he said, 'a great and critical occasion in the history of the Six Counties, but not for the Six Counties alone, for everything which interests them touches Ireland, and everything which touches Ireland finds an echo in the remotest parts of the Empire'.[34]

In the period between George V's Belfast speech and the truce of 11 July 1921, Smuts actively helped bring both the British government and the Irish nationalist leaders to the negotiating table. He even travelled incognito to Dublin – as 'Mr Smith' – in order to meet de Valera.[35]

'My belief', wrote Smuts to de Valera, 'is that Ireland is travelling the same painful road as South Africa, and is destined to achieve the same success.'[36] Success, however, is a relative term, and Smuts was a little premature in using it. In any case the close identification of interests between Irish and Afrikaner nationalists within a British imperial context did not survive independent Ireland's progressive disengagement from the British imperial system. Yet at the turn of the twentieth century the Irish 'pro-Boers' had been in the van of nationalist opinion and their opposition to the 1899–1902 war powerfully boosted the development of militant separatism in Ireland.[37] Irish sympathy for the Boers was not confined to extremists. When General Sir William Butler, a Catholic Home Ruler from Tipperary, was appointed the British army Commander-in-Chief in South Africa in October 1898 he found himself out of sympathy with the expansionist ambitions of men such as Cecil Rhodes and in disagreement with the High Commissioner, Sir Alfred Milner, concerning the inevitability of war with the Boers. By the summer of 1899 his position had become untenable and he was obliged to resign since the War Office held the view that 'imperial interests would suffer' if he remained in post.[38]

What the Irish and the Afrikaners (and French Canadians, too) shared was a sense of nationality with no *British* provenance. Speaking in Adelaide in 1884 in a celebrated speech during which he first coined the phrase 'commonwealth of nations', Lord Rosebery had argued that Australia was becoming a nation in its own right. 'Does this fact of your being a nation ... imply separation from the Empire?', he asked, 'God forbid! There is no need for any nation, however great, leaving the Empire, because the Empire is a commonwealth of nations.'[39] Nevertheless, while Australia and other white dominions might *become* nations, Ireland was already one. From the nineteenth-century nationalist perspective Ireland was not a nation of 'settlement', but a nation conquered; closer, then, to parts of the Indian and colonial empire, than to Australia or Canada. This fact was appreciated by some Irish Home Rulers. In 1882 Frank Hugh O'Donnell, MP for Dungarven, County Waterford, told the British House of Commons that the Irish Party were the 'natural representatives and spokesmen of the unrepresented nationalities of the Empire'. Two years later O'Donnell declared that 'English tyranny in Ireland was only a part of that general system of the exploitation of suffering humanity which made the British Empire a veritable slave empire'.[40] Among the strongest links were those forged with Indian nationalists. The India Reform Society, founded in the early 1850s, 'included a powerful contingent of Irish MPs'.[41] In 1883 O'Donnell promoted a scheme to obtain an Irish seat in Parliament for Dadabhai Naoroji, a pioneer Indian politician and early President of the

[8]

Indian National Congress. Parnell is said to have 'liked the plan very much', but feared it might not be understood in Ireland.[42] Perhaps this Irish support for Indian nationalism was little more than a parliamentary *mariage de convenance*, but some Irish MPs displayed a genuine interest in the advance of self-government within the Empire. Willie Redmond (MP for Wexford), John Redmond's brother, speaking in a debate on Jamaica in 1884, supported more liberal government for the island on the grounds that Irish members were charged to support self-government not only in the case of Ireland 'but in the case of people all over the world who were asking that right'. For similar reasons Lysaght Finigan, the member for Ennis, County Clare, in 1881 said he would vote for Transvaal independence.[43]

The Irish model for parliamentary and extra-parliamentary pressure was watched and, to a certain extent, followed by Indian nationalists. In 1876 Surendranath Banerjea, a Bengal politician, said, 'Let us have political associations on the model of the Catholic Association of Daniel O'Connell'.[44] In 1886 the Viceroy of India, Lord Dufferin, an Anglo-Irish peer, was warning London about the dangers consequent on 'the importation *en bloc* from England, or rather from Ireland, of the perfected machinery of modern democratic agitation'.[45] In his memoirs, Jawaharlal Nehru, later the first Prime Minister of independent India, recalled that while he was a student in England before 1914 he had visited Ireland where he was attracted by the early beginnings of Sinn Fein.[46] The Irishwoman Annie Besant, who founded the All-India Home Rule League in 1915, based her agitation in part on the Irish model and in May 1916 her journal *New India* incurred official displeasure by justifying the 1916 Rising in Ireland.[47] In May 1917 Sir Satyendra Sinha, one of the Indian representatives at the Imperial War Conference, spoke about the dangers of delay in introducing political reform in India, warning Lloyd George that 'it might be the same for you in India as in Ireland if you wait too long'.[48]

In India, however, the Irish model of guerrilla warfare which developed in 1919–21 was not followed. Nevertheless, during the 'Anglo-Irish War' the Irish Republican Army (IRA) demonstrated (as Boer commandos had done twenty years before) that comparatively small but highly motivated irregular forces could present a formidable challenge to the armed might of the British Empire.[49] The lessons of the 1919–21 conflict were appreciated by Zionist opponents of the British Empire. Eliahu Bet Zouri, one of the Stern Gang assassins of Lord Moyne (who coincidentally came from an Anglo-Irish family) in November 1944,[50] had been brought up to admire the success of the IRA.[51] Michael Collins, indeed, has been called 'the chief pioneer of urban guerrilla warfare'.[52] One observer has claimed that 'the struggle that led to the

[9]

R.T.C. LIBRARY
LETTERKENNY

(still conditional) independence of Cyprus was almost blow for blow a repetition of "the troubles" that had freed Catholic Ireland from the English rule more than three decades earlier'.[53]

In terms of the official *response* to armed challenge, the Irish experience undoubtedly had imperial ramifications. Traditionally the nineteenth-century Irish police force, the Royal Irish Constabulary (RIC), has been held up as the model for colonial police organisation throughout the empire.[54] Unlike the British forces which were being established more or less contemporaneously, the Irish police were controlled by the central government, they were armed, and organised along distinctly military lines. The paramilitary, or gendarmerie, approach which was adopted in Ireland reflected circumstances where the state was likely to come under armed challenge. In more distant parts of the Empire a paramilitary force – such as the Royal Canadian Mounted Police or the Cape Mounted Rifles – suited the 'frontier' conditions which frequently obtained and (by no means an unimportant consideration) was certain to be much cheaper than the alternative of regular troops.

In an important essay Richard Hawkins has challenged this broad view,[55] arguing that the Irish influence on British colonial policing has never properly been tested. Furthermore, 'the constabulary system developed in Ireland so thoroughly in response to local circumstances that one might easily be sceptical of its having any real common ground with forces in other parts of the world'.[56] Yet the 'official mind' of imperial policing continued to believe in some correspondence between Ireland and the Empire. From 1907 all officers of colonial police forces had to attend the RIC Depot in Dublin for training. After the RIC was disbanded in 1922, London asked the Royal Ulster Constabulary (RUC) to continue to provide training and this service was offered at least until the 1940s.[57] During the Jewish insurgency in Palestine following the Second World War, Sir Charles Wickham's experience as Inspector-General of the RUC from its formation in 1922 was evidently judged appropriate for him to be commissioned to report on the Palestine police in 1946.[58] The perceived 'colonial dimension' of policing in Northern Ireland surfaced in the late 1960s when the RUC was reformed after it proved unable to cope with widespread civil disturbances without military help. Although the intention of the changes was to remove the RUC's paramilitary characteristics and reorganise it along the lines of a fully civilian English police force, the first Chief Constable under the new dispensation,[59] Arthur Young, was in part selected for his colonial experience. Although he was Commissioner of the City of London Police when he was appointed to the RUC, he had been Chief of Police in Malaya during the 'Emergency' in the early

1950s, and subsequently Chief of Police in Kenya (where he was less of a success) during the Mau Mau unrest. In 1969 the Prime Minister, Harold Wilson, specially wanted Young for the Belfast job because of his experience of dealing with terrorism in Malaya.[60]

Far from the RIC being the most appropriate model for the tough paramilitary duties of imperial or colonial policing, it could be argued that the experience of 1919–21 actually demonstrated how *unsuited* the Irish police were to dealing with a serious violent challenge. Recent work on the RIC has identified a progressive 'domestification' of the force, to such an extent that by the turn of the twentieth century (and even more so by 1919) 'its ability to use force was greatly diminished'.[61] It was *force majeure* following 1919 which brought changes to the RIC that effectively transformed it into a more 'colonial' type of police force than it had in fact become. In response to the challenge of the IRA, the RIC was concentrated in more heavily fortified barracks than hitherto; it was reinforced by considerable numbers of ex-soldiers (colloquially known as 'Black and Tans'); the force was well supplied with mechanical transport and its weaponry was improved. Finally in 1920 an archetypical paramilitary force – the 'Auxiliary Division' of the RIC – was established to supplement the regular police. If a 'colonial model' of policing be sought in Ireland, it may be found in the 'Auxies' and the Black and Tans. 'Undoubtedly', wrote a 1930s critic of empire, 'the Black and Tans in Ireland were the lineal descendants – politically speaking – of the punitive police we had been employing for so many years in India.'[62] So appropriate, apparently, were the Black and Tans for colonial service that when the RIC was disbanded in 1922, significant numbers of the force (including the Irish Chief of Police, General Sir Henry Tudor) transferred into the Palestine Gendarmerie, and others enlisted in the armoured car companies supplementing the Royal Air Force's air policing scheme in Iraq. In the autumn of 1922, having taken command in Jerusalem, General Tudor told his old friend and current political master Winston Churchill that Palestine was 'a rest cure after Ireland'.[63]

There was also an imperial side to the military expertise (such as it was) which was developed in 'counter-insurgency' tactics in Ireland, though some British army opinion felt that Ireland was too sensitive a case for study in preparation for colonial security work. This was the view of General Sir Charles Gwynn, author of *Imperial Policing*, the standard text-book used at the British Staff College. He 'thought it inadvisable to draw on experiences in Ireland, instructive from a military point of view as many of them are'.[64] Gwynn had been born in County Donegal, and as a grandson of the nationalist leader William Smith O'Brien, was well aware of the passions that could be aroused by discussing Irish affairs. By contrast, H. J. Simson, the author of a contemporary work on what he called 'sub-war', had no compunction about including Ireland among his references. 'Since 1918', he wrote in 1937, 'sub-wars have been rather common in territories under British rule. Perhaps the best example of all, and the one most skilfully managed by the other side, was the Sinn Fein campaign in Ireland in 1920–21.'[65] Simson identified two main lessons from the British experience. The first was 'the need to deal promptly with resort to force in the interests of peace and of the submission of disputes to judgment'. 'It is better to win first and then give, as we did in South Africa, than do as we did in Ireland in 1921 and are doing now in Palestine.' The second lesson was the need for co-ordination, especially between the military and the civil power.[66]

It is clear that the direction of the British campaign in Ireland was seriously hampered by the overlapping and sometimes conflicting responsibilities of the civil and military authorities. Between 1919 and 1921 the division of responsibility between the police administration and the military high command was never clearly sorted out. Similar confusion and incoherence handicapped subsequent British campaigns, and it was arguably not until a fully co-ordinated policy was adopted during the Malayan Emergency (1948–60) – especially under Sir Gerald Templer (a general of Anglo-Irish lineage) – that a British counter-insurgency campaign had even a passing chance of success.[67] Even, however, with a wealth of experience unmatched by any other twentieth-century state, the British security effort in Northern Ireland after renewed 'troubles' broke out in 1969 was characterised – initially at least – by a largely uncoordinated approach. Yet in this late-flowering 'north-west frontier' of the British Empire colonial expertise was brought to bear in the person, for example, of Sir Frank Kitson, perhaps the leading British counter-insurgency theorist, who served in Kenya, Malaya, Oman and Cyprus before commanding a brigade in Northern Ireland and going on to head the Staff College.[68] Among other things, the incoherence of successive British counter-insurgency campaigns, in Ireland and elsewhere, reflects the difficulty of striking a balance between coercion and conciliation, between a purely military response and a more sophisticated political strategy, especially in circumstances (such as Ireland) where the higher decision-makers themselves have no very clear idea what their ultimate policy objectives are. In a celebrated and much-quoted phrase during a series of lectures on 'the expansion of England', Sir John Seeley remarked: 'we seem, as it were, to have conquered and peopled half the world in a fit of absence of mind'.[69] It might be argued that 'absence of mind' has equally accompanied the twentieth-century contraction of England.

Ireland and the 'Irish example' posed the greatest danger for the stability of the Empire during the years 1919–22, a period identified by John Gallagher as one of particular imperial crisis. 'Once the British Empire became world-wide,' he wrote, 'the sun never set upon its crises.' In 1919–22 'nationalisms' provoked 'a new and more elaborate set of crises' which 'marched indefatigably on through the body politic of Empire, like gout through the enfeebled frame of a toper'.[70] Militant, anti-imperial nationalism, dramatically demonstrated in Ireland, seemed to spring up throughout the post-war Empire. Sir Maurice Hankey, the British Cabinet Secretary, complained in January 1921 about the pernicious influence of President Woodrow Wilson's 'impossible doctrine of self determination. The adoption of this principle at the peace conferences has struck at the very roots of the British Empire all over the world from Ireland to Hong Kong, and has got us into a hideous mess.'[71] Nationalist unrest in Egypt in the spring of 1919, and the search for a constitutional settlement over the following three years, inevitably drew comparisons with Ireland. When discussions with moderate Egyptian leaders threatened to break down in October 1921, H. A. L. Fisher, a member of the Cabinet committee on Egypt, urged concessions on Lloyd George. 'All I am concerned with', he wrote, 'is to send Redmond back with a good offer for fear that we may have to deal with a Michael Collins'.[72]

In a typically striking phrase John Gallagher drew together the linked imperial crises of the period. 'But for us', he said, 'the road to Asia lies through the swing doors of the Gresham Hotel in Dublin, one of the cover headquarters of the revolutionary Irish Government.'[73] In 1920 the Secretary for India, Edwin Montagu, again drew an Irish parallel when going to the heart of the post-war imperial dilemma. Concerned about the possibility of internal unrest he warned the Cabinet that

> if any of my colleagues think of the isolation of Europeans in India, of the smallness of the British force in India, and realise that a campaign comparable to the Sinn Fein campaign in Ireland would be almost impossible to deal with except by punishment and revenge, certainly not by prevention, they will understand the danger of the situation which has been caused by the assertion of a force we do not in reality possess in preference to a doctrine of goodwill.[74]

Arguably, it was precisely the increasingly desperate assertion of force that Britain did not in reality possess in Ireland which finally alienated moderate nationalist opinion and ensured the progressive secession of independent Ireland from the Empire-Commonwealth.

Ireland contributed to two constitutional stratagems associated with the end of Empire: federation and partition. The history of the British Empire and Commonwealth is littered with the wreckage of failed federal constitutions. At one time federation was regarded as the great panacea to the challenge of devolving power within the Empire. From the mid-nineteenth to the mid-twentieth century British politicians responded to problems of imperial control – especially those arising from conflicting local and metropolitan needs and aspirations – by proposing federal or federalist arrangements. Some of these, like 'imperial federation', simply never got off the ground. Some, in the Caribbean and Africa, collapsed after a short life. Others, such as Malaysia and Canada, stagger on, though not necessarily in great health. Australia, by contrast, has been a comparative success. One of the reasons, no doubt, why the British have been so taken with federations is that they themselves have never experienced this form of government.

The federal option, however, was proposed for the 'mother country' on a number of occasions since it seemed to offer a solution to the 'Irish question'. Canadian and South African federation, went one argument, had succeeded in accommodating and reconciling former enemies of the British within an imperial framework; why, then, could it not work for Ireland? Yet the adoption of a federal British constitution was in itself never very likely to assuage Irish nationalist demands. A. V. Dicey, who for over forty years was a vigorous opponent of any form of Home Rule, aptly observed in 1882 that federalism would 'impose on England and Scotland a constitution which they do not want' and offer Ireland one 'which Ireland is certain to dislike', having 'none of the real or imaginary charms of independence'.[75] So it was that federation remained no more than an impractical vision (as on the whole it was in other parts of the Empire) of how political irreconcilables might be reconciled within the British 'family of nations'.

Partition was a much more ruthlessly pragmatic solution to the problems of irreconcilable groups. During the twentieth century British imperial policy-makers adopted a partitionist approach in Ireland, Palestine and India in order to facilitate the devolution of power in each place.[76] Partition was one of the mechanisms with which – in A. J. P. Taylor's celebrated phrase – Lloyd George 'conjured' the Irish problem 'out of existence' in 1921.[77] For almost fifty years the stratagem seemed to work; apart from the occasional regrettable outbreak peace appeared to have been secured in Ireland; the devolved administration in Belfast was firmly established; and, above all, Irish political concerns had been taken off the British political agenda. Why, then, should not a similar solution work in other parts of the Empire? But a more pessimistic reading of the Irish experience would note that the 1921 Treaty which entrenched partition had been followed by a bloody civil war in the

Irish Free State, while both popular irredentism in independent Ireland and actual republican violence in the North threatened the existence of what was in any case an unstable and artifical political entity.

The parallels with Palestine were obvious (though we may pass in silence over the presence of the Black and Tans): as Sir Henry Wilson put it, the 'Palestine problem' was 'exactly the same as the Irish – two different sets of people living in a small area, each hating the other "for the love of God"'.[78] But for the most part the 'lessons' drawn from Ireland did not favour partition,[79] and the British resisted its attractions right up to their withdrawal from Palestine in May 1948, after which partition was imposed by Jewish *force majeure*. As is noted below,[80] analogies were drawn between the Catholic–Protestant divide in Ireland and that between Hindu and Muslim in India. During the Second World War Churchill observed to the Canadian premier, Mackenzie King, that 'the Moslems ... declare they will insist upon Pakistan, i.e. a sort of Ulster in the North'.[81]

The notion of an 'Ulster in the North' conveys an image of embattled perseverence characteristic of Ulster Protestantism,[82] and one which provides other points of contact between the Irish and the imperial experience. The tradition of valiant resistance handed down from the 1689 siege of Derry apparently sustained Ulster-born soldiers during the Indian rebellion of 1857.[83] In 1912 Bonar Law, a Canadian of Ulster Presbyterian descent, evoked the events of 1689 at a Unionist demonstration in Belfast: 'Once more you hold the pass for the Empire. You are a besieged city.'[84] After the 1921 Treaty, Sir Henry Wilson held that the future of the Empire depended on Ulster. England, he predicted, would lose Egypt and India as it had lost Ireland. 'We shall be left with Ulster, and from there we shall have to start again and build an empire. Don't laugh,' he enjoined, 'because bear in mind that Portugal once had an empire, and even Venice.'[85] In a wider Irish sense the siege theme was picked up and placed within an imperial context by the writer J. G. Farrell in his 'Empire Trilogy' of novels which treat situations in which the apparently enduring values of British civilisation and the British Empire are threatened by (as it were) barbarian outsiders in Ireland, India and South Asia.[86]

While Ireland's contribution to the constitutional practice of the Empire has been mixed, the Irish experience can clearly provide evidence to support some of the general theories concerning the working of the British imperial system. Twentieth-century Ireland can certainly be fitted into the Robinson and Gallagher 'informal rule where possible, formal rule where necessary' dictum.[87] In their work on the partition of Africa, Robinson and Gallagher went on to stress the strategic imperative – the defence of the vital imperial route between Britain and India – which underpinned the acquisition of territory in east and south Africa.[88] Both scholars developed the notion of 'collaboration' between imperial rulers and imperial ruled.[89] Every colonial power, they argued, depended upon local collaborators who, like the rank and file party workers in a general election, have the task of delivering support for the political 'bosses' – in this case the colonial administrators. 'The imperial croupier', remarked Gallagher, perhaps stretching a point somewhat, 'never found any shortage of colonial subjects ready to place bets with him at the table, though they usually staggered up from the table in some disarray.'[90]

It could be argued that by 1921 the costs of direct British rule at least in nationalist Ireland had come greatly to exceed the benefits. But the constitutional changes which accompanied the 1920–25 'Anglo-Irish settlement'[91] merely marked stages in a progressive shift from formal rule to more informal influence. The strategic requirements which were at the core of Anglo-Irish relations – the pressing need to secure Great Britain's maritime defence – and which lay behind the Union of 1801 were met in the defence clauses of the 1921 Treaty.[92] Although the 'treaty ports' were given up by Britain in 1938, the impact of their loss in the Second World War was mitigated by the retention of bases in Northern Ireland together with advances in aeronautical technology. Although independent Ireland remained neutral during the war, in 1945 the British Dominions Secretary acknowledged that the Dublin government had been very helpful indeed and 'willing to accord us any facilities which would not be regarded as overtly prejudicing their attitude to neutrality'.[93] Informal modes of assistance, in other words, helped sustain the British imperial war effort more successfully than any formal re-annexation of Ireland might have done.[94] In economic terms the links with Britain remained binding for a long time after 1921, despite the so-called 'economic war' of the 1930s. Ireland's apparent independence from British domination was not matched by any equivalent monetary autonomy, at least until the parity of the Irish pound with sterling was broken in 1979. In reality de Valera's notion of 'external association' was no more than a synonym for 'informal' empire.

Ireland, too, can provide successive groups of people who could be fitted into a collaborative framework. By this analysis, Anglo-Irish, Protestant ascendancy, 'Castle Catholics', constitutional nationalists, Redmondites, pro-Treatyites and others have taken their place at the imperial gaming table. Donald Akenson, moreover, has argued that Irish settlers in the overseas Empire themselves constituted 'ideal prefabricated collaborators'[95] who helped to sustain the British imperial edifice.[96] For the late eighteenth and early nineteenth centuries, C. A. Bayly has identified 'the critical role of the Irish within British imperial expansion'. It is anachronistic, he maintains, to equate nationalism with anti-imperialism. 'Irish patriots', he asserts, 'were desperate to reap the benefits of imperial expansion while Irish soldiers and savants were in the front line of empire-building. In short, Irish nationalism arose from Ireland's perceived exclusion from empire, not her inclusion within it.'[97]

Of all the categories of Irish people for whom the Empire provided opportunities, perhaps it was the declining Ascendancy class who benefited most, finding a *raison d'être* in imperial service progressively denied to them at home. In this way – as a sort of imperial Junker class – their experience might confirm Joseph Schumpeter's depiction of imperialism as 'atavistic' in character, stemming 'from the living conditions, not of the present, but of the past'.[98] There was, too, an economic motivation to service in the Empire since military and civil administration stipends could help offset a shrinking income from the land at home.[99] While imperial service might shore up the precarious finances of a declining social group, it could also boost the fortunes of the rising Catholic middle class. One study has noted the increasing proportion of Catholics among Irish recruits to the Indian Civil Service. In the 1850s less than 10 per cent of the Irish were Catholic, but by the eve of the First World War this had risen to 30 per cent.[100]

Although the most extensively studied aspect of the Irish relationship with the British Empire concerns the Irish diaspora, much academic work remains to be done in order both to establish the actual extent of Irish migration and also its impact, at home and abroad.[101] It is comparatively easy to compile a catalogue of Irish people who achieved great distinction within the Empire, whether as administrators, soldiers, clergy, business people, scholars, or whatever. Among the most outstanding was Sir Peter Freyer, a Galway-born and educated doctor who worked in the Indian Army Medical Service, and whose pioneering of the prostatectomy has been a great boon to mankind [*sic*].[102] But such a catalogue may not materially advance our understanding. Indeed it may simply be a contribution to the 'just fancy that' school of history. What needs persistently to be addressed is the question of whether the *Irishness* of imperial servants and settlers, both individually and as a group, made any specific difference to their experience and service. Some of the ways in which the imperial context of Anglo-Irish relations affected the political and constitutional debate have been discussed above, but the long-term impact of imperial matters has been small indeed.

One of the themes which emerges from the studies in this volume is the *irrelevance* of the Empire to some Irish concerns. Philip Ollerenshaw has shown that hard-nosed Belfast businessmen saw no particular merit in concentrating their efforts exclusively on the Empire. No doubt this reflected the comparative insignificance of much of the late nineteenth-century Empire to the British economy as a whole.[103] Belfast businessmen were successful enough to think in terms of a global market, rather than one limited by the frontiers of the British Empire. A neat illustration of this exists on the walls of Messrs Robinson and Cleaver's palatial 'Royal Irish Linen Warehouse' erected in Belfast in 1886–8. The building is decorated with sculpted heads 'emblematic of the business relations of the firm with all the countries of the world'. 'Canada' and 'Australia' are here, to be sure, as is Queen Victoria and the Maharajah of Cooch Behar, but so are George Washington and the Emperor and Empress of Germany: two empires (at least) are represented, but only one of them British.[104]

Other imperial resonances are to be found in the Irish built environment. Belfast, like other nineteenth-century industrial cities in the British Isles, is well supplied with imperial street names: Kitchener Street is next to Soudan Street, Cawnpore Street intersects with Kashmir Road, and Empire Street itself runs into Milner Street.[105] But Kansas Avenue, Luxor Gardens and Bosnia Street testify to a wider world-view. Dublin, by contrast, has virtually no specifically imperial street names.[106] Only two have been identified: Bengal Terrace and Ontario Terrace, the former, ironically, adjacent to the Irish nationalist necropolis of Glasnevin Cemetery.[107] Statues of British monarchs and heroes in the Irish Republic have suffered from the attentions of nationalists. Lord Nelson, on a 120-foot column in the centre of Dublin, was blown up in March 1966, while the recent disinterment of a statue of Queen Victoria, buried in the grounds of University College Cork in 1945, provoked a controversy over the appropriateness of restoring and displaying 'imperial' monuments in modern Ireland.[108]

After the substance of Empire has largely passed away it may be that its most lasting legacy – more enduring than bronze indeed – is chiefly intangible. If we take D. K. Fieldhouse's characterisation of imperialism as a form of 'social hysteria',[109] the traces which the British Empire has left in Ireland – and which Ireland has left in the British Empire – may most abundantly be found in social and cultural resonances, rather than in any concrete constitutional, political or even economic structures. Suitably, therefore, this collection of essays begins with a discussion of myths and stereotypes and a consideration of what might be termed the 'imagination' of Ireland and Empire.

Notes

1 For example, Nora Robertson, *Crowned Harp*, Dublin, 1960; and Lionel Fleming, *Head or Harp*, London, 1965; both Anglo-Irish memoirs.
2 Engels to Marx, 23 May 1856, in *Marx-Engels Selected Correspondence*, Moscow, rev. edn, 1975, p. 86.
3 See the illuminating discussion in Richard Koebner & Helmut Dan Schmidt, *Imperialism: the Story and Significance of a Political Word, 1840–1960*, Cambridge, 1965.
4 The address was discovered by David H. Hume and is quoted in his Chapter 6 below.
5 In the House of Commons on 21 May 1917 Lloyd George announced the formation of an Irish Convention to prepare 'a constitution for the future government of Ireland within the Empire' (*Hansard*, 93 H.C. Deb 5s, col. 1996).
6 Bishop's presidential address at Synod of the Diocese of Down and Connor and Dromore, 30 October 1917, in *Report of Diocesan Synod, 30 & 31 October 1917*, pp. 7–8 (Down & Dromore Diocesan Archives, Belfast).
7 A number of other sports, such as hockey, rowing and bowls, still stage 'home' internationals between England, Ireland, Scotland and Wales. The impact of 'British' games such as these is discussed in Chapter 2 below. For a Scottish perspective on the imperial relationship see John M. MacKenzie, 'On Scotland and the Empire', *International History Review*, XV (1993), pp. 714–39.
8 Leaving 'Ireland' (the Irish Football Association), who won the championships that year, as permanent holders of the trophy.
9 Although in 1921 the southern-based 'Football Association of Ireland' broke away from the 'Irish Football Association' (which had its headquarters in Belfast), teams for the British Championships continued to be selected on an all-Ireland basis. The policy broke down after one player with nationalist sympathies refused to play for 'Northern' Ireland in a match against the British army. There is a most useful discussion of Irish sport and politics in John Sugden & Alan Bairner, *Sport, Sectarianism and Society in a Divided Ireland*, Leicester, 1993.
10 Even the term 'Anglo-Irish' is problematic: 'I was brought up to think myself Irish without question or qualification,' wrote Stephen Gwynn, 'but the new nationalism prefers to describe me and the like of me as Anglo-Irish', quoted in J. C. Beckett, *The Anglo-Irish Tradition*, London, 1976, p. 148. 'Anglo-Irish', moreover, is not a wholly appropriate designation for that other 'British' group on the island of Ireland, the Ulster-Scots.
11 Beckett, *Anglo-Irish Tradition*, p. 96.
12 As might be asserted for Ulster Protestants in more recent times.
13 In South Africa Irish sectarian tensions only began seriously to emerge among the expatriate community at the time of the third Home Rule Bill crisis, 1912–14. Donal P. McCracken, 'Irish settlement and identity in South Africa before 1910', *Irish Historical Studies*, XXVIII (1992–93), pp. 140–1.
14 John S. Galbraith, 'The Empire since 1783', p. 61, in Robin W. Winks (ed.), *The Historiography of the British Empire-Commonwealth: Trends, Interpretations, and Resources*, Durham, NC, 1966, pp. 46–68. Other such words will readily suggest themselves: 'Ulster' or 'Come on Ireland', as shouted at any sporting occasion, spring to mind.
15 Koebner & Schmidt, *Imperialism*, pp. xiii, xxv.
16 Nicholas Mansergh, *The Irish Question 1840–1921*, London, 3rd edn, 1975, p. 142.
17 Koebner & Schmidt, *Imperialism*, p. 146.
18 Or even 'English' as well, as noted in Chapter 4 below.
19 See Joseph P. O'Grady, 'The Irish Free State passport and the question of citizenship, 1921–4', *Irish Historical Studies*, XXVI (1988–89), pp. 396–405.
20 David Harkness, *The Restless Dominion: the Irish Free State and the British Commonwealth of Nations, 1921–31*, London, 1969. For a contrary view, see Ged Martin, 'The Irish Free State and the evolution of the Commonwealth, 1921–49', in Ronald Hyam & Ged Martin, *Reappraisals in British Imperial History*, London, 1975, pp. 201–23. Aspects of Ireland and the imperial relationship are also covered in Deirdre

94'.5091

McMahon, *Republicans and Imperialists: Anglo-Irish Relations in the 1930s*, New Haven & London, 1984; and R. F. Holland, *Britain and the Commonwealth Alliance, 1918–39*, London, 1981.

21 P. S. O'Hegarty, *A History of Ireland under the Union, 1801 to 1922*, London, 1952, p. 774.

22 See Ian McCabe, *A Diplomatic History of Ireland, 1948–9: the Republic, the Commonwealth and NATO*, Dublin, 1991.

23 Nicholas Mansergh, *The Commonwealth Experience*, London, 1969, pp. 210–11. In 1917, ironically, the only Sinn Fein supporter at the Irish Convention, Edward MacLysaght, had declared that 'Sinn Fein can be won over if it can be persuaded that national freedom is possible within the empire' (R. B. McDowell, *The Irish Convention 1917–18*, London, 1970, p. 113).

24 Mansergh, *Commonwealth Experience*, pp. 196–7.

25 Harkness, *Restless Dominion*, p. 13.

26 Erskine Childers, *The Framework of Home Rule*, London, 1911, pp. vii, 189.

27 W. K. Hancock, *Smuts: the Fields of Force, 1919–1950*, Cambridge, 1968, p. 5.

28 *Ibid.*, p. 49.

29 Memo by Smuts, *c.* May 1921, *ibid.*, p. 44.

30 Among those pressing Smuts to use his considerable influence towards a solution of the Irish crisis were Sir Horace Plunkett and Roger Casement's brother, Tom.

31 14 June 1921, Hancock, *Smuts: the Fields of Force*, p. 53. The full text of the letter is reproduced in Thomas Jones, *Whitehall Diary*, III, *Ireland 1918–25* (ed. Keith Middlemas), London, 1971, pp. 74–5

32 Jones, *Whitehall Diary*, p. 247.

33 'The true key to his [Grigg's] life was his almost fanatical devotion to the Empire', *The Times*, 2 December 1955.

34 Jones, *Whitehall Diary*, pp. 75–9. See also Harold Nicolson, *King George V: His Life and Reign*, London, 1952, pp. 348–54, which largely confirms the account in Jones.

35 See Hancock, *Smuts: the Fields of Force*, pp. 55–60. Smuts's role is also covered in Tim Pat Coogan, *Michael Collins*, London, pbk edn, 1991, pp. 213–16.

36 4 August 1921, Hancock, *Smuts: the Fields of Force*, p. 59.

37 See Donal P. McCracken's excellent *The Irish Pro-Boers 1877–1902*, Johannesburg, 1989. Aspects of this point are discussed in Chapters 4, 5 and 8 below.

38 For Butler's time in South Africa, see Sir W. F. Butler, *Sir William Butler: an Autobiography*, London, 1911, pp. 385–455. Butler's moderate nationalist sympathies were shared by his wife, Elizabeth, Lady Butler, the celebrated artist. See, for example, her painting 'Evicted' (1890), and the discussion of her work in Paul Usherwood & Jenny Spencer-Smith, *Lady Butler, Battle Artist*, London, 1987.

39 Mansergh, *Commonwealth Experience*, p. 19.

40 O'Donnell and others are discussed in Mary Cumpston, 'Some early Indian nationalists and their allies in the British parliament', *English Historical Review*, LXXVI (1961), pp. 279–97. There is a useful note of work on aspects of India and Ireland in Scott B. Cook, '"The Irish Raj": social origins and careers of Irishmen in the Indian Civil Service, 1855–1914', *Journal of Social History*, XX (1986–87), pp. 507–29, at p. 524 n. 6.

41 M. E. Chamberlain, *Britain and India: the Interaction of Two Peoples*, Newton Abbot, 1974, p. 87.

42 Anil Seal, *The Emergence of Indian Nationalism*, Cambridge, pbk edn, 1971, p. 258. Naoroji was later elected as a Liberal for the London constituency of Central Finsbury (1892–95).

43 Cumpston, 'Some early Indian nationalists', p. 286. For a general discussion of Irish nationalists and the Empire, see H. V. Brasted, 'Irish nationalism and the British Empire in the late nineteenth century', in Oliver MacDonagh, W. F. Mandle & Pauric Travers (eds), *Irish Culture and Nationalism, 1750–1950*, Dublin, 1983, pp. 83–103.

44 Chamberlain, *Britain and India*, p. 171.

45 Seal, *Emergence of Indian Nationalism*, p. 179. See also the discussion of Dufferin by T. G. Fraser in Chapter 3 below.

46 Jawaharlal Nehru, *An Autobiography*, London, 1936, p. 25.

47 H. F. Owen, 'Towards nationwide agitation and organisation: the Home Rule Leagues, 1915–18', in D. A. Low (ed.), *Soundings in Modern South Asian History*, London, 1968, pp. 159–95.

48 *The Political Diaries of C. P. Scott, 1911–28* (ed. Trevor Wilson), London, 1970, p. 288. Various instances of Ireland as an exemplar for India are noted in Sir Algernon Rumbold, *Watershed in India, 1914–22*, London, 1979.

49 Charles Townshend, *The British Campaign in Ireland, 1919–21*, Oxford, 1975, is an indispensable account of this conflict. See also Townshend, 'The Irish Republican Army and the development of guerrilla warfare, 1916–21', *English Historical Review*, XCIV (1979), pp. 318–45, which provides a corrective to over-idealised accounts of the IRA's organisation and achievements. The place of the IRA in revolutionary warfare is rather uncritically discussed in Michael Elliott-Bateman, John Ellis & Tom Bowden, *Revolt to Revolution: Studies in the 19th and 20th Century European Experience*, Manchester, 1974.

50 Moyne (Walter Guinness) was the British Minister of State Resident in the Middle East at the time.

51 Robert B. Asprey, *War in the Shadows: the Guerrilla in History*, London, 1976, p. 832n. See also Robert Taber, *The War of the Flea: Guerrilla Warfare, Theory and Practice*, St Albans, 1970, p. 92.

52 In the entry on Collins in John Keegan & Andrew Wheatcroft, *Who's Who in Military History*, London, 2nd edn 1987, p. 77. See also Tom Bowden, *The Breakdown of Public Security: the Case of Ireland 1916–1921 and Palestine 1936–1939*, London, 1977, where Collins is described as 'an Irish Lenin' (p. 11).

53 Taber, *War of the Flea*, p. 92. The Greek Cypriot leader, General George Grivas-Dighenis, however, makes no mention of the Irish example in either his *Guerrilla Warfare and Eoka's Struggle*, London, 1964, or *The Memoirs of General Grivas* (ed. Charles Foley), London, 1964. As noted by Donal Lowry in Chapter 8 below, the Belfast *Protestant Telegraph* identified the IRA as the inspiration for African terrorism in Southern Rhodesia in the 1970s.

54 The classic exposition of this view is in Sir Charles Jeffries, *The Colonial Police*, London, 1952, pp. 30–1.

55 'The "Irish model" and the empire: a case for reassessment', in David M. Anderson & David Killingray (eds), *Policing the Empire: Government, Authority and Control, 1830–1940*, Manchester, 1991, pp. 18–32.

56 *Ibid.*, p. 31.

57 W. F. Murphy, 'Official government sources regarding the history of the Royal Ulster and Ulster Special Constabularies, 1920–56', unpublished M.A. dissertation, Queen's University, Belfast, 1989, p. 56.

58 David A. Charters, *The British Army and Jewish Insurgency in Palestine, 1945–47*, London, 1989, p. 242, n. 101; Charles Townshend, *Britain's Civil Wars: Counterinsurgency in the Twentieth Century*, London, 1986, pp. 114, 119.

59 In keeping with the 'civilianising' of the RUC, the title chief constable replaced the more military 'inspector-general'.

60 W. D. Flackes & Sidney Elliott, *Northern Ireland: a Political Directory, 1968–1993*, Belfast, 3rd edn, 1994, pp. 357–8.

61 W. J. Lowe & Elizabeth Malcolm, 'The domestification of the Royal Irish Constabulary, 1836–1922', *Irish Economic and Social History*, XIX (1992), pp. 27–48, at p. 27.

62 Lt. Col. A. Osburn, quoted in V. G. Kiernan, *European Empires from Conquest to Collapse, 1815–1960*, London, 1982, p. 178.

63 Keith Jeffery, *The British Army and the Crisis of Empire, 1918–22*, Manchester, 1984, pp. 73, 129. See also Douglas V. Duff, *May the Winds Blow!*, London, 1948, one of several autobiographical volumes by a Catholic British ex-patriate, born in Argentina, a godson of Sir Roger Casement, who joined the RIC in 1921 and transferred to the Palestine Gendarmerie in 1922.

64 Charles Gwynn, *Imperial Policing*, London, 2nd edn, 1939, p. 8.

65 H. J. Simson, *British Rule, and Rebellion*, Edinburgh, 1937, p. 37.

66 *Ibid.*, pp. 331, 119. Bernard Law Montgomery drew on his experience serving in Cork in 1921 when he was General-Officer-Commanding-in-Chief (GOC) Palestine during the Arab rebellion in 1939. See Nigel Hamilton, *Monty: the Making of a General, 1887–1942*, London, 1981, pp. 280–306. Service in Ireland during the 'Troubles' threw a shadow over more unlikely areas of British life, such as film censorship, as noted in Chapter 1 below.

67 There is a growing literature on the topic of counter-insurgency. Among the relevant works which discuss the 'Irish experience' are those by Townshend cited in nn. 38 and 47 above; Ian F. W. Beckett (ed.), *The Roots of Counter-insurgency: Armies and Guerrilla Warfare, 1900–1945*, London, 1988; Ronald Haycock (ed.), *Regular Armies and Insurgency*, London, 1979; Thomas R. Mockaitis, *British Counterinsurgency, 1919–60*, London, 1990; and Keith Jeffery, 'Intelligence and counter-insurgency operations: some reflections on the British experience', *Intelligence and National Security*, II (1987), pp. 118–49.

68 The most important of Kitson's books is *Low Intensity Operations: Subversion, Insurgency and Peacekeeping*, London, 1971. For a sharply critical view of his work, see Roger Faligot, *Britain's Military Strategy in Ireland: the Kitson Experiment*, London & Dingle, 1983.

69 Sir J. R. Seeley, *The Expansion of England*, London, 2nd edn, 1895, p. 10.

70 John Gallagher, 'Nationalisms and the crisis of empire, 1919–1922', in *Power, Profit and Politics: Essays on Imperialism, Nationalism and Change in Twentieth-Century India*, ed. Christopher Baker, Gordon Johnson & Anil Seal, special issue of *Modern Asian Studies*, XV (1981), pp. 355–68, at p. 355; also published by Cambridge University Press, 1981. See also Gallagher's inimitable treatment of these years in his 1974 Ford Lectures, *The Decline, Revival and Fall of the British Empire*, Cambridge, 1982, pp. 86–99. My own *British Army and Crisis of Empire* was to a very large extent inspired by Gallagher's analysis. The Irish impact on imperial policy during this period is also discussed by another of Gallagher's pupils: John Darwin, *Britain, Egypt and the Middle East: Imperial Policy in the Aftermath of War, 1918–22*, London, 1981.

71 Quoted in Jeffery, *British Army and Crisis of Empire*, p. 161. Sir Keith Hancock's magisterial *Survey of British Commonwealth Affairs, I: Problems of Nationality, 1918–36*, Oxford, 1937, discusses the impact of 'self determination', including that of Ireland, on the Empire-Commonwealth.

72 Jeffery, *British Army and Crisis of Empire*, p. 119.

73 The printed version of this phrase is even more striking, since through an error, it reads '… through the swing doors of the *Grafton* Hotel in Dublin …' (Gallagher, 'Nationalisms and the crisis of empire', p. 359).

74 Jeffery, *British Army and Crisis of Empire*, p. 104.

75 John Kendle, *Ireland and the Federal Solution: the Debate over the United Kingdom Constitution, 1870–1921*, Kingston & Montreal, 1989, pp. 22–3. This is a definitive survey of the topic.

76 T. G. Fraser, *Partition in Ireland, India and Palestine: Theory and Practice*, London, 1984, is the best guide.

77 A. J. P. Taylor, *English History 1914–45*, Harmondsworth, 1970, p. 213.

78 Keith Jeffery (ed.), *The Military Correspondence of Field Marshal Sir Henry Wilson, 1918–22*, London, 1985, p. 273.

79 For British and American analogies drawn between Ireland and Palestine see W. R. Louis, *The British Empire in the Middle East, 1945–51*, Oxford, 1984, pp. 448, 496–7.

80 By T. G. Fraser in chapter 3.

81 Quoted in Nicholas Mansergh, *The Prelude to Partition: Concepts and Aims in Ireland and India* (1976 Commonwealth Lecture), Cambridge, 1978, p. 52.

82 As exemplified (not least by the title) in the most articulate contemporary exposition of Ulster unionism: Arthur Aughey, *Under Siege: Ulster Unionism and the Anglo-Irish Agreement*, Belfast, 1989.

83 See Chapter 3 below, and for the 'Ulster' military tradition, Chapter 4.

84 *Belfast News-Letter*, 10 April 1912.

85 Jeffery, *Military Correspondence of Sir Henry Wilson*, pp. 317–18.

86 *Troubles*, London, 1970; *The Siege of Krishnapur*, London, 1973; and *The Singapore Grip*, London, 1978.

87 First propounded in John Gallagher & Ronald Robinson, 'The imperialism of Free Trade', *Economic History Review*, 2nd ser. VI (1953), pp. 1–15 (reprinted in Gallagher, *Decline, Revival and Fall of the British Empire*, pp. 1–18).

88 See Robinson & Gallagher, with Alice Denny, *Africa and the Victorians*, London, 1961; and 'The Partition of Africa', *New Cambridge Modern History*, XI, Cambridge, 1962, pp. 593–640 (reprinted in Gallagher, *Decline, Revival and Fall of the British Empire*, pp. 19–72).

89 The significance of local circumstance – whether exemplified by resistance or collaboration – was first raised in 'The imperialism of Free Trade', and amplified by Gallagher in the 1974 Ford Lectures (cited nn. 87 and 70 above). For a sophisticated development of the idea, see Ronald Robinson, 'Non-European foundations of European imperialism: sketch for a theory of collaboration', in Roger Owen & Bob Sutcliffe (eds), *Studies in the Theory of Imperialism*, London, 1972, pp. 117–40.

90 Gallagher, *Decline, Revival and Fall of the British Empire*, p. 152.

91 Nicholas Mansergh (in *The Unresolved Question: the Anglo-Irish Settlement and its Undoing, 1912–72*, New Haven & London, 1921) has valuably argued that the Anglo-Irish settlement should be understood as covering the whole period from the 1920 Government of Ireland Act to the 1925 Boundary Commission Report.

92 See Jeffery, *British Army and Crisis of Empire*, pp. 91–2.

93 Ronan Fanning, *Independent Ireland*, Dublin, 1983, pp. 124–5. The reality of wartime co-operation contrasts vividly with Churchill's public excoriation of Irish neutrality after VE Day in 1945.

94 This was contemplated on a number of occasions. See Robert Fisk, *In Time of War: Ireland, Ulster and the Price of Neutrality 1939–45*, London, 1983.

95 Ronald Robinson's phrase, in 'Non-European foundations of European imperialism', p. 124.

96 Donald Harman Akenson, *The Irish Diaspora: a Primer*, Toronto & Belfast, 1993, pp. 141–51. See also Hiram Morgan, 'Empire-building: an uncomfortable Irish heritage', *Linen Hall Review*, X, no. 2 (Autumn 1993), pp. 8–11.

97 C. A. Bayly, *Imperial Meridian: the British Empire and the World, 1780–1830*, London, 1989, p. 12.

98 Joseph A. Schumpeter, *Imperialism and Social Classes*, Oxford, 1951, p. 84.

99 J. C. Beckett once put it to the author that 'Indian pensions' rescued the Irish minor gentry from total oblivion.

100 Cook, '"The Irish Raj"', p. 517.

101 It is only possible to mention a selection of the literature. The best introductory guide is Akenson, *The Irish Diaspora*. See also his other relevant works, especially: *The Irish in Ontario: a Study in Rural History*, Kingston & Montreal, 1984; *Half the World from Home: Perspectives on the Irish in New Zealand, 1860–1950*, Wellington, 1990; *Occasional Papers on the Irish in South Africa*, Grahamstown, 1991. In addition, for Australia, see Patrick O'Farrell, *The Irish in Australia*, Kensington, NSW, 1987; Oliver MacDonagh & W. F. Mandle (eds), *Ireland and Irish-Australia: Studies in Cultural and Political History*, London, 1986. For Canada, Cecil J. Houston & William J. Smyth, *Irish Emigration and Canadian Settlement: Patterns, Links and Letters*, Toronto, 1990. For South Africa, Donal P. McCracken, 'Irish settlement and identity' (cited n. 13 above).

102 For Freyer, and other Irish exiles, see Gerald Griffin, *The Wild Geese: Pen Portraits of Famous Irish Exiles*, London, 1938.

103 See S. B. Saul, *Studies in British Overseas Trade, 1870–1914*, Liverpool, 1960.

104 C. E. B. Brett, *Buildings of Belfast, 1700–1914*, London, 1967, p. 47; Marcus Patton, *Central Belfast: a Historical Gazeteer*, Belfast, 1993, p. 107.

105 There is also a Colenso Parade which local tradition, no doubt apocryphally, maintains was erected after December 1899 by a nationalist builder with a wicked sense of humour.

106 This definition excludes clearly British names, such as Victoria, Wellington and Raglan, which have no direct imperial connotation.

107 As the Empire, in place names, can be found in Ireland, so too can Ireland be found in the Empire. One example will suffice: the Harare suburb of Avondale, named after Parnell's property in county Wicklow by O'Connell Farrell, who occupied the farm estate (as it then was) in 1890 (R. Cherer Smith, *Avondale to Zimbabwe: a Collection of Cameos of Rhodesian Towns and Villages*, Salisbury, n.d., p. 1).

108 See Aengus Ó Snodaigh, 'Erecting political ghosts from our statued past', *Sunday Business Post*, 8 January 1995. A related debate has continued for some time in Ireland concerning Georgian architecture, seen by some as emblematic of English cultural imperialism.

109 D. K. Fieldhouse, '"Imperialism": an historiographical revision', *Economic History Review*, 2nd ser. XIV (1961–62), p. 209.

CHAPTER ONE

Ireland, the Empire and film

Jeffrey Richards

Myths and stereotypes are the essential elements of popular culture. They are far easier for audiences to identify and absorb than complex analyses of issues and historical problems. The myths and stereotypes of Ireland and Irishness are as potent and indeed politically influential as any. They have a long history and the cinema is only the latest vehicle for their dissemination.

In cinematic terms, the image of Ireland has been largely in the hands of the British and American film industries. For Ireland experienced on an even greater scale the problems Britain faced in seeking to establish a native film industry: chronic under-investment, technical backwardness and the overwhelming dominance world-wide of Hollywood. Periodically an Irish-made feature like *The Dawn* (1935) would be hailed as the great breakthrough but it always proved a false dawn. There were schemes from the 1930s onwards for an Irish film studio. When Ardmore, Ireland's first and only permanent studio, eventually opened in 1958, it began promisingly enough with a series of adaptations of theatrical hits featuring the celebrated Abbey players. But it soon became, like many British studios, merely a rented facility for use by foreign film companies rather than the heart of a native Irish film industry. Indeed until the 1970s the silent era represented the most sustained period of indigenous Irish film-making both in quantity and quality. The creation of the Irish Film Board in 1980, film funding by the Irish Arts Council and the involvement of the broadcasting network RTE led to an Irish film-making renaissance not dissimilar to the British one, fuelled by Channel 4 funding.[1]

Nevertheless in America, Britain and Ireland alike the same images of Ireland and Irishness have been purveyed. They are based on a cultural construction of Irishness in which the Irish themselves have happily collaborated. The figure of 'Paddy', the Irish stereotype, goes back at least to the sixteenth century.

[25]

L. P. Curtis Jr has argued that 'Paddy' was defined in the nineteenth century specifically as the mirror image of John Bull. So the ideal Englishman was defined as a sober, law-abiding, mature, straightforward, phlegmatic, clean, rational gentleman, individualistic and private. But by contrast the Irishman was depicted as a drunken, lawless, unstable, emotional, dirty, devious, childlike, superstitious, lazy, vengeful and irrational peasant, clannish and tribal. In particular the Irish were violent: so a 'paddy' became a colloquial term for a rage, a 'hooligan' a description of mindless violence after a legendary family of brawling London Irish, and a 'donnybrook' became a generic term for a free-for-all fight after the notoriously combative encounters at the eponymous fair.[2]

Prejudice against the Irish spread right across society from Benjamin Disraeli ('this wild, reckless, indolent, uncertain and superstitious race'), Charles Kingsley ('human chimpanzees') and James Anthony Froude ('the most superstitious, the most imaginative and inflammable people in Europe') to the working classes of Lancashire.[3] It was a prejudice that was partly racial, reinforced by the new 'science' of racism which graded human beings according to a scale of race and civilisation; partly religious (Protestant prejudice against Catholics); partly class (urban industrial progress against peasant backwardness); and partly imperial (as a subject people, the Irish were automatically inferior and in need of good government).

All of this is true up to a point, particularly in the nineteenth century. But Curtis's view has been modified and nuanced by Sheridan Gilley, who counters the prejudices of Disraeli, Kingsley and Froude with the sympathetic comments of Anthony Trollope ('good humoured, clever, the working classes very much more intelligent than those in England'), Thackeray ('I have met more gentlemen there than in any place I ever saw, gentlemen of high and low ranks') and Matthew Arnold who praised 'Celtic sensitivity and sensibility, eloquence, and gift for music, quickness of spirit and poetic genius'.[4] Gilley argues that 'Paddy' was the creation of both Englishmen and Irishmen and popular with both, particularly in the eighteenth century when the Irish were better liked in England than the Scots. 'Paddy' before the nineteenth century was a feckless, reckless, devil-may-care, hard-drinking, hard-fighting peasant, generous, hospitable and immensely brave, and as such celebrated in popular ballads in both England and Ireland. Gilley admits that a more hostile view emerged in the nineteenth century as a consequence of the increasing resort to violence to achieve independence. But he concludes that rather than the one-dimensional view adumbrated by Curtis:

It would be truer to say that Englishmen had drawn from their long experience of the Irish a national stereotype which had both its good points and its bad: as good and bad points were defined by the Irish themselves. So the English invoked the good points or the bad according to their temperament, moment or mood. Thus an Irish riot or rebellion typified Celtic lawlessness, though Irish military valour always came in for English praise; the remittances which poured into Ireland from overseas were in English eyes the hallmark of Celtic family loyalty, as the railways were monuments to Irish industry, although a single drunken Irishman proved all Irishmen drunkards, as the idleness of unemployed Irishmen in a slum established Irish indolence. The one observer might consider both industry and indolence equally Irish and happily hold either opinion on different occasions without resolving the contradiction, for it is the very nature of an idea of 'national character' that as often as it aspires to consistency it leaves contradictions of this kind unresolved.[5]

Gilley argues that the principal opposition to the Irish was due to a view of their nationalism as narrow and parochial against the supranationalism of the British Empire. It is this comment which gives us the imperial context; the idea of Ireland judged in relation to its attitude to the Empire. The imperial dimension is a vital element in the construction and evaluation of the Irish character.

The English domination of Ireland was the context from which the cultural images of Irishness sprang. The stage Irishman was developed in the sixteenth and seventeenth centuries.[6] In English plays set in England the Irishman appeared usually as a servant or a soldier, accurately reflecting the reality of the Irish presence in England. The Irishman was associated with distinct dress (tight trousers, cape, short dagger) and diet (potatoes, bonny-clabber (clotted cream), watercress and whiskey), with song and dance, Catholicism and a stage brogue. These two characters evolved during the eighteenth century, often in the hands of Irish playwrights, into familiar but attractive archetypes: the whimsical but faithful and resourceful servant frequently and generically called 'Teague' and classically embodied in the genial innkeeper Dennis Brulgruddery in George Colman's play *John Bull* in 1803, and the penniless, high-living, amorous, roistering gentlemanly soldier of fortune epitomised by Sir Lucius O'Trigger in Sheridan's *The Rivals* (1775). Both were regarded with affection, for as J. O. Bartley writes of the eighteenth century: 'There is no doubt that the Irish had come to be generally quite well liked in England. In 1760 they had long ceased to be a threat and were no longer even a nuisance.'[7]

These character archetypes survived in the nineteenth century when the era of mass-produced popular culture regularly reworked them to write them into the popular consciousness. The nineteenth century novels of Charles Lever and Samuel Lover embodied both the soldier and the servant. Lever's novels like *Charles O'Malley* (1841) and *Harry Lorrequer* (1839) were 'rollicking pictures of military life and of the hard-drinking, fox-hunting Irish society of his days' and were enormously popular. Samuel Lover created the gallant tragic hero Rory O'More in ballad, novel and play, but he also celebrated the accident-prone, blarneying servant 'Handy Andy Rooney' in his novel *Handy Andy* (1842). The principal difference from the eighteenth century is that these characters were now observed in an Irish setting. The same was true of the stage. The dress of the Irish characters was Anglicised, references to diet and religion disappeared and there was greater individualisation of the archetypes within a given range of Irish charac-teristics which now included eloquence, pugnacity, superstition, blarney, resourcefulness and a fondness for women and whiskey, song and dance. In this vein the plays of John Baldwin Buckstone, such as *Presumptive Evidence* (1828), *The Boyne Water* (1831) and *The Irish Lion* (1838), combined Romantic Irish landscape, sentimental plots and humanised character types.

The new literary and dramatic interest in Ireland was a product of the Romantic movement. Ireland, like Scotland, had become a prime location and preoccupation for the creative imagination of artists, poets and balladeers, who saw in the 'emerald isle' the elemental wild-ness and primitive picturesqueness that so appealed to Romantics and which in Ireland took the form of caves and cliffs, ruined castles, rugged landscape, ghosts, moonlight and fair colleens. This image was reproduced on stage in the work of scene-painters who provided an evocative background to Irish melodramas, directly reflecting the interest embodied in the rash of books of engravings of Irish scenes in the 1830s and 1840s.[8] A celebration of the Romantic Irish landscape was to become one of the enduring features of Irish films.

The Romantic spirit also permeated the work of the Irish Catholic poet Thomas Moore, whose ten volumes of *Irish Melodies* (1807–35) made a major contribution to the construction of a Romantic Irish identity. The same Moore who was the friend of Robert Emmet, biogra-pher of Irish rebel Lord Edward Fitzgerald and author of a four-volume history of Ireland was also Registrar of the Admiralty Prize Court, Bermuda, was married to an English Protestant, was a leading figure in London literary society and cultivated the friendship of Whig grandees. His career demonstrates that ambiguous relationship between national-ists and the Empire that runs through the history of Ireland.

But the songs, in which Moore provided words for traditional airs, were enduringly popular. As Miriam Allen De Ford writes:

Up to fifty years ago at least, nearly every English speaking person, from operatic stars to members of the family gathering around the piano knew and sang 'Believe me, if all those endearing young charms', 'The Last Rose of Summer' and 'The Harp that once through Tara's halls' ... Just as the more topical of the songs became hymns and political rallying calls in embattled Ireland, soldiers on both sides in the American Civil War ... sang them together in camp. They were popular songs in the truest sense.[9]

The songs which stress loss, tears, sorrows, battle and death became an integral part of the nationalist sensibility and run through the plays of Dion Boucicault and the films of Ireland, binding them together. A snatch of one of them is sufficient to evoke a picturesque and troubled past, whose legacy is still being lived through. In that cross-fertilisation that is so characteristic of nineteenth-century popular culture, Tom Moore himself became the hero of a play, Buckstone's *The Irish Lion* (1838) where he was depicted as a proto-Shaughraun, a singing, dancing, blarneying ladies' man.

The tradition of the lyrical Irish ballad survived well into the twentieth century, notably in the career of John McCormack. One early Hollywood sound film, *Song o'My Heart* (1930), partly filmed on location in Ireland, was virtually a filmed McCormack concert, with him singing eleven ballads. He also sang in the first British Technicolor feature, *Wings of the Morning* (1937), perpetuating the image of a Romantic and Arcadian Ireland.

A standard Irish play emerged in the nineteenth century which usually involved a romantic triangle with a villain seeking to discredit the hero and take over his land and his sweetheart, and a comic subplot usually involving the violent humiliation of some minor English functionary. The genre was comprehensively denounced by George Bernard Shaw in a review of a revival of Boucicault's *The Colleen Bawn*:

To an Irishman who has any sort of social conscience, the conception of Ireland as a romantic picture, in which the background is formed by the Lakes of Killarney by moonlight, and a round tower or so, while every male figure is a 'broth of a bhoy' and every female one a colleen in a crimson Connemara cloak, is exasperating ... The occupation of the Irish peasant is mainly agricultural; and I advise the reader to make it a fixed rule never to allow himself to believe in the alleged Arcadian virtues of the half-starved drudges who are sacrificed to the degrading, brutalizing, and, as far as I can ascertain, entirely unnecessary pursuit of scientific farming. The virtues of the Irish peasant are the intense melancholy, surliness of manner, the incapacity for happiness and self-respect that are the tokens of his natural unfitness for a life of wretchedness. His vices are the arts by which he accommodates himself to his slavery – the flattery on his lips which hides the curse in his heart; his pleasant readiness to

[29]

settle disputes by 'leaving it all to your honor', in order to make something out of your generosity in addition to exacting the utmost of his
legal due from you; his instinctive perception that by pleasing you he can
make you serve him; his mendacity and mendicity; his love of stolen
advantage; the superstitious fear of his priest and his Church which does
not prevent him from trying to cheat both in the temporal transactions
between them; and the parasitism which makes him, in domestic service, that occasionally convenient but on the whole demoralizing human
barnacle, the irremovable old retainer of the family. Of all the tricks
which the Irish nation have played on the slow-witted Saxon, the most
outrageous is the palming off on him of the imaginary Irishman of
romance. The worst of it is, that when a spurious type gets into literature,
it strikes the imagination of boys and girls. They form themselves by
playing up to it; and thus the unsubstantial fancies of the novelists and
music-hall song-writers of one generation are apt to become the unpleasant and mischievous realities of the next.[10]

From this countervailing view of Ireland, Shaw constructed his play
John Bull's Other Island, a play commissioned but rejected by the
Abbey Theatre on the grounds of difficulty of casting and staging but in
Shaw's view because 'it was uncongenial to the whole spirit of the neo-
Gaelic movement which is bent on creating a new Ireland after its own
ideal, whereas my play is a very uncompromising presentment of the
real old Ireland'.[11]

But Richard Allen Cave has argued persuasively that the standard
Irish play format was consistently and successfully subverted in the
nineteenth century to create sympathy for rather than mockery of the
Irish stereotype, against a new background created by the Catholic
Emancipation Act (1829), the extending of parliamentary representation in the Irish Reform Bill (1832) and a more liberal attitude to Ireland. So plays written by and for Tyrone Power and later Dion
Boucicault created much more rounded and sympathetic characterisation. Thus Power's character assumes the guise of the stage Irishman
(with his blarney, his blather and his booze) to fool opponents in
Eugene McCarthy's stage version of Lever's *Charles O'Malley* (1838)
and Samuel Lover's stage version of his own *Rory O'More* (1837) or by
episodes in which the English or other non-Irish visitors are confronted
with their preconceived notions of the Irish and thus sent up (Anna
Maria Hall's *Groves of Blarney*, 1838; Lover's *The White Horse of the
Peppers*, 1838).

The most celebrated exponent of the strategy was Dion Boucicault,
whose Irish plays *The Colleen Bawn* (1860), *The Shaughraun* (1875)
and *Arrah-na-Pogue* (1865) were continuously popular and played with
success in England, Ireland and the United States from their first
appearances. They had romantic settings, exciting incident and engaging

heroes (Myles-na-Coppaleen, Shaun the Post, Conn the Shaughraun) who were daring, loyal, quick-witted, and able to use the stage Irish persona to fool the English. There is no doubting Boucicault's passionate Irish nationalism. He articulated it clearly in *The Fireside Story of Ireland* (1881). But he achieved greater success in presenting a sympathetic picture of Ireland to the English with his melodramas, blending comedy, romance and drama, than in the violent and bitter *The Rapparee* (1870), set at the time of the Battle of the Boyne, which failed in London, and the powerful, tragic, *Robert Emmet* (1884), which failed in the United States. His Irish melodramas appealed to the universal sentiments of the age, linked Irish and English by common adherence to gentlemanliness and dramatised the Irish problem in such a way as to awaken sympathy for the Irish without alienating the English audience. But there is no doubting that Irish sympathy.[12]

Yet, this same writer penned the classic imperial melodrama, *Jessie Brown* (1858), dramatising the siege of Lucknow, drawing on the widespread horror in Britain and America at the massacres of English people, particularly women and children, and ending with a patriotic tableau of the relief of Lucknow by General Havelock. There is little evidence of sympathy here with the sepoys. Furthermore one of the leading characters, the Irish Private Cassidy, roundly abuses the mutineers ('black devils'), Nana Sahib the rebel leader is shown seeking to enslave Mrs Campbell and slaughter her children, and the British hero, Lieutenant Randal MacGregor declares: 'Freedom was never won by murder, for heaven never yet armed the hand of an assassin' – not exactly a Fenian sentiment. Yet there is hardly an English character in the play. Most of the British characters are Scottish or Irish, the myth and imagery of the Scottish soldier is freely used and a key role is even played by a letter in Gaelic, used to deceive Nana Sahib. It is as if Boucicault found himself much more in sympathy with the Celtic characters but also endorsed the racial hierarchy of the day and the general horror at the massacres, certainly not equating the Irish and Indian struggles for independence but endorsing the role of the Irish soldier in defence of the British Empire.[13]

But the play is as much a hymn to fighting as the Empire, with Jessie Brown the heroine, daughter of the regiment, curing Geordie McGregor of cowardice, the chaplain Blount overcoming his revulsion from fighting, and the Scots and Irish demonstrating their fighting qualities to the full. It highlights an ambivalence inevitably created by the existence of the Empire and felt by some in Ireland, Scotland and Wales; a desire for emancipation from it at home but a willingness to participate in it abroad. What is common to both is a love of fighting, which brings us back to the stereotype of 'Paddy'.

[31]

Throughout all the cultural manifestations, three continuing images have attached themselves to Ireland: violence, humour and communality. An Irish association with violence is as old as England's association with the island. As early as the twelfth century the chronicler Giraldus Cambrensis described Ireland as 'barren of good·things, replenished with actions of blood, murder and loathsome outrage'.[14] Fighting mercenaries have long been a prime Irish export. It was Shaw who said, not without some justice, that the best comedies in the English language had been written by Irishmen (Congreve, Farquhar, Goldsmith, Sheridan, Wilde and himself). They are all marked by a love of language, quick wits and high spirits, which in a negative sense – loquacity, blarney and fecklessness – have also been attached to Irishness. The communality, product of a peasant society, is the mirror image of the bourgeois individualism and imperial supra-nationalism of England. The informer, the perennial Irish hate figure, is the quintessential individualist in the Irish context.

The Irish melodrama is important to cinema as silent films appropriated melodrama wholesale. There were a large number of Irish dramas of a romantic nationalist tinge made in Hollywood in silent days. Among the earliest depictions of Ireland on film were a series of classic adaptations, filmed in Ireland by the Kalem Company and directed by a Canadian of Irish parentage, Sidney Olcott: *Rory O'More* (1911), *The Colleen Bawn* (1911), *Arragh-na-Pogue* (1911) and *The Shaughraun* (1912). This demonstrates the continuity to be found everywhere between the melodrama stage and the cinema, and the persistence of an essentially Victorian sensibility in the mass cinema-going public up until the 1940s.[15]

The violence, humour and communality already mentioned figure strongly in cinematic depictions of Ireland. But in the imperial context it is struggle and violence that characterise Ireland in cinema. The crimson thread running through the long and tangled story of Anglo-Irish relations is the Irish fight for independence, which has been imbued with a romantic aura as the classic struggle of a simple, united, rural people against imperial military might. Even in melodrama, plays were often set at the time of rebellion: *Arragh-na-Pogue* in 1798, *The Shaughraun* in the context of the Fenian troubles in the 1860s; other Victorian melodramas featured pre-Fenian groups such as the Peep O'Day boys, the White Boys, the Ribbonmen. The recurrent tropes are the use of violence, the role of the hated informer and communal solidarity. These myths, as Kevin Rockett has pointed out, mean that the cinema has consistently ignored inter-class rivalries and internal Irish conflict in favour of the communal solidarity necessary for sustaining the hallowed myth of united struggle.[16]

But the desire to dramatise the Irish struggle for freedom brought film-makers into conflict with the censors. The cinema in both Britain and America operated under the tight control of the censors, whose aim was to maintain moral rectitude and eliminate political controversy. While Ireland remained in the Empire, there was anxiety to avoid films stirring up ill-feeling. Sidney Olcott, who had directed the film versions of the Boucicault plays in 1910–12, returned to Ireland in 1914 to film *Bold Emmet, Ireland's Martyr*, which was banned in 1915 by the authorities on the grounds that it interfered with the recruiting drive in Ireland. In this it shared the fate of Frank Marshall's play *Robert Emmet*, commissioned by Sir Henry Irving, but banned by the theatrical censor, the Lord Chamberlain, in 1879. Irving subsequently handed the manuscript over to Boucicault who reworked it as a powerful nationalist melodrama and staged it in the United States without success.

Ireland a Nation, directed by Walter MacNamara, met the same fate as *Bold Emmet*. Based on the 1798 and 1803 rebellions, it was initially passed for showing in 1916 by the censor with the removal of six scenes (including the execution of Emmet). Even so, when it was shown, it generated so much audience enthusiasm that the authorities deemed it prudent to ban it completely and it was not shown again until after independence.[17]

Even after independence, the British censors were for some years chary of allowing films about the Irish rebellion. The film *Irish Destiny* (1926), released to coincide with the tenth anniversary of the Easter Rising, told a love story set against the struggle between the IRA and the Black and Tans, reconstructing the events of 1920–21 with many of the actual participants recreating their roles.[18] It was banned in Britain by the British Board of Film Censors (BBFC). But time healed the old wounds and when in 1936 Irish cinema produced *The Dawn*, it was passed by the BBFC for showing in Britain. Directed and co-written by Thomas Cooper, who also played IRA Commandant O'Donovan, *The Dawn* is a truly dreadful propaganda feature, technically crude, badly acted and appallingly heavy-handed. It is a celebration of the IRA ('the boys'), highlighting the brutality of the Black and Tans and featuring the taint of informing, described as the one sin an Irishman can never forgive. In 1919 Brian Malone falls under suspicion of informing, is expelled from the IRA and in bitterness joins the Royal Irish Constabulary (RIC). But appalled by the brutality of British forces, he deserts and rejoins the IRA, helping them to ambush a Black and Tan column. At the end he discovers that his brother Billy, generally regarded as an anglicised snob and coward, is in fact secretly the IRA Intelligence chief and the brains behind their activities. Billy is killed, receives a burial with full military honours and the IRA march off into the future.

Although after several years of conflict, Ireland had been partitioned in 1921 with the six counties of north-east Ulster remaining part of the United Kingdom (as 'Northern Ireland') and the remaining twenty-six counties becoming a self-governing dominion, (the 'Irish Free State') there had been civil war in the Free State in 1922–23 and outbreaks of IRA activity in England in the 1930s. Under these circumstances, J. C. Robertson, historian of the BBFC, observes that 'potentially the greatest source of friction between the BBFC and American and British studios from 1919 to 1939 was Ireland'.[19] In addition, T. P. O'Connor, veteran journalist and parliamentarian, and a former Irish nationalist MP in the British Parliament, was president of the BBFC from 1916 to 1929; Edward Shortt, BBFC President 1929–35, had been Chief Secretary for Ireland in 1918–19, and Colonel J. C. Hanna, Vice-President of the Board and Chief Script Examiner throughout the 1930s had served with the army in Ireland in the period 1918–22. So there was considerable interest and expertise in Irish matters on the British Board.

The BBFC records show details of seven projects submitted at script stage and allow us to assess the reaction of the authorities to them. In 1933 the synopsis of an unproduced play, *The Man with the Gun* was submitted by the writer Temple Thurston, presumably with an eye to sale of film rights. It was a love story set against the background of the Anglo-Irish War. Colonel Hanna commented:

> The whole story is written around the political troubles in Southern Ireland in 1921, and in the opinion of the Board is too recent history to be a suitable subject for a film. It is a very controversial period and I strongly urge that the sad and unpleasant memories which both sides to the conflict share are best left alone and not raked up through the medium of the screen.[20]

The film was not made.

In 1934 Universal Pictures submitted a synopsis called *Sir Roger Casement* covering his career from his appointment to the consular service in 1895 to his trial and execution in 1916. Colonel Hanna remarked:

> Naturally most of it is devoted to Casement's activities during the war. He is held up to admiration as an Irish patriot dying for his ideals, rather than as an insignificant traitor to his country who paid the ordinary penalty for his offence. The story is continued slightly after Casement's death to show the setting up of the Irish Free State. I have no hesitation in reporting that a film of this subject would be extremely undesirable in this country and would be unlikely to receive our certificate.[21]

It was not made.

When RKO Radio Pictures submitted Sean O'Casey's play, *The Plough and The Stars* in 1935, Colonel Hanna was predictably appalled:

The language is impossible from a film standard. It is very coarse, full of swearwords and most of the political speeches would be prohibitive from our point of view. The play is clever, cynical and bitter. Excellent character studies of unpleasant characters. The rebellion in Easter Week 1916 evokes many sad and painful recollections and will always prove highly controversial. I am strongly of the opinion that it is undesirable to rouse these feelings through the medium of the cinema. The corporal and sergeant are not well-drawn types and rather tend to discredit the English army.[22]

But the company was anxious to proceed. Radio Pictures' representatives met with representatives of the Board, the President was consulted and it was agreed that the subject in itself was not prohibitive (the Easter Rising was nearly twenty years in the past) but the language must be cleaned up. In due course John Ford's film *The Plough and the Stars* emerged and was certificated for showing.

The kind of approach the BBFC preferred was exemplified by the Samuel Goldwyn production *Beloved Enemy*. A synopsis was submitted by United Artists in 1936 under the title *Covenant With Death*. It centred on the love of an Irish rebel leader for the daughter of an English negotiator at the time of independence. The censors concluded that if the love interest remained central and no details of the conflict between the two sides were shown it would be acceptable. A scenario now called *Love Your Enemy* was submitted on August 20, 1936 and the censor reported: 'I find nothing objectionable in this story. In spite of it being taken from recent history, the names are fictitious and in my opinion there is nothing to which the British or Irish Free State authorities could take exception.'[23] It was duly filmed and released in 1936 under the title *Beloved Enemy*.

Although handsomely produced the film was dubbed by one American reviewer: '*The Informer* in evening clothes'.[24] It emerged as a highly romanticised version of the career of Michael Collins grafted onto a fictional love story. Brian Aherne played the dashing Irish rebel leader Dennis Riordan who meets and falls in love with Lady Helen Drummond (Merle Oberon), daughter of the British peace negotiator. Their secret love affair runs parallel with the end of the rebellion, and when in 1921 Riordan is instrumental in securing a treaty which partitions Ireland and sets up the Free State, he is accused by hardline colleagues of selling out the republican cause. Campaigning for peace in Dublin, he is shot by his closest friend, and dies in the arms of Lady Helen. Concern at audience dissatisfaction led the studio to shoot an alternative happy ending, in which Dennis is wounded but survives. Although the original release print featured the unhappy ending, it is the happy ending which has been used in television prints of the film.

Basically it is the age-old 'Romeo and Juliet' theme, set against a recent political problem and arguing for peace and reconciliation.

In 1936 MGM submitted the scenario of *Parnell*. Colonel Hanna thought it 'undesirable'. But Miss Norah Shortt, fellow scriptreader and daughter of Edward Shortt, thought it acceptable as long as relatives of the people involved did not object.[25] The film was then passed uncut in 1937. But it became one of Hollywood's legendary flops: a lavishly staged but dull, lifeless and stodgy biopic, hamstrung from the first by the gross miscasting of two highly modern actors, Clark Gable, who plays Parnell with a broad American accent merely as Clark Gable, and, to a lesser extent Myrna Loy, whose long-suffering nobility as Kitty O'Shea was not what fans of her wise, witty and sophisticated wife in *The Thin Man* series wanted. The film foregrounds the love of Parnell for Kitty O'Shea and the scandal and divorce which ended his career. But it also covers the campaign for Home Rule, parliamentary encounters with Gladstone, battles within the Irish Party at Westminster and the Pigott forgery case. It also, however, includes several set-piece speeches in which Parnell denounces violence and urges the peaceful constitutional road to self-government. He dies to the strains of 'The Minstrel Boy' and is clearly depicted as a romantic hero vexed by the conflict of love and duty. It cost $1,427,000 to make and made a net loss of $637,000.[26]

In 1938 a synopsis for a film called *The Rising* about the Fenian Uprising in 1866–7 was submitted by a Miss Myrtle Whittaker.[27] No objection was raised to it, possibly because it was historical. Costume seems regularly to have blinded the censors to the existence of political comment, such as when having regularly banned films denouncing anti-Semitism when they were set in the present day, the censors passed the film *Jew Süss* which denounced anti-Semitism in eighteenth century Württemberg.

In 1939 a film treatment was submitted by Warner Bros. The story, set against the background of IRA resistance to the Free State, involved informing, a daughter discovering that her father is the IRA leader and an ambush wiping out the rebels. Colonel Hanna opposed it: 'An unhappy page of Irish history and I think it would be quite unpopular with the Free State government. Personally I strongly advise against production of this story as a film.' Miss Shortt, now Mrs Crouzet, saw no objection. A third scriptreader was brought in, perhaps to arbitrate, and thought it similar to two or three other films already passed, but wondered 'whether it would be advisable to publish a film of this subject while the recent outbreak of IRA outrages in Great Britain persist'.[28] Neither this film nor *The Rising* was made.

There is no record of RKO Radio Pictures submitting a scenario for perhaps the most celebrated Irish film of the 1930s, John Ford's *The Informer*. But Robertson indicates that 'RKO undertook extensive indirect consultations with the BBFC prior to production and cut over 4 minutes from the running time of the released version on June 6, 1935'.[29]

Significantly of the seven projects submitted to the Board at script stage, five were from Hollywood companies and the two British submissions were by individuals rather than film companies. This suggests that there was very little interest by the British film industry in Irish stories in the 1930s. The success of *The Informer* generated a flurry of interest in Hollywood but the box office failure of *The Plough and the Stars*, *Parnell* and *Beloved Enemy* rapidly put an end to Hollywood's interest.

The general attitude of the Board seems to have been a grudging willingness to accept the Irish 'Troubles' as a background as long as a personal story, usually a love story, was foregrounded. This remained the approach most favoured by Hollywood. The little known and rarely revived *The Key*, shot in 1933 and released in 1934, was directed by Michael Curtiz for Warner Bros. Set in Dublin in 1920, it featured undercover intelligence activity, hostage taking and Black and Tan brutality, but centred on a philandering British officer (William Powell) having an affair with the wife (Edna Best) of an intelligence officer (Colin Clive). He helps free the husband, taken hostage by the IRA, at the cost of a prison sentence for himself.

The formula of love story against tangled political background remained a popular approach as late as David Lean's *Ryan's Daughter* (1970), a kind of *Brief Encounter* with sex set against the background of the 'Troubles'. Ryan's daughter (Sarah Miles) is the unsatisfied wife of a local Irish schoolmaster (Robert Mitchum). She has a passionate affair with a shell-shocked British officer (Christopher Jones), which ends when he is killed. The film shows communal support for the IRA in a spectacular scene in which a whole village turns out to help bring smuggled arms ashore, but it depicts the darker side of communality in the revenge of the villagers against Rosie Ryan who is stripped and cropped by them for her sins before leaving the village with her forgiving husband.

Between 1841 and 1925, 4¾ million Irish people emigrated to the United States and the substantial Irish-American community that resulted never lost its hatred of British rule and its romantic memory of the 'Old Country'. There was a sizeable Irish-American element in Hollywood: writers, producers, directors, actors. Film was the ideal medium for them to dramatise their interpretation of Irish history. But the film industry traditionally sought to avoid controversy and, more seriously, Britain was the biggest market outside America for Holly-wood films, and films that were too overtly anti-British were deemed to be potentially bad box-office. Even after Ireland gained independence, the continued existence of the British Empire provided a potent image of the status quo which Hollywood usually sought to endorse.

But one of the most persistent of Irish-American directors in seeking to bring Ireland to the screen was John Ford. Born Sean O'Fearna in Cape Elizabeth, Maine, he was pure Irish on both sides of his family and retained a love of Ireland and hatred of British rule that he was to seek with considerable tenacity to translate into film.

Six films, made between 1926 to 1957, encapsulate Ford's vision. It was a vision of two Irelands: the Ireland of the 'Troubles', of darkness, suffering, tyranny and death, the Ireland of the struggle, the sacred just cause; and the Ireland of exiles' memories and poets' dreams, a peace-ful, happy, pastoral, communal, tradition-steeped, sun-lit Erin. The first Ireland is depicted in *Hangman's House*, *The Informer* and *The Plough and the Stars*; the second in *The Shamrock Handicap* and *The Quiet Man*, with the three-part *Rising of the Moon* linking the two and summarising his Irish world.[30]

Hangman's House (1928) is basically a melodrama about a forced marriage and its consequences, set during the 'Troubles'. The English are present but Ford neatly sidesteps their role by making his villains renegade Irishmen who serve the English interest. Ford can make his point about the occupation just as forcefully through them.

The hangman of the title is 'Hanging Judge' O'Brien. He dies, haunted by memories of cruelty and death, his malign presence reach-ing out from the grave to condemn his daughter Conn to a loveless marriage. His hold is at last broken when his castle, the symbol of the power he exercised in the name of the oppressor, goes up in flames and there is a vivid shot of his portrait eaten away by the fire to underline the final exorcism of his influence. The man chosen as Conn's hus-band, as someone acceptable to the English who can maintain her in the state to which she belongs, is John D'Arcy, a suave, slimy cosmo-politan ('From Paris, Madrid, Moscow – anywhere but the Ireland that bore him'). When he discovers that she really loves fresh-faced young patriot, Dermot, he shoots her horse after it has won a race. The incensed crowd of spectators turn on him and he has to be rescued by the English. But when he informs on the fugitive patriot, Hogan, he is thereafter shunned both by his countrymen and the English. Ulti-mately he is consumed by the fire that destroys the castle.

In contrast to the inflexible tyrant and rootless informer who repre-sent Irish collaborationism, the Irish patriot and Fordian hero par excel-lence is Denis Hogan (Victor McLaglen). There is something of that later Fordian hero Ethan Edwards of *The Searchers* in Hogan, exile, soldier, outlaw, who comes home for a while but leaves again at the end. In the opening scene of the film he is in North Africa, drinking and joking with his comrades in the officers' mess of a Foreign Legion fort, but the arrival of a letter announcing that his sister has been seduced and abandoned by a cad and has died prompts him to request a leave of absence. The cad inevitably turns out to be D'Arcy and justice is done on him.

Although Hogan has found a congenial place in a military unit, a typically Fordian home for homeless heroes, his longing for his real homeland makes his exile profoundly tragic. It prompts the most moving scene in the film. Having exacted his vengeance and united the star-crossed lovers Conn and Dermot, Hogan prepares to leave Ireland. The pale moon silvers the sea in the little fishing village where he will take ship. He bids Conn and Dermot farewell and the film ends with a long, expressive close-up of Hogan gazing after them as they leave. His face mirrors the deep melancholy, emphasised by the obvious happiness of the lovers, that he feels at having to leave the cool, green land he loves to return to the heat and sand of the desert. Visually the film is stunning, lit and photographed by George Schneidermann to give the constant impression of just that Ireland which Ford had in mind, the Ireland of bardic lore and Celtic myth, floating otherworldly in a sea of mist. Love of country and love of family are extolled and are seen as the casualties of the lurking English presence, casting its long shadow over this paradise.

A different sort of informer from D'Arcy is the central figure of one of Ford's most celebrated films, *The Informer* (1935). It is a film he had long wanted to make, and which he eventually persuaded RKO to agree to, following his surprise success with another offbeat film, *The Lost Patrol* (1934). The studio head, another Irish American and Anglophobe, Joseph Kennedy, was relucant to approve it. But Ford was able to shoot it in three weeks for under $250,000 using RKO contract players, standing sets and fog to cover any gaps. It functions on several levels at once, all of them revealing of aspects of Ford's thinking. It is at once a tale of the 'Troubles', an Expressionist drama of fog and shadow whose basic story is timeless and universal, and a Catholic parable of redemption and forgiveness.

The story, based on a novel by Liam O'Flaherty, was substantially altered in a way that clearly demonstrates Ford's priorities in depicting the Irish rebellion. As George Bluestone comments: 'What do these deletions, additions and alterations amount to? In general, they endow the characters with a nobility, honesty and reasonableness which the originals do not possess.'[31] IRA Commandant Dan Gallagher, who in

R.T.C. LIBRARY
LETTERKENNY

the book is a pitiless, sadistic despot, feared and mistrusted by his own organisation ('I believe in nothing fundamentally. And I don't feel pity.'), becomes in the film a handsome, upright, fair-minded, pipe-smoking and respected leader, who seeks justice and not vengeance. He is also in love with Mary McPhillip, and a couple of short, tender love scenes, although disliked by the critics, help round out his character and confirm its heroic transformation. The Katie Madden of the book is a drug addict and degenerate revelling in her degradation and wilfully betraying the informer Gypo to his pursuers; in the film she is a prosti- tute sympathetically treated in the tradition of Ford's fallen women, driven to the streets by poverty, genuinely loving Gypo and betraying him unwittingly. The Frankie McPhillip of the film, a likeable, clean- cut, fugitive patriot, who returns to Dublin to see his mother, is a distinct contrast to the brutalised murderer of the book who returns seeking money to finance his escape.

Even more interesting than the character changes are the two major structural changes, which are quintessential Ford. He moved the period of the film back in time from the 1922 Civil War to 1920 and the last years of British rule. The communists of the novel became the IRA and Ford was at pains to stress the regular military nature of this secret army. Men are addressed by their ranks, a full dress court martial is held for Gypo, the IRA headquarters with its row of rifles has the appearance of a genuine field post, and military discipline is enforced. Ford could have it no other way. Undisciplined revolt or sheer anarchy were no part of his world-view. If he were a rebel, as he claimed, Ford was a conservative one. For him the 'Irish rebellion' was a war of inde- pendence and he depicted it accordingly.

The killers of Frankie in Ford's version are the hated Black and Tans. For it is easier for Ford to tell a story in which the Irish fight the English rather than one in which the Irish fight the Irish. Though the story of Gypo Nolan, who betrays his friend to the British and is then tracked down and executed by the IRA, holds the foreground, the alien British presence remains threateningly in the background. One little scene early on contrives eloquently to convey the tragedy of 'occupied Ire- land'. On a street corner, a shabbily dressed tenor sings 'The Rose of Tralee', watched by a crowd of his countrymen. A British patrol passes, stops to frisk the singer and as they march off a solder flips a coin into his hand. Continuing his song, the singer twirls round and contemptu- ously flings the coin away. The melancholy lyricism of the song and the simple reflex act of defiance set against the search, the presence of the armed men and the poorly clad crowd of onlookers continue to symbolise the poetic soul of Ireland, oppressed but not crushed by foreign occupation. Thereafter the shadowy presence of British patrols remains a permanent but never obtruded reminder of this occupation, emerging into the foreground only once, when on information received they break into the McPhillip house and shoot the escaping Frankie. But even then a touch of humanity is permitted in the obvious distaste with which the English officer hands over the blood money to the treacherous Gypo.

The opening statement of the film makes it clear that the story also has a definite religious dimension. 'Then Judas repented himself and cast down the thirty pieces of silver and departed.' The story that follows charts the torment and confusion and eventual repentance of 'Judas' Gypo. The other characters take on analogous New Testament roles: Katie as Mary Magdalene, Frankie as Christ and Mrs McPhillip as the Mother of Christ.

While the film's themes are quintessential Ford, the style is broodingly Expressionist, giving it the dimensions of a universal predicament. Low-angle shots, low-key lighting, many close-ups and everywhere shadows and fog, giving the story a moody fatalism and teutonic intensity. But the menacing presence of the British troops throughout, the lyrical, melancholy thread of Irish melodies and the heroisation of the IRA never let the audience forget the Irish dimension.

It is interesting to compare Ford's film with the unjustly neglected silent British version of O'Flaherty's novel, directed in 1929 by the German film-maker Arthur Robison. Ironically Ford's version is far more Expressionist than that of Robison, himself the arch-Expressionist creator of *Shadows*. But like Ford's film, it is a work of pure cinema, making little use of dialogue titles. Robison employs a vividly fluid camera style and crisp, authoritative editing but there is no fog and little shadow.

Robison duly sets his film during the 1922 Civil War and although he includes many of the same episodes as Ford (the betrayal and shooting of Frankie, the visit to the wake, the betrayal of Katie, and Gypo's death in the church while seeking forgiveness), the motivations of the characters are different and the whole ambience of the film is at variance with Ford's. It is not a film about the 'Troubles'. It is not a Catholic parable. It is not even an exploration of the informer's psyche. It is a very characteristically Germanic drama of Fate, sexual passion and revenge. Concerned as he is with human emotions, Robison has no need to justify the legality of IRA activities and the 'execution' of Gypo. So he conspicuously omits the trial, which is the high point of Ford's film and legitimises the IRA's activities. Robison's protagonists are simply members of a faction in the Irish Civil War, carrying out vengeance on one of their number who has turned traitor.

Lars Hanson's Gypo is a very different figure from Victor McLaglen's pathetic, half-comprehending, brute-man. Hanson's Gypo is a flashing-eyed Byronic figure, a Romantic anti-hero dogged by Fate and doomed to an unhappy end, blood brother to Hanson's earlier and more celebrated incarnation of the title role in *Gosta Berling's Saga*. In the memorable finale, he emerges from Katie's room and descends the stairs to face his pursuers, pointing dramatically at his heart. They fall back in awe until Gallagher arrives to shoot him. This is in marked contrast to Ford's Gallagher who not only does not kill Gypo himself but comforts Katie as the sound of shooting is heard.

Throughout the film the motivations of the characters are different from those of Ford. Gypo and Frankie are rivals for Katie's affections in Robison's version. Gypo betrays Frankie when he believes Katie intends to go away with him. Katie betrays Gypo when she in turn believes that he plans to leave her for another prostitute. Robison uses an almost identical church and forgiveness finale as Ford but with none of the religious build-up and Christian analogy leading up to it.

The style and emphasis of Robison's film only serve to point up the distinctively Fordian characteristics of Ford's *Informer*. In *The Informer* these characteristics provide strength and coherence but when he stressed many of the same elements in *The Plough and the Stars* (1936), the result was one of his few resounding failures. The reasons for the film's failure tell us a lot about Ford. As it stands, *The Plough and the Stars* has none of the dramatic power of *The Informer*, the affectionate observation of *The Quiet Man* or the visual beauty of *Hangman's House*. Tradition has it that the film's failure was due in part at least to the casting of Preston Foster and Barbara Stanwyck in the leading roles, the price Ford allegedly had to pay for importing the Abbey Theatre players Barry Fitzgerald, Eileen Crowe, F. J. McCormick and Arthur Shields for supporting roles. In fact the two stars have little to do with the film's real failure, both turning in quite competent performances. The film collapses under the weight of the inherent ambiguities resulting from the Fordian conception of O'Casey's play.

The studio presumably sanctioned the film as a follow-up to the success of *The Informer* which had garnered ecstatic reviews and won four Oscars. *The Plough and the Stars* certainly employed many of the same technical crew and actors as the earlier film. The censors demanded a toning down of the language and the box office demanded the softening of criticism of the British role in the Easter Rising. But the film's real failure lies in the way Ford has subverted the play for his own nationalist purposes. O'Casey's play has humanity, warmth and humour, backed by a raw tenement realism, the feel of life in the backstreets as the rebellion rages. But Ford and his scenarist Dudley Nichols, in cutting the text and opening out the action, disastrously shift the play's emphasis. The 1916 Easter Rising, which is the background to O'Casey's play, is in the foreground of Ford's film and this cannot but express his personal preoccupation with the 'Troubles'. He could not resist the opportunity to dramatise the central myth of the Irish struggle, and so grafted it on to a play which could not accommodate it within its own terms of reference. The Easter Rising is depicted unequivocally in terms of heroism, sacrifice and the homeland. Events which are simply reported in the play are shown in the film: the proclamation of the Republic by Padraig Pearse, the siege of the General Post Office, the execution of James Connolly.

Yet, as in *The Informer*, Ford shows himself to be a conservative rebel, concerned to legitimise the Rising as a war of liberation. In a stirring and characteristic sequence Ford depicts the gathering of the rebel army. It is done with all the pageantry usually associated in Ford's world with the US cavalry. Soldiers march in, bearing flags; boy pipers play 'The Wearing of the Green'; the troops, drawn up in ranks, give the Republican salute. Even the women and children who watch are arranged in ranks, conveying the impression of the entire population under arms, fighting for freedom. They listen to a rousing speech from 'General' Connolly. Connolly, in fact a union leader, is depicted throughout in exclusively military terms. Never seen without his uniform, always addressed as 'general', he is played as a soldierly archetype and photographed from the apotheosising low-angle which Ford always reserved for his great men and leaders. Catholic imagery and symbols are deployed to sanctify the struggle: the priest with his cross in the Post Office, the Madonna-like shawled women in their posed attitudes of mourning, and most vividly, the death of a boy sniper, shot from the roof by British troops and sliding down from it, arms outstretched like a suffering Christ.

The box office dictated that in some way the British must be exculpated. But Ford could not forgive. So he undercuts each conciliatory gesture towards the British. Connolly is courteously treated by the British as he is led out to be shot, forgives his enemies as they fire but is taken to his death in a wheelchair, an image which transcends all the mutual soldierly courtesies. When the socialist Covey denounces the British troops searching the tenement, a British corporal replies: 'I'm a socialist myself. But I have to do my duty. A man's a man and he must fight for his country.' But this is offset by Fluther's passionate defence of sniping as the only recourse of a handful of unarmed patriots against the armed might of an empire.

The uncompromising tragic ending of the play, with both Jack Clitheroe and Mrs Burgess killed, is transformed by Ford into an optimistic finale. Jack and Mrs Burgess survive. The film instead ends with the funeral of the young girl Mollser, which comes to symbolise the dead hopes of the Rising. But as Jack and Nora follow the coffin, they see the Tricolour being torn down from the roof of the Post Office and flung into the streets. Nora asks 'When will it all end' and Jack returns 'This is only the beginning. We'll live to see Ireland free.' It is a defiant and noble ending, totally at odds with the tenor of the play but in keeping with Ford's heroic view of the Irish struggle for independence.

Yet what glory is there in a group of drunken, cowardly braggarts, Fluther, Uncle Peter and the Covey, who sit around playing cards, who plunder shops and for all their talk do not lift a finger to help the cause? In the context of the play, there is nothing wrong for this is their normal way of life and the great events were reported and not seen. But in the context of the film, there is. Funny as some of the incidents are, the humour seems ill-timed. The characters seem suddenly stage Irish stereotypes, the knockabout, the drunkenness, the pub brawls and the 'Oirish' banter seem trivial when set against the great events now being seen and not merely reported. For once, and this is rare in Ford, the humour seems intrusive and obtruded, not growing naturally out of characters and action as it does in *The Quiet Man*. Perhaps after all humour was out of place when Ford was dealing with a subject so tragic and so close to his heart as the Easter Rising. Equally, perhaps, the very absence of humour, which Ford latterly thought a weakness, is one of the strengths of *The Informer*.

To be true to the play and to provide an internal coherence to the film, *The Plough and the Stars* would need to be closer in conception to *The Informer*, with the private drama of the protagonists holding the centre of the stage. But again this was difficult, for Ford was clearly out of sympathy with the predicament of the leading characters, Jack and Nora Clitheroe. Nora's behaviour is at odds with Ford's fundamental conception of a woman's role and duty. The film opens with her trying to persuade Jack not to go to the meeting of the Citizen Army. When the Rising begins and Jack reports for duty, she denounces it and runs hysterically through the streets looking for him until halted and denounced at the barricades by Irish women, who are quietly standing by their husbands and effacing their own feelings in the interests of their country. Nora finally becomes tiresome, her personal concerns petty beside the great issues at stake around her. Ford defines the roles of men and women earlier in the film in a speech not in the play: 'A woman is never happy unless she has a man beside her. It's a woman's nature to love, just as it's a man's nature to fight and neither can help it more than the other.' But is it not also, in Ford's cosmology, a woman's duty not to interfere with a man's desire to fight? This is what Nora does and Ford has little sympathy with her.

A similar and even stronger ambiguity lies in the looting episode. Ford has consistently attacked mob violence in his films, yet in this film he compromises his principles by treating the looting episode simply as a lovable and comical manifestation of the Irish character. But this places a visible strain on the sequence, which typifies the strain evident throughout the film in the unresolvable differences between Ford's world-view and that of O'Casey, and in the dictates of plot and character which Ford finds in some places embarrassingly unsympathetic. The film finally disintegrates under the strain of these opposing tendencies and the likelihood is that even without casting, cutting and censorship problems, it would have done so.

When the film was completed, RKO executives were dissatisfied with it. While Ford was away on holiday, they sought to improve the film by making Jack and Nora unmarried lovers. Contract director George Nicholls Jr was called in to reshoot scenes involving Foster and Stanwyck to make this point. Ford was furious but was powerless to do anything. RKO showed their revised version in the United States; but Ford's version was shown in Britain and Ireland and this version is the one that has survived and is now shown on television.[32]

The third and final episode of the three-part *Rising of the Moon* (1957) is based on Lady Gregory's eponymous play. Originally a short dialogue piece between a policeman and a fugitive on the quayside, it is developed by Ford and his scenarist Frank Nugent into a dramatic episode constituting Ford's final statement on the 'Troubles'.

The first part of this episode, not in the original play, details the escape of the Irish prisoner and does so with a stress, as in *The Plough and Stars*, on the Catholic nature of the struggle and the sanction leant to it by the faith and the concept of the total popular participation. Outside the prison a line of men and women shuffle in endless procession, telling their beads and praying for Sean Curran, the patriot hero held by the British. He escapes disguised as a nun, the veil functioning almost as a mystical means of preserving him. Sean, disguised now as a ballad singer, incarnation of the precious Irish heritage, is recognised on the quayside by a police sergeant (Denis O'Dea), who talks to him about the song 'The Rising of the Moon' and then strolls away singing the song, allowing Curran to escape to the waiting ship and demonstrating that he is one with the struggle.

The other side of the image of Ireland, the positive side, is the Old Ireland first evoked in *The Shamrock Handicap* (1926). Its plot is a familiar one: impoverished Irish nobleman and daughter travel to America, enter their horse in the eponymous race, win a fortune and return to Ireland. The opening section is a loving, sentimentalised evocation of Old Ireland, a land drenched in tradition and *noblesse oblige*.

It is an idealised land of penurious but good-hearted aristocratic land-lords, innocent young lovers, faithful retainers and loyal tenants. Community feeling is encapsulated in the bustling details of market day in the little country town. The picture is one of a peaceful, traditional, agrarian society, slightly run down (several ruins are in evidence) and sometimes in debt (a condition common to lord and tenants) but happy in shared traditional values, the beauties of the landscape and the feeling of belonging. There is no sign of any alien English presence to mar the Arcadian idyll.

It was this image to which Ford returned in *The Quiet Man* (1952) and which marked the first occasion on which he actually went to Ireland to shoot. It is the ultimate celebration of an unchanging rural Ireland: white-painted cottages, rolling hills and verdant meadows studded with reminders of the past like the venerable Celtic cross. Over all pours a cascade of Irish folk melody.

Significantly the Quiet Man, Sean Thornton (John Wayne) is an American, making the transition from the free and easy democratic society of the United States to the strongly ritualised and traditionalist society of his forebears. He acquires the family cottage and marries a story-book Irish colleen, Mary Kate Danaher (Maureen O'Hara). The society he enters is agrarian and communal. There are no real leaders. In so far as guidance is needed, it is provided by the Catholic priest. It is a male-dominated world. The women invariably stand aside in shawled groups; one of them hands Sean a stick 'to beat the lovely lady with' when Mary Kate rebels. Mary Kate herself is defined by her role as home-maker.

Drinking and fighting become ritual elements affirming rather than destroying community spirit. Drinking is used to seal bargains, to cement friendships, to welcome friends and visitors. Sean is willing to participate in the drinking but refuses to fight. His reason is that he killed a man in a fight in America but he does not explain his reluctance and it is interpreted as cowardice. But Ford makes it clear that there are occasions when a man must fight – here to preserve his marriage, threatened when his brother-in-law 'Red Will' Danaher (Victor McLaglen) withholds Mary Kate's dowry. Sean fights, but not vindictively. He fights in defence of a tradition and in accordance with the Marquis of Queensberry rules. Ford handles the fight as a comic marathon donnybrook, in which the protagonists gleefully knock seven bells out of each other to the strains of an Irish jig and as a community ritual, participated in by the village and presided over by the priest. The fight is the film's triumphant high-point, a rousing and irresistible justification of community, tradition and masculinity. It signals Sean's final integration into the community.

[46]

Jim Sheridan's *The Field* (1990), based on John B. Keane's play, is almost precisely the dark mirror image of *The Quiet Man*. The visiting American (Tom Berenger), known as the 'Yank', is not integrated into the community. He remains an outsider, seeking to acquire the land long rented by 'Bull' McCabe (Richard Harris), who puts him in the same category as previous exploitative outsiders – the English – whom Bull helped to drive out. In the big fight, unlike the one played by Ford for laughs, Bull kills the Yank. Bull is the equivalent of Red Will Danaher, here obsessed to the point of madness with the land and despising the rootless tinkers who lost their land, the invading English who sought to take over the land and the Yank who wishes the acquire his field. The priest, who in Ford's community is a leader and a full participant in community rituals, is here an outsider – 'just passing through' says Bull. He sides with the Yank and locks the congregation out of the church after the murder. The widow who owns the field, unlike her counterpart in Ford who marries Red Will, is here hounded out of the village by a campaign of persecution by Bull's son Tadgh. Tadgh is eventually killed too, and Bull now has no family to whom to hand over the land for which he has fought and killed. This is a grim, tragic, relentless story, without humour, of a land cursed by its past (famine, emigration, English occupation, poverty). It is also almost the cinema's Shavian riposte to Ford's Boucicaultian vision.

Ford's final Irish film, also made in Ireland, was *The Rising of the Moon* (1957). It was narrated by Tyrone Power, film star great-grandson of the eponymous actor who helped to transform the Irish stereotype. It was a minor and unsuccessful work, made by Ford as a labour of love: 'I made it just for fun and enjoyed it very much'.[33] In addition to Lady Gregory's short play, it also included adaptations of Frank O'Connor's story 'The Majesty of the Law' and Michael McHugh's play *A Minute's Wait*. Like *The Quiet Man*, these stories stress the importance of tradition, ritual, communality, drink and reverence for the Church. It is interesting and significant then that in March 1958 Limerick County Council unanimously approved the suggestion of one of its members, Mr D. P. Quish, that the Irish government should 'contact all countries with which Ireland has diplomatic relations and have *The Rising of the Moon* withdrawn from exhibition'. The reason for this motion was that 'the film is a vile production and a travesty of the Irish people'.[34]

By one of those ironies with which the history of Hollywood is replete, Ford, while making his celebrations of Irish freedom-fighting for RKO Radio Pictures, was contractually obliged by 20th Century-Fox to make a trilogy of films celebrating the British Empire in India: *Black Watch* (1929), *Wee Willie Winkie* (1937) and *Four Men and a Prayer* (1938), the first two of which starred Victor McLaglen who, though frequently cast as an Irishman, particularly by Ford, was in fact not Irish at all. According to his autobiography *Express to Hollywood* (1934), he was born in Tunbridge Wells, the son of a South African bishop who spent most of his life doing missionary work in the East End of London. McLaglen served in the British army during the First World War and was Assistant Provost-Marshal in Mesopotamia after the fall of Baghdad in March 1917. Both before and after the war he travelled extensively in the Empire, working as a gold prospector in Canada, a pearler in the South Seas, a boxing coach in India and a hunter in Africa. But his first love was boxing. He fought as a prize-fighter all over North America and eventually in England where he was spotted by a film producer and signed up to act in films in 1920. Before long, he was established in Hollywood where he became a fixture in films. While on the one hand in Hollywood he played the Irish free-dom-fighter in *Hangman's House*, the hapless Gypo in *The Informer* and later 'Red Will' Danaher in *The Quiet Man*, he also played with evident authenticity a tough professional soldier in the armies of the Empire in *The Lost Patrol*, *Wee Willie Winkie* and *Gunga Din*.[35]

Ford's involvement with the Empire goes back to the earliest days of his film career. He assisted his elder brother Francis Ford, director and star of two now lost films with intriguing imperial settings. In 1915 Francis Ford directed *The Doorway of Destiny* in which he played Colonel Patrick Feeney, with John Ford as his brother Edward. It told the story of an Irish regiment sent on a suicide mission by the British in India and assaulting a sepoy citadel waving an Irish flag, made by Feeney's mother. In the same year *The Campbells Are Coming* appro-priated the plot of Boucicault's *Jessie Brown*, with Francis Ford playing Nana Sahib and the heroic Scots regiments relieving Lucknow.

But just as he subverted his Irish stories to stress his heroic vision of the Irish rebellion, so Ford in *The Black Watch* and *Wee Willie Winkie* slanted his imperial films away from the English and towards the Scots, with whom he could feel greater sympathy. Both films featured Scot-tish regiments, highlighted the regimental ritual, military comradeship and service that meant so much to Ford, and utilised musical scores of traditional Scottish airs.

Four Men and a Prayer, one of Ford's least favourite films, is an incredible thriller, in which four sons chase off across the world seek-ing to clear the name of their murdered father, an English colonel, cashiered from the Indian army for gun-running. Ford said of it: 'I just didn't like the story or anything else about it ... I kidded them slightly'.[36] In fact he kidded them more than slightly, sending the film up unmercifully wherever possible. But he responds warmly to one epi-sode when two of the brothers arrive in India to interview their father's batman, who turns out to be Corporal Mulcahy (Barry Fitzgerald). Someone calls Mulcahy an Englishman and he starts a fight which rapidly develops into a saloon brawl, carried on to the strains of an Irish jig.

Ford's own feelings about British imperialism were made much clearer in two other films. In *Mary of Scotland* (1936), he celebrates the Catholic Scottish Queen Mary as a martyr to Protestant and English imperialism and intolerance. *The Hurricane* (1937), though ostensibly about a South Sea island under French rule, is a deeply felt indictment of colonial rule and by implication, British imperialism, with the island of Manikura functioning as a substitute Ireland.

The British cinema's equivalent of Ford as a director returning regularly to Irish themes is Brian Desmond Hurst. Hurst was a Belfast-born Protestant who worked with Ford in Hollywood in the silent days before returning to Britain to launch his own directorial career in 1932. Despite working in a wide variety of genres which include adaptations of Dickens (*Scrooge*) and Ivor Novello (*Glamorous Night*), he managed a number of Irish subjects, including adaptations of Synge (*Riders to the Sea* (1935) and *Playboy of the Western World* (1962)), and *Irish Hearts* (1934), a drama about a small town Irish doctor fighting a typhus epidemic.[37]

In 1936 he was asked by the Head of Production at British International to take over at short notice *Ourselves Alone*, a production which had run into difficulties under director Walter Summers. Hurst brought in Irish playwright Denis Johnston to rework the script, and took over and completed the film. It emerges as a Fordian drama of the 'Troubles', garnished with Irish songs sung by popular balladeer Cavan O'Connor. It conforms to the preferred BBFC model of foregrounding a love affair: RIC inspector John Hannay (John Lodge) and army Intelligence officer Captain Guy Wiltshire (John Loder), are both rivals in love for Maureen Elliott of Castle Elliott. In the end Hannay resigns her to Guy, taking on responsibility for shooting her brother (actually shot by Guy) and earning the admiration of his sergeant who says he's done a wonderful thing: 'You've seen a miracle in Ireland – two people out of three who are going to be happy'.

The film seeks to strike a balance between the sides. On the British side, the gentle, pipe-smoking gentleman Wiltshire who is reluctant to be in Ireland is contrasted with Inspector Hannay, keen to pursue the IRA ruthlessly and played in such a bad-tempered and brusque manner by John Lodge as to evoke no audience sympathy. On the IRA side, hardline Commandant Connolly (Clifford Evans), who believes 'Hell itself could be no worse than Ireland under English rule' and favours total war against the English, is contrasted with Maureen's brother, Terence Elliott, who is the legendary IRA commander 'Mick O'Day', preferring to tie up rather than shoot captured British soldiers and wishing to spare civilians from the consequences of IRA violence. The title itself becomes an ironic commentary on the Irish situation as Wiltshire tells another officer: 'Sinn Fein – "Ourselves Alone". It ought to be our motto – we're the ones who are alone.' But sympathy tilts towards the Irish: emphasised by the successful hunt for the obligatory informer, Hennessy, and the characterisation of dedicated patriot Mick O'Day, charming and likeable, fighting for love of Ireland and freedom and seeking to avoid unnecessary bloodshed but killed by the English.

After the war, Hurst directed an adaptation of Daphne du Maurier's nineteenth-century Irish family saga, *Hungry Hill* (1946). Constructed within the conventions of the three generation family saga and including romances, marriages, deaths and separations, it is almost an allegory of Ireland intertwining the fortunes of the wealthy Protestant ascendancy family the Brodricks and the dispossessed Catholic Irish peasant family the Donovans. The tension between them and their mutual dependency run through the film.

The Brodricks of Clonmore Castle take over and exploit the copper deposits on Hungry Hill, claimed by the Donovans as their own. 'Copper John' Brodrick (Cecil Parker) denounces the Donovans for failing to exploit the resources and highlights the difference of outlook: Protestantism, work, wealth, progress, exploitation of natural resources against Catholicism, tradition, contentment, ecology. It leads to violent confrontation when Old Donovan stirs up the people against the mine and a gunpowder explosion at the mine kills both him and Copper John's younger son. Eventually 'Wild John', Copper John's grandson, (Dermot Walsh), wants to close down the mine when it begins to fail. But the locals, who now depend on it for a livelihood, want to keep it open and a Donovan leads the opposition to closure. In the ensuing violence, Wild John is killed. But the faithful family retainer Old Tim persuades his mother Fanny in the interests of reconciliation not to demand Sam Donovan's hanging. She expresses hope for peaceful reconciliation and co-existence of the Donovans and Brodricks in future, and by extension of Catholics and Protestants in Ireland.

There is one particularly memorable scene at a wedding at which the English are waltzing sedately with the locals looking on from the door. A fiddler arrives, strikes up a jig and suddenly everyone lets rip, spilling out onto the lawn and dancing wildly until they drop – conventions, differences forgotten, English and Irish, Catholic and Protestant carried away by the native music of Ireland. It is an exhilarating moment.

But then by the same paradox as befell Ford, Hurst at the same time as tackling Irish subjects was also caught up in the cinematic celebration of Empire. In the 1930s he had been set to direct Alexander Korda's

epic film version of *Lawrence of Arabia* showing Lawrence as an imperial hero, a film cancelled due to unrest in the Middle East and objec-
tions from the Turkish Embassy to the depiction of the Turks.[38] He
produced in 1950 the definitive film version of Thomas Hughes's
classic *Tom Brown's Schooldays* about the education of the archetypal
Victorian imperial gentleman in 1850. He directed *Simba* (1955), an
unsparing denunciation of Mau Mau atrocities in a Kenya struggling
for independence.

Violence has been integral to the Irish myth. Even comic films stress
its centrality to the Irish psyche. The entire action of *The Quiet Man* is
based on the idea that 'a real man' fights and it ends with a marathon
donnybrook. Mario Zampi's comedy *Happy Ever After* (1954) centres
largely on the attempts (bungled and unsuccessful) of the villagers of
Rathbarney to kill off a caddish new squire (David Niven), who has
stopped poaching, called in debts, ejected tenants and disbanded the
hunt. Old Mother Riley, in fifteen popular slapstick comedies (1936–
52), celebrated the combative Irish washerwoman as comic anti-heroine.
The persona was developed from a classic stage sketch 'Bridget's Night-
Out' in which a violent row between mother and daughter resulted in
the smashing of all the crockery on the kitchen. Arthur Lucan, who
plays Old Mother Riley, though English-born took his name from a
Dublin dairy, was popular in Ireland and of course formed a team with
his Dublin-born wife Kitty McShane, who played his daughter in the
act.

Violence has inevitably run through films. Chronologically perhaps
the earliest is *The Private Lives of Elizabeth and Essex* (1939), which
includes a brief Irish section, in which Queen Elizabeth I (Bette Davis),
after learning of the massacre of the English army by Irish rebels, toys
with the idea of abandoning Ireland, only to be reminded that if she
does, Spain will use it as a base against England. This reinforces the
very real strategic justification for English rule over Ireland. Elizabeth
memorably replies that it is not worth the effort involved in holding 'a
few acres of fever-smitten bog and a handful of tattered peasants who
only want to be left in peace to cut each others' throats'. But she is
persuaded to send Essex who is outgeneralled and outwitted by the Earl
of Tyrone, played by Alan Hale as a blarneying stage Irishman with a
broad Hollywood Irish brogue.

The Fighting Prince of Donegal (1966), a Walt Disney swashbuckler
filmed in Ireland and based on a novel by Robert T. Reilly, featured the
campaign of Red Hugh O'Donnell, Prince of Donegal (Peter McEnery)
against the forces of Elizabeth I. Within the conventions of the swashbuckler, this film is uncompromising. Negotiation is no good; oppression must be fought. Hugh plans negotiation but the Viceroy tells him

'Actions speak louder than words in politics', and he learns from this that one must fight and he does 'for a belief, a faith, a necessity'. But even within the structure of Irish freedom-lovers under traditional aristocratic leadership against English oppression, the Irish are still depicted as booze-loving, dog-loving and combative, the final celebratory banquet ending as a massive punch-up.

Douglas Sirk's elegant and exciting *Captain Lightfoot* (1955), a Hollywood film shot on location in Ireland, centres squarely on Irish resistance to English occupation. The screenplay by W. R. Burnett and Oscar Brodney presses all the romantic apparatus of the classic highwayman drama into the rebel cause (gentleman highwaymen robbing the rich to give to the poor, coach hold-ups, daring disguises, narrow escapes, the playful outwitting of the dunderheaded authorities). But it is effortlessly blended with the classic ingredients of Irish resistance drama (communal support, violence, the role of the informer) and calls for activism. The impulsive hero, Michael Martin, nicknamed Captain Lightfoot (Rock Hudson), embodies this activism. He quarrels with the leader of the local patriot group Regis O'Donnell (Denis O'Dea) who believes in passive resistance, and goes to Dublin where he joins forces with the head of the Irish resistance, Captain Thunderbolt (Jeff Morrow). But it is Regis rather than Michael who is converted. For when Michael is captured and imprisoned, Regis is responsible for breaking him out after fighting off the English guards.[39]

Both *Lightfoot* and *Donegal* uncompromisingly endorse armed resistance. But an historical setting has always been seen – quite erroneously – to distance a film from contemporary problems by implying that it is all in the past. Myths are fed by history, and history is often rewritten to conform with myths. In British films since independence, Ireland has come to be almost synonymous with the IRA, which has figured as a locus of violence. The IRA has tried intermittently since 1921 to seek to reunite the two parts of Ireland by violence and this has coloured almost all depictions of Ireland. The message, however, has been consistently the liberal democratic one of rejection of violence with *Odd Man Out* (1947) and *The Gentle Gunman* (1952) tracing the destructive effects of violence, and *Shake Hands with the Devil* (1959) and *A Terrible Beauty* (1960) showing the IRA leaders as psychopaths and centring on individual IRA members redeemed by love and renouncing violence. Recent British films set in the 1920s have been strongly informed by post-colonial guilt and have stressed the violent consequences of the English presence in Ireland: thus, for instance, *Ascendancy*, *The Dawning* and *Fools of Fortune*. Launder and Gilliat's excellent *Captain Boycott* (1947) celebrated the constructive alternative to violence. It tells the story of Captain Boycott (Cecil Parker), highlighting the evils of landlordism in such a way as to endorse the non-violent alternative which succeeds in defeating and routing him. The Land League of Parnell, which seeks change in Ireland by peaceful means, is represented in the village by the publican and the priest, the potent alliance of Church and pub, the twin centres of the community. The hero, farmer Hugh Davin (Stewart Granger), who is first seen train- ing men for violence, is converted to peaceful methods by a powerful speech from Parnell (Robert Donat), urging ostracism of those who take over cottages of evicted tenants. The film seeks to be fair to everyone. The commander of the British troops indignantly tells Boycott: 'You cannot make British soldiers fight for what any fool can see is an unjust cause'. Even Boycott in the end helps Davin save threatened tenants. But the message is clear: non-violence is the way.

It is fighting which provides the link with the rest of the Empire. For the Irish soldier was ubiquitous in the armies of the Empire. Irish soldiers participated in the army at every level from celebrated generals to private soldiers. H. J. Hanham points out that 'Ireland throughout the nineteenth century supplied more than its share of the army'.[40] The army was seen as a major source of employment for the Irish, and the Irish soldier has been a figure of popular cultural myth from Shake- speare's MacMorris, who participates in the army of Henry V, to Kipling's 'Soldiers Three', one of whom is the Irishman Mulvaney. The Irish soldier has been a common feature of imperial epics. In *Soldiers Three* (1951), a direct adaptation of Kipling, he was played by Cyril Cusack, in *Four Men and a Prayer* (1938) by Barry Fitzgerald and in *The Lost Patrol* (1934) by J. M. Kerrigan, for instance.

Links with Ireland stretched to other parts of the Empire. Thorold Dickinson's *The High Command* (1937), a neat imperial thriller, opens in Ireland in 1921 with Major Sangye shooting in self-defence a fellow officer who has accused him of being his wife's lover. The death is passed off as the work of the IRA but years later when the major is General Sir John Sangye V.C. and commanding British forces in a West African colony, the past comes back to haunt him. In *Sword in the Desert* (1949), a vigorous Hollywood action picture celebrating the Jew- ish resistance in Palestine after the Second World War, the British are shown as an army of occupation and the Jews are assisted by a comical IRA terrorist (Liam Redmond), gleefully planting landmines while indulging in the broadest 'Oirish' blarney. Fortunately he is killed off in a raid on a British army camp.

Elsewhere, Irish rebellion is displaced into Australia. One of Holly- wood's rare excursions into Australian history, *Captain Fury* (1939), featured a transported Irish rebel Michael Fury (Brian Aherne) who organises a band of bushrangers to challenge the tyranny of a local land-

lord (George Zucco). Billed as 'the story of a pioneer who fought to preserve the integrity of a nation which had condemned him', the film is
basically an Australian western which legitimises the rebellion when
the Governor pardons Fury for having exposed the machinations of the
tyrant.

Ned Kelly (1970) had Mick Jagger as an effete, Irish-accented bush-
ranger mincing his way unconvincingly through the role of a Marxist
Robin Hood, robbing the rich to give to the poor, burning mortgages
and planning a Free Irish Republic in New South Wales. The police are
brutal and repressive, the law unjust, the upper classes greedy and
oppressive. The crude caricatures and heavy-handed dialectic mingled
uneasily with visual lyricism and the inherent mythic power of the
story.

There has been cultural continuity between the Ireland projected in
the stage melodramas, popular ballads and novels, and the Ireland of
the cinema. But throughout that image has been conditioned by the
presence of the Empire, whether Ireland is seen as part of it or struggling to escape from it. There have been two prevailing, complemen-
tary images: a peaceful, pastoral, rural, traditional and communal Ireland,
an Arcadian image idealised because it is untainted by the English presence, and a darker – literally, since it often takes place at night – more
violent and often urban Ireland, struggling against English occupation.
Of Irishness, there have been several predominating characteristics,
but often seen, as Gilley suggested, from different perspectives. Pre-
eminent is violence, which can be viewed positively as freedom-fighting or negatively as terrorism, comically as an expression of natural
high spirits or in gender terms as a manifestation of masculinity, but
also imperially, as a displacement of a racial characteristic into a
totally different arena whether (as in India) to support the empire or (as
in Australia) to undermine it. Then there is humour, which can be
deployed against the Irish in the form of the booze and blarney 'thick
paddy' stereotype or by the Irish against the English as a quick-witted,
high-spirited subversion of stereotype. Finally there is communality,
usually seen positively, whether as supportive of traditional social
structure or resistance to the British, but sometimes negatively, as hostile to outsiders. However they are interpreted, the characteristics
remain constant and, as Shaw suggested, are taken up and perpetuated
by each new generation as the correct way to behave and to express
their Irishness. That is the power of popular culture.

Notes

1 On Irish cinema and depictions of Ireland in cinema see Kevin Rockett, Luke Gibbons & John Hill, *Cinema and Ireland*, London, 1987; and Anthony Slide, *The Cinema and Ireland*, Jefferson, NC, and London, 1988.
2 L. P. Curtis Jr, *Anglo-Saxons and Celts*, Bridgeport, CT, 1968.
3 The quotations are taken from *ibid.*, pp. 51, 84–5. On the attitudes in Lancashire see Neville Kirk, *The Growth of Working Class Reformism in Mid-Victorian England*, London, 1985; and Steven Fielding, *Class and Ethnicity: Irish Catholics in England*, Buckingham, 1993.
4 Sheridan Gilley, 'English attitudes to the Irish in England 1780–1900', in Colin Holmes (ed.), *Immigrants and Minorities in British Society*, London, 1978, pp. 81–110
5 *Ibid.*, p. 85
6 On the stage Irishman see G. C. Duggan, *The Stage Irishman*, Dublin, 1937; J. O. Bartley, *Teague, Shenkin and Sawney*, Cork, 1954; and Annelise Truninger, *Paddy and the Paycock: a Study of the Stage Irishman from Shakespeare to O'Casey*, Berne, 1976.
7 Bartley, *Teague, Shenkin and Sawney*, p. 167.
8 Michael R. Booth, 'Irish landscape in the Victorian Theatre', in Andrew Carpenter (ed.), *Place, Personality and the Irish Writer*, New York, 1977, pp. 159–89.
9 Miriam Allen De Ford, *Thomas Moore*, Boston, 1967, p. 33.
10 George Bernard Shaw, *Our Theatres in the Nineties*, II, London, 1932, pp. 29–30.
11 George Bernard Shaw, *The Prefaces*, London, 1934, p. 439.
12 Richard Allen Cave, 'Staging the Irishman', in J. S. Bratton *et al.*, *Acts of Supremacy: the British Empire and the Stage 1790–1930*, Manchester, 1991, pp. 62–128.
13 'Jessie Brown', *Plays by Dion Boucicault* (ed. Peter Thomson), Cambridge, 1984, pp 101–32.
14 Charles Townshend, *Political Violence in Ireland*, Oxford, 1983, p. 1.
15 Slide, *The Cinema and Ireland*, pp. 99–108
16 Rockett, Gibbons & Hill, *Cinema and Ireland*, p. 23.
17 *Ibid.*, pp. 12–16.
18 In the majority of the films, discussed, the 1919–21 conflict is characterised as one between the IRA and the 'Black and Tans', although the latter, British ex-service recruits to the Royal Irish Constabulary, only constituted a part of the Crown forces. See Charles Townshend, *The British Campaign in Ireland 1919–1921*, Oxford, 1975, p. 94.
19 J. C. Robertson, *The British Board of Film Censors*, London, 1985, p. 86.
20 BBFC Scenario Reports 1933, no. 128.
21 BBFC Scenario Reports 1934, no. 349. A silent film, *Whom the Gods Destroy* (1916), which was loosely based on Casement's career, had run into problems with the British censors.
22 BBFC Scenario Reports 1935, no. 415.
23 BBFC Scenario Reports 1936, no. 40.
24 Alvin H. Marrill, *Samuel Goldwyn Presents*, London, 1976, p. 172.
25 BBFC Scenario Reports 1936, no. 77.
26 H. Mark Glancy, 'MGM film grosses, 1924–1948', *Historical Journal of Film, Radio and Television* XII (1992), microfiche.
27 BBFC Scenario Reports 1938, no. 65.
28 BBFC Scenario Reports 1939, no. 28.
29 Robertson, *British Board of Film Censors*, p. 88.
30 On Ford, see Tag Gallagher, *John Ford: the Man and his Films*, Berkeley & Los Angeles, 1986; Peter Bogdanovich, *John Ford*, Berkeley & Los Angeles, 1978; Dan Ford, *The Unquiet Man*, London, 1979; Lindsay Anderson, *About John Ford*, London, 1981; John Baxter, *The Cinema of John Ford*, London, 1971; Andrew Sinclair, *John Ford*, London, 1979. There would have been a seventh film, *Young Cassidy* (1965),

recreating the Dublin youth of Sean O'Casey, but Ford shot only ten minutes before falling ill. The film was completed by Jack Cardiff.

31 George Bluestone, *Novels into Films*, Berkeley & Los Angeles, 1968, p. 77.
32 Al DiOrio, *Barbara Stanwyck*, London, 1984, p. 91.
33 Bogdanovich, *John Ford*, p. 143.
34 Slide, *The Cinema and Ireland*, p. 83.
35 On the context of imperial cinema see Jeffrey Richards, *Visions of Yesterday*, London, 1973.
36 Bogdanovich, *John Ford*, p. 69.
37 On Brian Desmond Hurst, see Brian McIlroy, 'British film-making in the 1930s and 1940: the example of Brian Desmond Hurst', *Film criticism*, XVI (1991–92), pp. 67–83.
38 The scripts of films likely to offend 'friendly foreign governments' were regularly submitted to the relevant London embassies. See Jeffrey Richards, *Age of the Dream Palace*, London, 1984, p. 122.
39 On Celtic fringe swashbucklers, see Jeffrey Richards, *Swordsmen of the Screen*, London, 1977, pp. 141–8.
40 H. J. Hanham, 'Religion and nationality in the mid-Victorian army', in M. R. D. Foot (ed.), *War and Society*, London, 1973, pp. 161–2.

The author is grateful to Bill Fuge and Anthony Slide for advice and assistance.

CHAPTER TWO

Ireland, sport and empire

Alan Bairner

Until quite recently, there has been a widespread tendency in academic circles either to ignore completely the place of sport in the development of modern society or at least to underestimate its importance. This failing, as Lincoln Allison suggests, resulted from two competing and equally erroneous assumptions, namely 'that sport was both "above" and "below" the political dimensions of social life'.[1] According to the former misconception, the world of sport is an autonomous realm capable of transcending social and political divisions; according to the latter, sport is a trivial element of human society deemed to be unworthy of serious scholarly interest. In either case, the importance of sport to the formation and development of society was denied.

This elitist dismissal of sport was by no means confined to the conservative end of the political spectrum. Socialists and Marxists who might reasonably have been expected to take a greater interest in a sphere of activity which engages the attention of large numbers of ordinary men and women were equally, if not more, dismissive. In the first place, since sport belonged to the superstructural level which, according to orthodox Marxist teaching, was merely a reflection of the economic structure of a given society, it did not merit separate analysis. Secondly, for many on the political left, sport came to be regarded as simply the most recent in a long list of distractions, of which religion had been one of the earliest, which lured the working classes from the path of socialist politics. As such, it was seen in Britain, although to a much lesser extent in continental Europe, as not only ephemeral but also potentially harmful. Ironically, it was the implication revealed by this paradoxical assessment of the status of sport in modern society, as both trivial and, in a certain sense, important, that actually led to a reappraisal of the subject, first by Marxists and later more generally.

Inspired by Marxist thinkers such as Antonio Gramsci, Max Horkheimer and Theodor Adorno, intellectuals on the left began to recognise the significant role played by superstructural phenomena in the elaboration of consciousness. One area of study which benefited as a result was that of popular culture, including sport and leisure activity. In consequence, from the 1960s onwards there has been a marked proliferation in the amount of academic interest, Marxist and non-Marxist, in sport and this has been reflected in a number of disciplines, including anthropology, sociology, philosophy and social history, as well as in the study of politics.

For Marxists, the most immediate problem has been to explain how ruling elites maintain their political ascendancy with only limited recourse to coercion. Although numerous factors have been adduced to be of importance, it has become increasingly apparent that popular cultural activities, like sport, play vital roles in the mediation between social reality and consciousness, culminating in the form of political authority described by Gramsci as 'hegemonic'. This conclusion, for example, has been arrived at by way of analysis of the role of sport in Britain.[2] It can also be reached, however, through studies of the involvement of sport in the processes of imperialism.

According to analyses based on orthodox Marxist assumptions, imperialism was essentially an economic strategy supported by coercion and little distinction needed to be made between the techniques of different imperial powers. In the case of British imperialism, however, as Brian Stoddart observes, 'the military story in what became known as the White Dominions suggests the development of a confidence on the part of imperial authorities that the military presence was rather a small part of imperial culture'.[3] In other corners of the British Empire, of course, greater recourse to coercion was required, but even there considerable emphasis was placed on the need to establish some degree of cultural authority. This became increasingly important when it was recognised that at home, as Tom Kemp puts it, 'militarism and sabre-rattling were unpopular amongst wide sections of the middle class'.[4] Whilst they favoured the spread of the Empire, they demanded that, whenever possible, this should be achieved by peaceful means and thus sport, together with language, religion and educational practices, became vitally important to the growth of the British Empire. As Stoddart claims, 'through sport were transferred dominant British beliefs as to social behaviour, standards, relations, and conformity, all of which persisted beyond the end of the formal empire, and with considerable consequences for the postcolonial order'.[5] This view is endorsed by Harold Perkin who writes that 'in the case of Britain and its Empire in the last hundred years or so, sport played a part both in holding the Empire together and, paradoxically, in emancipating the subject nations from tutelage'.[6]

Given Britain's pioneering role in the modern development of sport, it is perhaps not surprising that this came to assume a high profile in the British Empire. Nevertheless, the extent to which sport became an instrument of imperial policy is astonishing. According to James Mangan, 'the formation of character was the essential purpose of Victorian *elitist* education – at home and overseas' and, for the export of character, it was necessary to have 'trainers of character, mostly from public school and ancient university, who used the games field as the medium of moral indoctrination'.[7] Not all the functionaries of the British Empire were sportsmen or even interested in the idea of using sport as a means of consolidating imperial power. The Sudan Political Service, however, was sufficiently exceptional in this regard to prompt the phrase, 'the land of Blacks ruled by Blues'. And, in the words of Richard Holt, 'as the Empire expanded in the late nineteenth century both the need for recruits and the increasing importance of athleticism combined to promote the cause of the sportsman'.[8] As a result, hardly any part of the Empire remained unaffected by British sporting traditions. According to David Vital, indeed, 'Jewish Palestine may have been the one little corner of the great British Empire in which no-one ever played cricket'.[9] Certainly the impact of British sport was by no means confined to the so-called white dominions, a fact recognised by Marxist and cricketer, C. L. R. James, who was also more conscious than most of the cultural package which accompanied British sport to such places as his native Trinidad.

> At school we learnt not only to play with the team. We were taught and learnt loyalty in the form of loyalty to the school. As with everything else in those days, I took it for granted. It was only long afterwards, after gruesome experience in another country, that I saw it for the specifically British thing that it was.[10]

Generation after generation of imperial administrators took British sports to every far-flung outpost of the Empire, first to amuse themselves, then to help cement relationships with indigenous elites and finally to introduce entire native populations not only to these sports but to the idea that the British way of life was superior and demanded their respect. Thus, as Stoddart claims, the contribution of sport to the maintenance of the Empire was impressive: 'At the height of empire, then, sport as a cultural bond had considerable force, conveying through its many forms a moral and behavioural code that bonded the imperial power with many if not most of the influential colonial quarters'.[11] However, not everywhere was affected in exactly the same way by the introduction of British sports as an element of the imperial process. In this respect, as in many others, for example, Ireland presents a more complex picture than that observable in other parts of the Empire. With specific reference to sport, the relationship between Britain and Ireland has been affected by three factors.

First, because of the geographical proximity of the two and the close links between their respective upper classes, it is more difficult than in other imperial contexts to draw a clear distinction between the imperial elite and the indigenous elite. Specifically, members of both groups had been educated at the same schools and universities and thus shared a common grounding in British sports. Second, there exists in the north-east corner of Ireland a large Protestant community, with origins in Britain and a continued loyalty to British traditions, which cannot easily be compared with native populations in other parts of the Empire. The adoption of British sports would be regarded by Ulster Protestants as part of their rightful inheritance rather than as the result of an imperialist imposition of an alien culture. Finally, in Ireland, unlike most other parts of the Empire, there existed a relatively organised native sporting tradition which pre-dated the emergence of modern sport and of the British Empire.

It has been claimed that the Irish held their own equivalent of the Olympics – the Tailteann Games – as early as 1169.[12] It is difficult, however, to be certain about the precise character of the indigenous Irish sporting tradition or, indeed, to establish the extent to which it was unique. For example, although various forms of football, including the game of Cad, were played in Ireland for centuries, it is impossible to state with any degree of certainty that these differed markedly from the rough-and-tumble games which were played throughout Europe.[13] Claims that other modern sports were first played in Ireland are equally difficult to substantiate. In his history of cricket, Rowland Bowen notes that, by the middle of the seventeenth century, 'the game evidently enjoyed an enormous popularity in Ireland, for Cromwell ordered the destruction of all bats and balls in Dublin, and large numbers were given up for burning in 1656'.[14] It is doubtful, however, if the game of 'krickett' proscribed by Cromwell's commissioners was an Irish invention and certainly by the eighteenth century, as Stanley Bergin and Derek Scott observe, 'whatever cricket was played in Ireland was confined essentially to the military, the gentry and members of the viceregal or Chief Secretary's staff and household'.[15]

Claims have also been made that golf was an Irish invention.[16] There is considerably more evidence, however, to support the view that the game first arrived in Ireland during the period of the Hamilton and Montgomery Plantation of Ulster which began in 1606.[17] Similarly, regardless of the Irish connections of William Webb Ellis who has acquired a quasi-mythical status as the inventor of rugby, the game itself became established in Ireland, as Gareth Williams asserts, 'as a colonial reflection of the structure and social context of the game in England'.[18]

Far less contentious than any of the above claims is the belief that a game resembling the modern sport of hurling was indigenous to Ireland. According to Trevor West, 'the game of hurley, or hurling, has been played in Ireland for over a thousand years, as evidenced by frequent references to the sport in Irish literature'.[19] Other sources suggest that hurling has been a distinctively Irish pastime for at least two thousand years.[20] More precisely, T. S. C. Dagg notes that there are records of hurling having been played as early as the thirteenth century and that the game's popularity became so great that it was proscribed by both the statutes of Kilkenny (1366) and the Galway Statutes (1527).[21] Even the status of hurling as a national Irish pastime, however, does not go unchallenged. As West points out, two distinct forms of hurling were probably played in Ireland until the nineteenth century – a southern version, *iomaín*, which resembles the modern game, and a northern version, *camanácht*, more closely related to the sport of shinty, still played in Scotland today.[22] The general point to be made is that, although hurling was certainly played in Ireland for many centuries, it was also played in other Celtic societies and cannot be regarded as exclusively Irish in its origins. Thus, whilst a native sporting culture undoubtedly existed in Ireland, its precise contours are impossible to determine. Furthermore, its most characteristic element, hurling, had more or less disappeared by the nineteenth century, when the foundations of the modern sporting world were being laid in Britain, and there was little initial opposition in Ireland to the introduction of British games.

Two influences were of considerable importance in the initial dissemination of British sports throughout Ireland: the army and educational institutions. Games like cricket, golf and hockey, for example, depended greatly for their early development in Ireland on the existence of garrison towns throughout the country and a particularly large military presence in Dublin. For example, the first recorded cricket match in Ireland took place in Dublin's Phoenix Park in 1792 between an 'All-Ireland' selection and a team representing the military garrison.[23] Similarly, Ireland's second oldest golf club was formed at the Curragh in 1883 by soldiers of the Highland Light Infantry (71st Regiment).[24] As for hockey, it quickly became established as a regimental game not only in Ireland but throughout the British Empire.[25]

However, the rapid growth in popularity of hockey and cricket as well as of another team sport, rugby, owed as much to the role of educational institutions in Ireland and in Britain as to the British military presence and, in this respect, the close ties between the Irish and British elites becomes crucial. Many of the children, particularly the sons, of the Irish upper classes were educated either at English public schools, which since the days of Thomas Arnold at Rugby had been so instrumental in the development of sport, or at schools in Ireland which had been modelled on their English counterparts. That they chose to take up British sports is, therefore, scarcely surprising. W. P. Hone identifies the role of schools, for example, in the spread of cricket in Ireland.

> It may be that boys coming by coach and ship from their English schools lamented that their favourite games could not be enjoyed during their summer holidays and that their fox-hunting parents, themselves hard put to know how to pass the summer months, saw in cricket a means of gratifying their gregarious instincts.[26]

In addition, schools in Ireland itself, such as St Columba's Church of Ireland College, began to play a prominent role in the development of Irish cricket.[27] Meanwhile, at least as important as that of schools, was the part played by universities – Oxford, Cambridge and, above all, Trinity College in Dublin – in the spread of British sport in Ireland.

A rugby club was established at Trinity College in 1854, making it the second oldest club still in existence anywhere in the world.[28] Indeed, the historian of sport at the university argues that 'the 1854 foundation date gives Trinity a substantial claim to be the oldest rugby club in continuous existence' since 'Guy's Hospital FC, which was founded in London in 1843 and played its football initially on Kennington Oval, is certainly older, but went into abeyance for some years in the nineteenth century'.[29] Many of the club's founding members had been educated at English schools and the first Honorary Secretary and Treasurer, Robert Henry Scott, although born in Dublin, had himself attended Rugby School.

Members of Trinity College were also largely responsible for resurrecting the northern form of hurling which, like its southern counterpart, had declined in popularity particularly during the famine years of the late 1840s. However, they quickly merged it with the game of hockey codified by the Hockey Association in England in 1886.[30] Cricket, too, was played enthusiastically by Trinity students and the university cricket club is thought to date from 1835.[31]

In no small measure due to the influence in sporting circles of Trinity College, but also because it was the seat of government, Dublin was the birthplace of the vast majority of bodies responsible for the organisation and propagation of British sports in Ireland. These included the Irish Rugby Football Union, formed in 1879 through the amalgamation of the Irish Football Union (1874) and the Northern Football Union (1875), the Irish Lawn Tennis Association (1877), the Golfing Union of Ireland (1891) and the Irish Hockey Union (1893).

As a result of Dublin's prominence, the north-east corner of Ireland, despite its large pro-British population, played a secondary role in the promotion of British games. For the most part, however, the reception of sports like cricket and rugby in Belfast and its surrounding area followed the pattern established in Dublin. From the 1830s onwards, cricket clubs were formed in Ulster, usually by former pupils of English public schools, and often these clubs also became instrumental in the development of rugby. For example, the North of Ireland Cricket Club, established in 1859, inspired the formation in 1868 of the North of Ireland Football Club, many of whose rugby playing members had been educated at English public schools. Despite the growing popularity of these sports in Ulster, however, Dublin remained the administrative centre of British games in Ireland, with one notable exception.

Although originally springing from the same sources as other British sports, namely the English public schools and ancient universities, association football in England and elsewhere in Britain became increasingly identified with working-class communities as the nineteenth century progressed. It was almost inevitable, therefore, that it received its most enthusiastic initial reception in Ireland in Belfast, the most industrialised part of the island. Again the existence of a substantial military presence was important but so too were the close ties between Belfast and the west of Scotland where football had rapidly established itself as the most popular sport amongst working-class men. The Irish Football Association was formed in Belfast in 1880 and, although clubs based in Dublin joined the ruling body, it was clear that the focal point of football in Ireland, unlike that of other British sports, was to be Belfast and, more generally, the counties of Ulster. Indeed, teams representing British army regiments enjoyed more conspicuous successes than Dublin clubs in the early years of competitive football in Ireland.[32]

In a variety of ways, therefore, the major British games established themselves in Irish society. Regardless of the precise character of the influences involved, however, the general impression to emerge so far is that the people responsible for the introduction and maintenance of these games expressed common anglophile attitudes. Whether they were soldiers, civil servants, members of Irish landed families or Protestant workers in Belfast, they shared a belief in the naturalness of the union of Britain and Ireland and a preference for British traditions as opposed to those of Celtic Ireland. It would be wrong to suppose, however, that the rest of the Irish population remained unaffected by the spread of British games in their country.

Two future leaders of the Irish nationalist movement, C. S. Parnell and John Redmond, played cricket as young men.[33] Kevin Barry, who was to die for the cause of Irish independence, was a member of the rugby club at University College, Dublin, and a future President of the Irish Free State, Eamonn de Valera, played rugby at Rockwell College and has been described as 'a full-back and centre of some calibre'.[34] Furthermore, the playing of British games was not confined to Protestant schools and rugby clubs were formed at the Jesuit colleges of Belvedere and Clongowes Wood.[35] At the latter, indeed, a game resembling cricket had been played as early as 1820 and it was under the guidance of the Jesuit masters there that Redmond and his brother Willie were introduced to the most quintessential of English sports.[36] At the other end of the social scale, Catholic workers in Belfast were almost as quick as their Protestant neighbours to take up association football.[37]

The threat of British sporting hegemony in Ireland was, by the last quarter of the nineteenth century, very real. Irish nationalists, thus, became increasingly concerned that these developments in sport both paralleled and complemented similar trends in other cultural realms, the result of which was the weakening of a sense of Irish identity and, with it, of the desire to pursue the cause of Irish independence. For them, there was an urgent need to revitalise Irish sports and pastimes and ally these to a broad cultural nationalist movement. Their immediate difficulty, however, was that in so far as Ireland possessed an indigenous sporting tradition, this had all but disappeared by the middle of the nineteenth century. Most of the sports being played in Ireland were of British origin and hurling had not been seen in Dublin since at least the 1830s.

In addition to the impact of the famine, another factor often used to explain the disappearance of Irish games and pastimes is modernisation. Thus, according to Holt, 'the rural isolation that had kept much of Ireland out of the grip of British culture was being eroded'.[38] Furthermore, the claims of more disciplined British games had received support from the Catholic Church, the leaders of which had been increasingly dismayed by the excessive behaviour which frequently accompanied traditional Irish pastimes and festivals. As Elizabeth Malcolm observes, 'the oppressed and weakened Catholic Church of the seventeenth and early eighteenth centuries may have been prepared to allow popular religious festivals to flourish, but as it gained strength it came increasingly to challenge such practices'.[39] Some Catholic clergymen, however, took an altogether different view of the substitution of Irish practices by English customs and traditions. Amongst these was Archbishop Croke of Cashel who was in no doubt concerning the damage being done to Ireland by the rapid proliferation of British goods and fashions and who denounced the ugly and irritating fact that we are daily importing from England, not only her manufactured goods ... but her fashions, her accents, her vicious literature, her music, her dances and her manifold mannerisms, her games also and her pastimes, to the utter discredit of our own grand national sports, and to the sore humiliation, as I believe, of every genuine son and daughter of the old land.[40]

A few Irish nationalists, including members of the Young Ireland movement, came to recognise the need to introduce forms of recreation which would be less rumbustious than the traditional practices, but would be, nevertheless, distinctively Irish.[41] Amongst them, there were those who saw a future in the recovery and codification, according to modern practices, of traditional Irish sports and in 1848, for example, Thomas Francis Meagher attempted to revive hurling in the city of Waterford.[42] Another pioneer in this respect was Charles J. Kickham who 'had a keen, if not fully articulated, awareness of the political significance of organised sport, and especially its affinity to the processes that go to make a nationalist movement'.[43] However, the major driving force behind the revitalisation of a distinctive Irish sporting tradition was Michael Cusack.

Between October 1877 and November 1887, Cusack, in the words of his biographer, 'made his mark on Irish education, played a decisive role in Irish athletics, revived the national game of hurling, took part in a seminal move to revive the Irish language, edited a new weekly newspaper, and founded what has been for over a hundred years the biggest and most successful of Irish sports bodies'.[44] In 1882, Cusack founded the Dublin Athletic Club and the Dublin (later Metropolitan) Hurling Club. His twin aims were democratisation of sport in Ireland and resistance to the spread of British games, including rugby which he himself had played and coached at Blackrock College and had introduced at his own Academy in Dublin. Ironically, it might not have been possible for Cusack to breathe new life into the game of hurling had it not been for the earlier efforts of hockey players at Trinity College. As Trevor West observes, 'Trinity had made a major contribution to Gaelic games by keeping a form of hurling alive when it was virtually extinct in the rest of the country'.[45] However, the growing links between the Trinity hockey players and their English counterparts combined with Cusack's efforts to restore hurling to the status of a native Irish sport to ensure that henceforth a clear distinction between the two sports would be made. Nevertheless, although Cusack's endeavours were consolidated with the formation in 1884 of the Gaelic Athletic Association for the Preservation and Cultivation of National Pastimes (GAA), the influence of British sporting traditions on the development of an Irish nationalist sporting movement should not be ignored. In a number of ways, as W. F. Mandle claims, 'Gaelic games followed paths that had been taken or were currently being taken by organised sports in other societies, particularly those across the Irish Sea'.[46] However, the Association's commitment to the cause of Irish nationalism was never in doubt.

'From its inception', writes Pádraig Puirséal, 'it [the GAA] constantly strove to mould the national outlook to its own ideals, to re-awaken a legitimate pride of race and to further the resurgence of the national spirit.'[47] A rather more extreme assessment is offered by Holt who comments that 'from the beginning the GAA was fiercely anti-British not just in cultural terms but in a quite specific political sense'.[48]

Despite its avowed nationalist aims, however, the GAA began life as a relatively broad social movement embracing not only former players of British games, including Cusack himself, but also Protestants, such as Douglas Hyde, Unionists, like the Reverend Maxwell Close, and a District Inspector in the Royal Irish Constabulary, St George McCarthy. On the other hand a number of members of the extreme nationalist body, the Irish Republican Brotherhood (IRB), were among the Association's founding members and the first few years of the GAA's existence were characterised by a struggle for control of its activities involving rival nationalist groups as well as the Catholic Church. This struggle was accompanied by a rapid decline in the number of Protestant members and from that point onwards the GAA's development has been inextricably linked with the fortunes of Irish nationalist politics.

Between 1886 and 1891, the Association was almost completely taken over by the IRB. The more it became a recruiting ground for those nationalists committed to the use of physical force, the less it was supported by constitutional nationalists or the Catholic clergy who were further alienated by the GAA's decision to join with the IRB in supporting Parnell in the aftermath of the O'Shea scandal.[49] As time wore on, however, the Association's leadership became increasingly adept at drawing together the different strands of Irish nationalism, including the Church, to support a body committed to the promotion of the Irish cause, but not to a particular political strategy. As a result, the GAA was able to come through such episodes as the Easter Rising and the Civil War more or less intact despite the fact that its individual members often found themselves on opposite sides of the political debate. Of one thing, however, they could all be certain – the implacable opposition of the Association not only to British sports but also to the British presence in Ireland.

The GAA's opposition to British sports was expressed through its Ban policy formalised in 1887.[50] This not only banned members of the

Crown forces from participating in Gaelic games (which in addition to hurling came to include Gaelic football, camogie and handball), but also prohibited GAA members from watching or taking part in 'foreign' games.[51]

The Association's opposition to British rule in Ireland was also clearly expressed and its history is punctuated with a series of anti-British actions. For example, in 1899, during Britain's involvement in war in South Africa, GAA conventions passed pro-Boer resolutions and toasts to Boer success were proposed.[52] In County Kerry, the Association welcomed a club called 'The Irish Brigade Transvaal'.[53] Other GAA clubs were renamed in honour of Boer leaders such as General De Wet.[54] Furthermore, beyond the baiting and taunting, the Association was deeply involved in nationalist efforts to resist British attempts to recruit Irishmen to fight in South Africa. Protestants in Ulster, on the other hand, were loyal in their support of the war effort and, at the symbolic level, took the step of christening the west terracing at Windsor Park, Belfast, home of Ireland's international association football team, as the Spion Kop to commemorate the battle of that name.

In the early years of the twentieth century, northern Protestants became increasingly alarmed about the possibility that the country might be given Home Rule and that the link with Britain would be greatly weakened. To resist this possibility, the Ulster Volunteer Force was formed in 1913. The immediate response was the formation of the Irish Volunteers to which the GAA made a significant contribution in terms both of membership and organisation.[55] Nevertheless, the Association did not formally endorse the Volunteer movement and again there loomed the possibility of a split along the traditional fault line of Irish nationalism, this time between Sinn Fein members, who represented the physical force tradition, and supporters of Redmond's constitutional nationalism.[56] This disagreement came to a head in 1916 with the Easter Rising, the importance of which was initially underestimated by the GAA leadership as well as by most other sections of Irish nationalist opinion.[57] Yet many members of the Association were involved in the Rising and its aftermath, a large number of them suffering as a result. 'The Gaels were to the fore, not alone in Dublin and the other areas where the Irish Volunteers went into action, but also in places where the countermanding of orders caused frustration among men no less willing to face danger and death than their brothers in arms.'[58]

Of the executed leaders of the Rising, Padraig Pearse had been Chairman of the Leinster Colleges GAA and Sean McDermott, Con Colbert, Michael O'Hanrahan and Eamonn Ceannt had all been members of the Association. Other Gaels whose death sentences were commuted to terms of penal servitude were J. J. Walsh, Chairman of the Cork County Board, Jack Shouldice, a Dublin all-Ireland footballer, Sean Etchingham and Con O'Donovan. Some other prominent GAA members received prison sentences, including Harry Boland, Austin Stack, Mick Collins and Jim Nowlan.[59] Indeed, so many Gaelic sportsmen were interned that it was possible for the 1916 final of the Wolfe Tone Tournament between Kerry and Louth to be played at Frongoch Prison Camp in Wales.[60]

In 1918, the issue of conscription to military service provided the GAA with an opportunity to declare its anti-Britishness. By that stage, Sinn Fein, the inheritors of the IRB mantle, had become a dominant influence in the Association[61] and when conscription proposals were mooted by the British government, it was inevitable that the GAA would assume a leading role in the opposition movement which received widespread popular support. 'Never, before or since', writes Pádraig Puirséal, 'did Ireland show such a united front and such determined but passive resistance.'[62] In response, the British authorities, who had kept a watchful eye on the GAA since its formation, banned all meetings, including sporting gatherings, in July 1918. Instead of applying for the special permits which would have allowed their matches to go ahead, the GAA's leadership organised a 'Gaelic Sunday' for 3 August.[63] On that day, nearly 1,500 games were played, watched by large crowds. There was only limited interference from the security forces, no doubt deterred by the sheer size of the protest. 'Gaelic Sunday' represented the coming of age of the GAA as a central pillar of Irish nationalism. As Marcus de Búrca comments, 'it not only found a place in the history of Gaelic games and of the GAA itself, but became notable as the greatest single act of defiance outside the purely political sphere between 1916 and 1922'.[64]

Another important episode in the GAA's history took place on 20 November 1920 when a body of members of the paramilitary Auxiliary Division of the RIC, as part of a search operation, entered the Association's national stadium, Croke Park, Dublin, and subsequently shot into the crowd which had gathered to watch a match between Dublin and Tipperary.[65] Thirteen people were killed, including the captain of the Tipperary footballers, Michael Hogan. The action itself came to be seen by nationalists as a direct response to assassinations earlier that day of sixteen members of the British security forces in and around Dublin, but it was also the logical product of the acrimony which had long soured relations between the authorities and the GAA and may even have played a part in precipitating the end of British rule in the major part of Ireland. The latter, however, was the result of a divisive treaty which meant that Ireland was partitioned, leaving the six Ulster counties under British jurisdiction and resulting in a bitter civil war, in which GAA members again found themselves in opposition to one another. That Irish independence was achieved at all, however, owed much to the organisational skill and the symbolic power of the GAA. According to Mandle, 'it is arguable that no organisation had done more for Irish nationalism than the GAA – not the IRB, so influential in its founding, but now dissolved; not the Gaelic league, its linguistic counterpart which had failed in its mission to restore the national language; not the Irish Parliamentary Party, which had been unable to adjust to the nationalist revival; not even Sinn Fein, which had broken apart under the impact of the Treaty'.[66]

After 1921 the GAA, as well as the various bodies which controlled British sports in Ireland, had to adjust to an entirely new situation. Thus, it is necessary to assess not only their differing roles in the period during which Britain exercised political control over the whole of Ireland, but also the legacy of sporting divisions in Ireland for which they were responsible. More generally, what lessons can be drawn from the Irish experience concerning the role of sport in the context of British imperialism?

According to David Daiches, there are two ways in which a people can respond to the loss of independence such as occurs during the process of imperialism. Either, 'it can attempt to rediscover its own national traditions and by reviving and developing them find a satisfaction that will compensate for its political impotence'. Or, 'by accepting the dominance of the culture of the country which has achieved political ascendancy over it, it can endeavour to beat that country at its own game and achieve distinction by any standard the dominant culture may evolve'.[67] Both types of response, together with combinations of the two, are discernible in the realm of sport, as in other areas of human endeavour, throughout the British Empire.

As Richard Holt asserts, 'the formation and early history of the GAA is arguably the most striking instance of politics shaping sport in modern history; it is certainly the outstanding example of the appropriation of sport by nationalism in the history of the British Isles and Empire'.[68] At least as instructive, however, is John Wilson's more general observation that 'the break-up of the British Empire is poignantly marked by the rise to supremacy of former colonies in international competition in games "exported" to colonies by Britain'.[69] In most corners of the Empire, the expression of sporting nationalism was more or less in accord with the second option suggested by Daiches. In the Indian subcontinent, the Caribbean, south and east Africa, Australia and New Zealand, British sports were taken up with enthusiasm and gradually became important indicators of the extent to which the colonies were acquiring self-esteem and becoming less psychologically dependent on their imperial overlords. Thus, C. L. R. James refers to the 'intimate connection between cricket and West Indian social and political life'.[70] Even if the initial adoption of the game of cricket signified a degree of submission to the values of British imperial rule, it quickly helped to awaken a radical political consciousness: 'Cricket had plunged me into politics long before I was aware of it. When I did turn to politics I did not have too much to learn.'[71] In the white dominions, too, British games helped to lay the foundations of an independent identity. For example, as Mandle suggests, 'there is a case for arguing that Australian nationalism and self-confidence was first and most clearly manifested in the late 1870s because of the feats of its sportsmen and particularly of its cricketers'.[72] In these examples, people turned to the traditions of the imperial power rather than to indigenous practices as part of the response to political impotence and, in general, according to Holt, 'nationalist opposition to Anglo-Saxon sports ... was limited and ineffective'.[73] There were, however, exceptions.

The United States, above all, were able to develop their own unique sporting culture, and Canada, largely because of its close proximity to the United States, but also due to other factors, including climatic conditions and the presence of a large French-speaking minority, also pursued a different form of sporting nationalism.[74] Even in Australia, an attempt was made, through the introduction of Australian Rules Football, to take a sporting option more consistent with the first possibility identified by Daiches, albeit by manufacturing rather than reviving a native sport. No single organisation, however, anywhere in the Empire made as great an effort as the GAA to react against imperialism by seeking to replace British games with native ones, including Gaelic football which ironically may have served as a model for the inventors of Australia's 'native' football code.[75]

The vehemence of the GAA's position cannot be explained simply in terms of the close proximity of Ireland to Britain and the consequent swamping of Ireland with British games. In Scotland and Wales, for example, nationalists were largely content to derive satisfaction from victories against England in what had originally been English games. Therefore, no major attempt was made in Scotland to develop a sporting nationalism based exclusively on the native game of shinty. Obviously the differing nationalist responses made by the various constituent elements of the United Kingdom can only fully be explained by reference to the different ways in which they had been incorporated into the Union. But what specific sporting factors, if any, can explain the extreme position taken by the GAA?

The most significant factor in this respect is the fact that the people

IRELAND, SPORT AND EMPIRE

who were most enthusiastic about British games in Ireland were precisely those who regarded themselves as British. Of course, as Holt points out, 'playing Anglo-Saxon games did not make all sportsmen reassuringly pro-British'.[76] He cites the example of the Boers who

> developed a keen interest in Rugby, which became a kind of ruling passion in the rural areas between the wars and a vehicle for a [sic] Afrikaner self-expression and identity ... The Springboks may have been playing an 'imperial' game but they were playing it to assert themselves as a proud and independent people, whose attitude to the British Crown was ambiguous to say the least.[77]

In Ireland, however, the overwhelming majority of those involved in the propagation of British sports were loyal to the Crown. Naturally they became patriotically Irish when teams representing Ireland faced opposition from England or elsewhere. Some of the participants in British games like the Reverend William Sewell, headmaster of St Columba's College, were even cultural nationalists.[78] A few, like de Valera himself, were political nationalists. As a general rule, however, British sports in Ireland were useful vehicles for the establishment of what Holt calls a 'loyalist culture'.[79] In such circumstances, it was inevitable that Irish nationalists would feel obliged to construct an alternative means by which to express sporting nationalism. The result was the formation of the GAA.

The main drawback of the type of sporting nationalism which is embodied in the GAA is that its exclusivity leads to isolationism. One cannot construct a unique sporting tradition and then expect to compete with other nations. 'Ourselves alone' thus becomes not only a general political slogan, but also a particularly apt description of the role of the GAA. Some attempts have been made to promote Gaelic games in countries with large Irish communities such as England, Australia and the United States and 'compromise rules' matches have been arranged involving Gaelic and Australian Rules footballers and also hurlers and shinty players. In general, however, whilst the GAA has played a significant part in securing a separate sense of identity for the Irish people, it has been unable to offer the Irish the opportunity, enjoyed by people throughout the world, to beat the former colonial masters at their own games and, indeed, by its overt hostility towards 'foreign' games, it has actually stood in the way of such an opportunity. Despite the removal of the ban on playing 'foreign' games in 1971, the GAA's resistance to collaboration has continued largely as a result of the dual function which it has served since partition.

In the six counties of Northern Ireland, the GAA has continued to play its traditional role as a channel for the expression of Irish nationalist aspirations. In the Republic of Ireland, however, and even in the early years of the Irish Free State, its role became that of a bulwark for the newly independent Ireland. Against the wishes of Sinn Fein, for example, the Association contributed significantly to the Free State government's revival of the ancient Tailteann Games which took place in 1924, 1928 and 1932.

> As a cultural exhibition with mass appeal they may be regarded as one of the early (and now largely forgotten) successes of the new state. That they were so successful was due largely to the leading role in the festival played by the GAA, in providing the main stadium and in lending some of its leading officials to the various organising committees.[80]

The games provided an early indication of the GAA's role in helping to construct a cultural package which would put flesh on the bare bones of political independence. To this day, all-Ireland Gaelic finals are celebrations of Irish national identity which demand the attendance of the leaders of Irish politics and society. By a curious twist of fate, however, the sports which, in terms of national self-expression, play an increasingly important role as the twentieth century draws to a close are arguably not the Gaelic ones which helped to forge an Irish identity, now largely unchallenged, but rather those which the British and their loyal adherents in Ireland first developed but which now provide Irish sportsmen and sportswomen with the chance to compete on the world stage.

Although some sports remain too closely associated with British imperialism to appeal to more than a handful of Irish people, others, most notably association football, have become so universally popular as to make it nonsensical to continue to dismiss them as 'British'. As a result sports like football and golf are viewed with much less suspicion even by the most diehard Gaels in Northern Ireland than cricket, hockey or rugby. In the Irish Republic, football, whilst popular since the end of the last century, has acquired the status of a national obsession since the 1980s. By an even more curious twist of fate, it has done so largely because of the success of the national team under the guidance of an English manager, Jack Charlton, and consisting of a number of players born not in Ireland but in various parts of the United Kingdom, a few of them with somewhat tenuous Irish connections. It is undeniable that much of the support for this team and its sport is due to the unprecedented success it has achieved, including qualification for the first time for the final stages of both the European Championships, in 1988, and the World Cup, in 1990. Nevertheless, the increased enthusiasm for football is also consistent with the efforts of the Irish political establishment to present their country as a mature member of the international community rather than as a nation still essentially preoccupied with its post-colonial relationship to Britain. To that extent, British sporting hegemony may ironically have provided Ireland with one of its potent weapons in the struggle to free itself once and for all from its ties with Britain and the legacy of the British imperial presence. Meanwhile, in Northern Ireland, the GAA, itself modelled on British sporting bodies and truer today than most of them to their original ideals of amateurism, fair play and muscular Christianity, continues to play the alternative nationalist role necessitated by the fact that part of Ireland remains British.

'Sport', according to Brian Stoddart, 'must be reckoned a most pervasive and enduring theme in the history of British imperialism'.[81] Nowhere is the truth of this statement more apparent than in Ireland. First, sport was used by the British in Ireland not only to engage the attention of those most supportive of the Union, but also in an attempt, less successful than in other parts of the Empire, to attract indigenous support. Second, whilst patriotic Irishmen enjoyed and continue to enjoy sporting successes against the British, played at their own games, political nationalists, themselves inspired by examples set by the British, opted for an exclusivist sporting nationalism which has played an important part in the modern history of Ireland. Specifically, the GAA has served both counter-hegemonic and hegemonic functions depending on the circumstances in which it has found itself. Finally, however, with independence secured and in spite of continued partition, the Irish have turned again to 'British' sports, particularly football, in order to take a more active, less protectionist, part in the international community. According to Michael Holmes, 'the Republic of Ireland football team has given a new sense of identity to many'.[82] However, it is too early to say with any degree of certainty that this development will survive a downturn in the Irish football team's fortunes just as it is too early to be certain that a concomitant revolution is taking place elsewhere in Irish society. But if a new Ireland is emerging, then sport may have proved itself yet again to be one of the most accurate indicators of social and political trends. To underestimate its importance in this instance, or indeed in any other, is not just elitist but downright foolish.

Notes

1 Lincoln Allison, 'The changing context of sporting life', in L. Allison (ed.), *The Changing Politics of Sport*, Manchester, 1993, pp. 1–14, at p. 5.
2 See, for example, John Hargreaves, *Sport and Popular Culture: A Social and Historical Analysis of Popular Sports in Britain*, Cambridge, 1986.
3 Brian Stoddart, 'Sport, cultural imperialism, and colonial response in the British Empire', *Comparative Studies in Society and History*, XXX (1988), pp. 649–73, at p. 650.

4   Tom Kemp, *Theories of Imperialism*, London, 1967, p. 90.
5   Stoddart, 'Sport, cultural imperialism, and colonial response', p. 651.
6   Harold Perkin, 'Sport and society: Empire into Commonwealth', in J. A. Mangan and R. B. Small (eds), *Sport, Culture, Society. International Historical and Sociological Perspectives*, London, 1986, pp. 3–5, at p. 3.
7   J. A. Mangan, 'Ethics and ethnocentricity: Imperial education and British tropical Africa', in W. J. Baker & J. A. Mangan (eds), *Sport in Africa. Essays in Social History*, New York & London, 1987, pp. 138–171, at p. 139–40.
8   Richard Holt, *Sport and the British. A Modern History*, Oxford, 1989, p. 206.
9   David Vital, 'Bread upon the waters. The legacy of the British in Jewish Palestine', *Times Literary Supplement*, 5 June 1992, pp. 6–7, at p. 7.
10 C. L. R. James, *Beyond a Boundary*, London, 1969, p. 50. For perceptive analysis of the relationship between cricket and politics in the Caribbean, see H. Beckles & B. Stoddart (eds), *Liberation Cricket. West Indies Cricket Culture*, Manchester, 1994.
11 Stoddart, 'Sport, cultural imperialism, and colonial response', p. 666.
12 Padraig Griffin, *The Politics of Irish Athletics 1850–1990*, Ballinamore, County Leitrim, 1990, p. 3.
13 Edmund Van Esbeck, *The Story of Irish Rugby*, London, 1986, pp. 7–11.
14 Rowland Bowen, *Cricket: A History of its Growth and Development throughout the World*, London, 1970, p. 28.
15 Stanley Bergin & Derek Scott, 'Cricket in Ireland', in E. W. Swanton (ed), *Barclay's World of Cricket*, London, 1980, pp. 508–10, at p. 508.
16 Robert Browning, *A History of Golf, The Royal and Ancient Game*, London, 1955, p. 7.
17 See W. H. Gibson, *Early Irish Golf. The First Courses, Clubs and Pioneers*, Naas, County Kildare, 1988, pp. 1–7.
18 Gareth Williams, 'Rugby Union', in T. Mason (ed), *Sport in Britain. A Social History*, Cambridge, 1989, pp. 308–43, at p. 321. Whilst it is true that his father served in the army in Ireland, Webb Ellis himself was almost certainly born in Manchester and his place in the history of rugby owes nothing to his father's experiences. Sean Diffley, *The Men in Green. The Story of Irish Rugby*, London, 1973, p. 19; Edmund Van Esbeck, *One Hundred Years of Irish Rugby*, Dublin, 1974, p. 3.
19 Trevor West, *The Bold Collegians. The Development of Sport in Trinity College, Dublin*, Dublin, 1991, p. 32.
20 Marcus de Búrca, *The GAA. A History*, Dublin, 1980, p. 1.
21 T. S. C. Dagg, *Hockey in Ireland*, Tralee, 1944, pp. 19–20.
22 West, *The Bold Collegians*, p. 33.
23 W. P. Hone, *Cricket in Ireland*, Tralee, 1956, pp. 3–4.
24 See Gibson, *Early Irish Golf*, pp. 40–1. According to Gibson, the oldest club is probably Royal Belfast although he recognises that this is a matter of some doubt. The club was formed in 1881.
25 Dagg, *Hockey in Ireland*, p. 67. On its disbandment in 1923, the 2nd Battalion of the Leinster Regiment presented the Leinster Regiment Cup to be awarded to the province winning the Inter-provincial hockey championship. The cup continues to be competed for.
26 Hone, *Cricket in Ireland*, p. 6.
27 *Ibid.*, p. 27.
28 Van Esbeck, *The Story of Irish Rugby*, p. 13.
29 West, *The Bold Collegians*, p. 25.
30 *Ibid.*, pp. 35–6.
31 West, *The Bold Collegians*, p. 13.
32 Malcolm Brodie, *100 Years of Irish Football*, Belfast, 1980, Ch. 1.
33 Hone, *Cricket in Ireland*, pp. 11–13, 23
34 Van Esbeck, *One Hundred Years of Irish Rugby*, p. 65. According to Sean Diffley, de Valera was once a substitute fullback for Ireland. Diffley, *The Men in Green*, p. 16.
35 Van Esbeck, *The Story of Irish Rugby*, p. 14.
36 Hone, *Cricket in Ireland*, p. 23.

37 See, for example, John Kennedy, *Belfast Celtic*, Belfast, 1989.
38 Holt, *Sport and the British*, p. 238.
39 Elizabeth Malcolm, 'Popular recreation in nineteenth century Ireland', in Oliver MacDonagh, W. F. Mandle & Pauric Travers (eds), *Irish Culture and Nationalism, 1750–1950*, London, 1983, pp. 40–55, at p. 46.
40 Quoted in Holt, *Sport and the British*, p. 238.
41 Malcolm, 'Popular recreation in nineteenth century Ireland', p. 49.
42 *Ibid.*
43 R. V. Comerford, *Charles J Kickham. A Study in Irish Nationalism and Literature*, Portmarnock, County Dublin, 1979, p. 185.
44 Marcus de Búrca, *Michael Cusack and the GAA*, Dublin, 1989, p. 36.
45 West, *The Bold Collegians*, p. 57.
46 W. F. Mandle, *The Gaelic Athletic Association and Irish Nationalist Politics, 1884–1924*, London & Dublin, 1987, p. 158.
47 Pádraig Puirséal, *The GAA in its time*, Dublin, 1982, p. 10.
48 Holt, *Sport and the British*, p. 240.
49 Mandle, *The Gaelic Athletic Association*, Chs 1–4.
50 Puirséal, *The GAA*, pp. 73–4; de Búrca, *The GAA. A History*, pp. 34–42.
51 During the 1890s, and the secretaryship of Dick Blake of County Meath, the Ban policy was temporarily set aside. Blake was dismissed from his post, however, in January 1898, almost certainly because he was suspected of being soft on nationalism. On this, see de Búrca, *The GAA. A History*, pp. 68–71.
52 Mandle, *The Gaelic Athletic Association*, p. 120.
53 *Ibid.*, p. 121.
54 Eoghan Corry, *Catch and Kick*, Dublin, 1989, p. 88.
55 Mandle, *The Gaelic Athletic Association*, pp. 161–7.
56 de Búrca, *The GAA. A History*, pp. 124–5.
57 *Ibid.*, pp. 129–30.
58 Puirséal, *The GAA*, p. 168.
59 *Ibid.*, pp. 168–9.
60 Corry, *Catch and Kick*, pp. 102–3.
61 Mandle, *The Gaelic Athletic Association*, pp. 181–2.
62 Puirséal, *The GAA*, p. 175.
63 de Búrca, *The GAA. A History*, pp. 141–2.
64 *Ibid.*, p. 142.
65 Charles Townshend, *The British Campaign in Ireland 1919–1921. The Development of Political and Military Policies*, Oxford, 1978, pp. 130–1.
66 Mandle, *The Gaelic Athletic Association*, p. 221.
67 David Daiches, *Robert Burns*, London, 1952, p. 8.
68 Holt, *Sport and the British*, p. 240.
69 John Wilson, *Politics and Leisure*, London, 1988, p. 155.
70 James, *Beyond a Boundary*, p. 217.
71 *Ibid.*, p. 71.
72 W. Mandle, 'Cricket and Australian nationalism in the nineteenth century', in T. D. Jaques & G. R. Pavia (eds), *Sport in Australia. Selected Readings in Physical Activity*, Sydney, 1976, pp. 46–72. p. 60.
73 Holt, *Sport and the British*, p. 218.
74 For an interesting perspective on sport in the United States, see A. S. Markovits, 'The other "American exceptionalism" – why is there no soccer in the United States?', *Praxis International*, VIII (1988), pp. 125–50. On Canada, see R. Gruneau, *Class, Sports, and Social Development*, Amherst, 1983, Ch. 3.
75 J. Hallows, 'Leisure and pleasure', in Jaques & Pavia (eds), *Sport in Australia*, pp. 121–39, at p. 128.
76 Holt, *Sport and the British*, p. 221.
77 *Ibid.*, p. 228.
78 See Hone, *Cricket in Ireland*, p. 28.
79 Holt, *Sport and the British*, p. 212.

80 de Búrca, *The GAA. A History*, p. 167.
81 Stoddart, 'Sport, cultural imperialism and colonial response', p. 673.
82 Michael Holmes, 'Symbols of national identity and sport: the case of the Irish football team', *Irish Political Studies*, IX (1994), pp. 81–98. at p. 97.

CHAPTER THREE

Ireland and India

T. G. Fraser

But for the British Empire there would have been little, if anything, to unite the fortunes of Ireland and India. Students of ethnic conflict might find some resonances between Ireland and Sri Lanka, both large islands lying off the Eurasian land mass trying to assert distinctive cultural identities in the face of divided populations. But India, with its sheer size and rich diversity, is a different matter. Yet for almost two hundred years Ireland and India formed part of the British imperial system and their fortunes were to become intertwined in a complex pattern which meant that within twenty-five years each was to become independent and partitioned along religious lines. Symbols of that relationship long remained. When President Radhakrishnan came to Dublin on a state visit in 1962 he was proudly shown by Eamon de Valera an engraved sword he had received in 1919 in San Francisco from the revolutionary Hindustan Ghadr Party; in August 1979 official flags in New Delhi were lowered to half staff in memory of the last British Viceroy and first Governor-General of independent India, Lord Mountbatten, who had been killed in Ireland by Irish republicans.

The relationship between Ireland and India developed over two centuries at many levels. Ireland helped sustain the British Raj in India in a manner out of all proportion to her size. The Anglo-Irish aristocracy was an integral part of the British elite which provided rulers for the Empire; hence, it comes as no surprise to find amongst the viceroys and governors-general of India, Lord Canning, Lord Mayo, Lord Dufferin and Lord Lansdowne. Even more significant were the sons of the Irish gentry and professional middle classes. Throughout the British period, service in India provided the mechanism for young men of education and ambition, but no great connections, to rise in the social hierarchy, and in this the Irish proved to be no exception. Lord Macartney in Madras in the 1780s, the three Lawrence brothers – who laid the foundations of British rule in the Punjab, and Sir Michael O'Dwyer, the tough and

[77]

highly controversial Lieutenant-Governor of the Punjab during the First World War, are only some of the most prominent examples of this phenomenon. The Indian Army, always separate from its British counterpart, fulfilled the same function in military terms. Able young officers without the means to sustain the social life in a British army mess could find a congenial home in one of the Indian regiments. This was particularly important for many of the sons of the Irish gentry, often compared with the Prussian Junkers, whose small estates pushed large numbers to seek a military career. The two greatest 'Indian' Field-Marshals, Lord Roberts and Sir Claude Auchinleck, fit exactly into this pattern.

In a quite different direction, India was an obvious outlet for Irish missionary endeavour, itself a notable aspect of Irish society since the time of St Columba. Despite official British disapproval of missionary work, Irish missionaries, chiefly Roman Catholic and Presbyterian, were active in education and in many aspects of medical and social work. Finally, the Irish were well represented among the rank and file of the British garrison in India, the 'steel frame' around which the Raj was built. For much of the nineteenth century some 40 per cent of the British army was recruited in Ireland and thousands of Irish soldiers, and their wives and families, spent a significant part of their lives in the steamy cantonments of north India, or tramping up the Grand Trunk Road to take part in the unceasing warfare against the Pathans, Afridis and Waziris of the frontier. It was no accident that Kipling chose the surname O'Hara for his hero Kim. Of their experiences, hopes and fears we know shamefully little, except when sympathy with political events back home caused them to take action, as some of them did in 1920.

And so to the other dimension of the Irish–Indian relationship, the links between their political development and ultimate fate, for Ireland did not just help to sustain the British Raj, it played some part in its destruction. For much of the nineteenth century, it can be argued, Ireland and India were the most important elements in the imperial system. Ireland, or at least parts of it, had been part of that system since the reign of Henry II when the Norman Conquest extended itself across the Irish Sea. Although historians debate the extent to which modern Ireland can be seen as a 'colonial' society, it is undeniable that as the nineteenth century developed Irish politics came increasingly to be dominated by the desire for some restoration of legislative independence from Westminster. By the 1880s, Home Rule was the issue of the day not only in Ireland, but in British politics as well. India was a much more recent part of the Empire. In the seventeenth century the East India Company had gone to trade in a sub-continent dominated by the

Mughal Empire, but when the power of the Mughals collapsed the Company became a contender for political power. After Robert Clive's victory at the battle of Plassey in Bengal in 1757, the Company increasingly became the major military and political power in India, a process which only concluded with the annexation of the Punjab in the 1840s. In 1857, the forces of traditional India attempted a final, but unsuccessful, challenge to British rule. The late nineteenth century saw India as the 'jewel' in the imperial crown, a vast market for British goods and source of raw materials, and the essential base for Britain's world power. But by then new forces were stirring to life amongst educated Indians who sought some element of reform in the autocratic nature of British rule. Such Indians, educated in western political concepts, looked to Europe for their inspiration and it was not surprising that their gaze took in Ireland. It was in August 1885 that Gladstone became convinced that Home Rule for Ireland was necessary; in December 1885 the first Indian National Congress convened at Bombay. For neither country was the process straightforward. Protestants in Ireland and Muslims in India came to assert a separate identity which in each case led to partition. This, then, is the other level on which the interaction between Ireland and India must be judged.

During the critical period in the eighteenth century when the East India Company was being transformed from a trading company to an engine of imperialism, three Irishmen, Laurence Sulivan, George Macartney and Edmund Burke, command attention for their distinctive contribution to the development of British control in India. Sulivan, from County Cork, was at first little different from many other ambitious young men who, if they could survive climate and fever in their first year, used service in India as the basis for subsequent wealth and advancement. Little is known of his origins or the nature of his early service in India, beyond the fact that he was in Bombay in the 1730s. Before leaving India for London in 1752, he rose steadily through the Bombay administration, holding the powerful position of Collector of the Company's Rents and Revenues and ending as a member of the Council. It was, however, in London with a reputation as an efficient and, by the rather generous standards of the time, honest Company servant that he advanced his career, becoming Chairman in 1758 the year after Clive's victory at Plassey. It was a difficult and controversial period. Not only had the Company's wars changed it from a trading company to a body administering large areas of India, but in doing so many of its servants were acquiring substantial fortunes which they did not hesitate to flaunt on their return. It became Sulivan's purpose to introduce good order into the affairs of the Company's territories in India and to curb the excesses of its servants, which were fast becoming

[79]

a public scandal. In doing so, he did not flinch from a long and enervating battle with Clive. For over quarter of a century Sulivan was to be the Company's most influential servant. In the 1770s his hopes for better standards of government in Bengal rested on Warren Hastings, appointed to the new office of Governor-General, and in 1780 Sulivan was an essential part of the coalition which saw his fellow-Irishman, Lord Macartney, elected as Governor of Madras. Sulivan's career was a remarkable example of how India could advance the fortunes of a man of relatively obscure Irish origins.[1]

Implicit in Sulivan's desire for more honest and effective government of the Company's Indian possessions was the extension of British control. In that sense he can be seen as one of those responsible for a steady imperial encroachment on indigenous Indian governments. This was to be even more marked in the period between 1781 and 1784 when Sulivan's protégé Lord Macartney was at Madras. Unlike Sulivan, George Macartney's origins were in the Scottish settlements in Ulster of the seventeenth century when his great-grandfather had crossed from Kirkcudbrightshire.[2] In 1780, with a career as Envoy to Russia, Chief Secretary for Ireland and Governor of Grenada behind him, he was the chosen candidate of Lord North's government and the Sulivan faction in the Company to become Governor of Madras. It was an inheritance which was to tax all Macartney's powers, for his administration was beset on all sides. The military threat seemed the most immediate. Not only had the American war brought the prospect of a French expedition, which appeared in 1782 under the brilliant Admiral de Suffren, but in July 1780 the territory had been invaded by the armies of Haidar Ali, the ruler of Mysore. But the real reason why Macartney had been chosen lay in the scandalous financial situation which had built up over the previous thirty years. Madras lay on the edge of the Carnatic, theoretically ruled by its Nawab, Muhammad Ali Walajah, who had steadily mortgaged his revenues to corrupt Company servants. 'The Nawab of Arcot's Debts' were to become the greatest financial scandal of the late eighteenth century and it was chiefly to address this problem that Macartney was sent out. Reminding him that the debts were 'of such a magnitude as to spread misery throughout the settlement', Sulivan directed Macartney to take over such revenues as were necessary to address the situation.

By the end of 1781, Macartney had such a mechanism in place. Control of the Carnatic's revenue was assigned to him; he had, in effect, taken control of the country. But in doing so he had offended against two powerful interests: those, like his superior Warren Hastings, who claimed to be opposed to an expansion of British power, and a powerful group of corrupt men who had much to lose from the establishment of honest government. It is a great pity that Hastings was persuaded to align himself with the latter for it brought him into bitter conflict with Macartney.[3] On 28 February 1785, Macartney's conduct was defended with brilliant forensic skill by Edmund Burke in his great speech on the Nawab of Arcot's debts. The Irish connexion was complete, for Burke's main source was Macartney's closest friend and fellow-Irishman, George Staunton, who had returned from Madras to plead his case.[4] Macartney's time in Madras marked a decisive phase in British imperial rule in India: it set a new standard of honest government which others were to follow, and it saw the implementation of the policy of replacing the power of Indian rulers with that of the British.

Once set upon this path, the expansion of British rule proved irresistible. One by one, the polities of India fell, so that by the 1840s the only independent power in the sub-continent was the Sikh empire in the Punjab. It had only been created in the 1790s by the great Maharajah Ranjit Singh, but as the Sikhs had been transformed by their tenth Guru, Govind Singh, into a powerful military brotherhood the British preferred as long as possible to leave them alone. The history of British rule in this critical province is inseparable from three Irish brothers, Henry, John and George Lawrence, who then went on to assume pivotal roles in the events of 1857. If the careers of Sulivan and Macartney illustrate how India could provide a forum for Irishmen of talent, the events surrounding the Lawrences show how an Irish upbringing could impact directly upon Indian affairs. Born outside Ireland of County Londonderry parents, the formative experience for the Lawrences was their schooling at Foyle College in Derry City, where they were joined by Robert Montgomery who was to become a close collaborator in India and give his name to a Punjabi district. At Christmas 1851, these men, now members of the Punjab Board of Administration, reminiscing about Foyle College, decided to send fifty pounds each to assist two impoverished elderly brothers who had been ushers at the school.[5] The city with its traditions of the greatest siege in Irish and British history marked them indelibly. One of John Lawrence's friends and biographers wrote:

> School did little for him. But the glorious associations of Derry seem to have produced an abiding impression on his mind. More than two centuries have passed since Derry made her glorious defence ... Its effect on the young schoolboy was deep and lasting. Long afterwards, in the height of his fame, when he revisited Lahore with the Viceregal mantle on him, Sir John Lawrence told, in a public address, how the blood of the old defenders of Derry warmed within him as he fought in India against fearful odds, and nerved him for his work.[6]

R.T.C. LIBRARY
LETTERKENNY

The Lawrences came to prominence in the aftermath of the first Anglo-Sikh war when Henry was appointed Resident at Lahore, still nominally independent, and John became Commissioner of the Trans-Sutlej States, which the British had annexed. This arrangement broke down and after the second Anglo-Sikh war, the entire Punjab came under direct British rule, placed under a Board of Administration. Henry Lawrence was President, with John Lawrence and Robert Montgomery as the two other members. Associated with them in the delicate business of taking over the recently conquered province were two other Irishmen, their brother George and John Nicholson. Henry Lawrence was, however, soon at odds with the new Governor-General, Lord Dalhousie, a rigid Scottish utilitarian unconvinced of the value of Indian institutions; with his long experience of the country Lawrence knew they had to be treated with sensitivity and respect. Dalhousie's policy of annexing Indian states was not one that Lawrence could support; in 1853 he quit the Punjab, leaving John as Chief Commissioner. The Governor-General's attacks on Indian traditions were fast driving key groups to revolt; on 10 May 1857 regiments of the Bengal army at Meerut mutinied and, marching on Delhi, they proclaimed the aged Mughal, Bahadur Shah, Emperor of Hindustan.[7]

The outbreak of revolt found the three Lawrences in key positions. George was Resident in Rajputana, John was still Chief Commissioner in the Punjab, and Henry had recently taken up appointment in Lucknow as Chief Commissioner of Oudh. The last was a post of rare sensitivity since Dalhousie's ill-judged annexation of the former kingdom of Oudh had been a prime cause of the outbreak. Had Henry Lawrence been spared more time he might have helped avert what happened, for tact and sympathy with Indian institutions had long marked his career. All he could do was prepare his positions, not least by winning over the sympathy of Indian soldiers not yet committed to the revolt and gathering supplies. On 1 July, the siege of the Lucknow Residency began. It was to become a Victorian epic, but Henry Lawrence was not to conduct it, for the following day he was mortally wounded. His dying instruction to the garrison echoed the words of Derry's defenders in 1688: 'No surrender! Let every man die at his post; but never make terms.'[8]

Notable though Henry Lawrence's stand at Lucknow was, it fell to John to take the steps which saved the British position in India. The situation in his own province was perilous enough. To confront a potentially hostile 36,000 men of the Bengal army, he had 10,500 British troops and 20,000 Punjabi irregulars, recruited from a province only recently brought under British rule. The bulk of the population waited to see how the British would react to the disasters they were encountering. Lawrence's policy was to disarm systematically the regiments of the Bengal army and win the active support of the Indian princes; his appeals brought the Maharaja of Patiala, the Raja of Kapurthala, the Raja of Jind and the Raja of Nabha with their troops into the field. At Peshawar John Nicholson, son of a Lisburn doctor, formed his movable column from British and Punjabi irregulars. Nicholson became a Victorian hero, a brilliant, ascetic and ruthless soldier, his movable column spearheading the revival of British fortunes. The situation was desperate and Nicholson's methods do not make comfortable reading, especially his demolition of the 55th Native Infantry, forty of whom were blown from cannons before the Peshawar garrison.[9] The temper of the time is caught in the correspondence of Dr James Graham, an Irish doctor based at Sialkot. 'Lawrence and his officers have established a reign of terror in the Punjab which Blacky appreciates!', he wrote on 4 July 1857.[10] On the 8th, he wrote that 'Nicholson and his movable column will make a desperate attempt to cut these rascals up. Mercy is a word not to be found in his vocabulary'; the following day Graham was killed when the Sialkot garrison rose.[11] Throughout these critical weeks Lawrence had been sending such troops as he could spare to reinforce the small British force holding the ridge above Delhi, and at the end of August he felt it safe to send Nicholson and his column. On 14 September, Nicholson was mortally wounded leading the main assault. Although serious campaigning followed, it is clear that the capture of Delhi marked the decisive change in British fortunes and that by their skill and resolution John Lawrence and John Nicholson had immeasurably contributed to that outcome. Of Lawrence, his secretary later recalled that 'in his hardest times he would recur to the defence of Londonderry'.[12]

There could be no greater contrast to the career of John Nicholson than the life and work of Amy Carmichael. Yet each was identifiably a child of the Irish evangelical Protestant tradition, the former a figure from the avenging traditions of the Old Testament, the latter consumed by the spirit of the New. Born into a prosperous mill-owning family in County Down in 1867, as a young girl in Belfast Amy Carmichael underwent a religious experience which led her first into missionary work amongst the underprivileged children of the city before feeling the call to service overseas. In 1895, she left Ireland for south India where she was to remain until her death fifty-five years later. The focus of her work ran directly counter to the thrust of British policy in India after the events of 1857. Convinced that what had happened had been in large measure provoked by the fervour of evangelicals and their perceived interference with Hindu and Muslim traditions, the government frowned on missionary work and any

tampering with established religious and social practices. While under-
standable from the viewpoint of imperial stability, it meant that various social ills went unchallenged until elected Indian members of the
new Legislative Assembly set to work in the 1920s, and many had to
await a sovereign Indian parliament. Amy Carmichael's vocation was
to work to defy convention by attacking one such problem, the so-
called Temple Children of south India. It was not uncommon for families to dedicate a child to the Temple; for example, to give thanks for
recovery from illness or simply for economic reasons. These girls then
entered into a system of what was, in effect, prostitution. From her concern to rescue such children came her creation of the Dohnavur Community, which still thrives, and lobbying government for legislation to
prevent the sale of children for immoral purposes. In 1919, her services
were officially recognised by the award of the Kaiser-i-Hind medal, she
died in 1951, in the country she had seen grow to nationhood.[13]

Amy Carmichael's response to India was that of an Irish Evangelical
Protestant whose faith in Christianity never wavered. More complex
was the reaction of Margaret Noble, a fellow Ulsterwoman from
Dungannon. In 1895, then a young headmistress in London, she met
the influential Indian religious teacher Swami Vivekananda, then on a
celebrated world tour which had taken him to the Parliament of Reli-
gions at Chicago. Attracted by the power of Vivekanada's message,
three years later she responded to his call to come to India to work with
Indian women. In order to do so she made a complete conversion,
becoming a Hindu, taking the vow of Brahmacharya or celibacy, and
changing her name to Sister Nivedita (the 'Consecrated One'). Ruthlessly purged by Vivekananda of her western values, she dedicated herself to the study and teaching of all aspects of Indian life and culture.
Unlike south India, Bengal in the early years of the century was a
stronghold of nationalism and it was unsurprising that she quickly
became involved in its politics. As Sister Nivedita, she became a key
figure in Bengal's political and cultural renaissance, writing of the
Hindu classics and becoming a leading figure in the province's elite.[14]
Her memory was to remain fresh in India as an Irishwoman who had
come to share the culture and aspirations of her adopted home.

Her close involvement in Bengali politics was but one facet of the
mutual interest of Indian and Irish nationalism in the late nineteenth
and early twentieth centuries. Despite their ferocity, the events of 1857
had not marked the first step towards national independence. To
understand how modern Indian politics sprang to life we must look
instead to the social groups which were emerging out of the western-
based educational system which the British had begun to create in the
1830s. It was a system which naturally appealed to important Hindu

castes which had previously supplied administrators, such as the bhadralok of Bengal or the chitpavan brahmins of Maharashtra. Although they were a small minority of the population, by the 1870s many amongst them were beginning to chafe under a system of government which excluded them from the decisions about their country's future, not least because the educational system had taught them concepts of liberalism and nationalism, then so fashionable in Europe. With the emergence of Charles Stewart Parnell's Irish Parliamentary Party in the 1870s, and the consequent demand for Home Rule, it was not surprising that politically aware Indians should look to Ireland for inspiration and a measure of sympathy.[15] Too much should not be made of this, for many Irish Home Rulers were also strongly imperial in sentiment, and many Indians were wary of the extremism which seemed such a distinguishing mark of Irish politics, but the connection was there.

Some links had existed earlier in the century. In 1839, Daniel O'Connell was amongst those who formed the British India Society, which helped focus attention on abuses in the East India Company's rule. Conversely, the great Bengali social reformer, Ram Mohun Roy, wrote in 1822 about the problems of Irish absentee landlords and tithes. From the mid-1870s, the main link between Irish and Indian politics was the somewhat maverick MP for Dungarvan, Frank Hugh O'Donnell. There was no mystery about O'Donnell's interest in the affairs of the subcontinent, for his brother was a member of the Indian Civil Service, with a keen interest in social questions. As such, O'Donnell felt indignant at moves to curtail the number of Irishmen entering the Indian service. Equally, there was no doubt about the sincerity of his concern for Indian affairs. A substantial section of his *History of the Irish Parliamentary Party* was devoted to his attempts to interest influential Indians in London in the possibility of political action. 'From the earliest days of my connexion with Parliament I had devoted myself to the grievances of India', he recalled, adding that 'was no year in Parliament in which I did not devote a large portion of my time to the defence of Indian interests'.[16] In 1875, O'Donnell and four other Irish MPs, together with two Indians living in London, J. C. Meenakshya and Gyanendramohan Tagore, formed the Constitutional Society of India. Although this failed to develop any momentum, O'Donnell continued his interest in Indian affairs. In 1883, he combined with another leading Irish politician, Justin McCarthy, to recommend to Indians in London that they form an association to press Parliament for reform. As a result of their initiative, the National Representation Committee was formed and did lobby MPs. It did not long survive, however. The best that can be said for O'Donnell's well-intentioned efforts is that he helped give focus to sentiments which were emerging among young Indians in London and although his efforts were appreciated it is clear that he was held at arm's length. By the 1880s he was pretty well estranged even from his own party colleagues who had termed him 'Cranky' O'Donnell. More significant was the feeling amongst educated Indians that their hopes for reform rested on a positive British response and that this would not be helped if their cause were to be identified with what one Indian newspaper described as 'Irish malcontents'.[17]

Indian politics began to assume their modern shape in 1885 with the foundation of the Indian National Congress. It was in no sense a revolutionary, nor even a nationalist, gathering. Those who attended came from the new western-educated sections of society and their message to the government was that they felt the time had come for them to have some say in the government of the country. To that end various moderate resolutions were passed and loyalty to the Empire emphasised. It was a crucial moment for the history of British India, for this first Congress was only a beginning. A national political platform for Indian hopes and grievances had come into being and much would now turn on how the British would respond. The tone of that response was set, not by an Englishman, but the man who had assumed the Viceroyalty in 1884, Frederick Temple Hamilton-Temple-Blackwood, Marquess of Dufferin, an Irish landlord and aristocrat with estates in County Down. Although Dufferin was appointed as a Liberal by Gladstone's government, his Liberalism was of a distinctive, and fast eroding, kind. As a landlord, he had been alienated by Gladstone's Irish Land Acts of 1870 and 1881; as a member of the Ulster ascendancy, he was instinctively repelled by his old chief's espousal of Home Rule.[18]

There is a persistent myth in Indian historiography that Dufferin actively assisted with the foundation of Congress. This is based on the story told by the first President, W. C. Bonnerjee, in his book *Indian Politics* that in 1885 Dufferin had met the leading British advocate of Indian political rights, A. O. Hume. Hume put to the Viceroy, Bonnerjee argued, a scheme for an annual meeting of Indian politicians to discuss social matters and Dufferin's response was that such a gathering should criticise government actions, fulfilling, as it were, the functions of an Opposition.[19] Dufferin's own account to the Governor of Bombay, Lord Reay, is rather different, and gives an important clue to his thinking on Indian politics: Hume and his friends, he reported, were proposing a convention 'on the lines adopted by O'Connell, previous to Catholic emancipation'.[20] In fact, from the start of his Viceroyalty the Irish–Indian analogy had never been far from his mind, reflecting his concerns over Gladstone's moves towards Home Rule. In February 1885, he gave the Secretary of State for India, Lord Kimberley, his view of the educated bhadralok of Calcutta, or, in the parlance of the time, the 'Bengali Baboo'. 'He has a great deal of Celtic perverseness, vivacity, and cunning, and seems to be now employed in setting up the machinery for a repeal agitation, something on the lines of O'Connell's Patriotic Associations'.[21] By the summer of 1886, with Gladstone now clearly wedded to Home Rule, Dufferin was referring to Congress as the 'Indian Home Rule movement'.[22] It was, of course, a far cry from the modest, almost supplicatory, tone of the first Congress; for Dufferin it had become 'the importation en bloc from England, or rather from Ireland, of the perfected machinery of modern democratic agitation'.[23] This obsession with Ireland lasted to the end of his term. In August 1888, he informed the Conservative Secretary of State, Lord Cross, that: 'Unless some definite line is taken in these matters, we shall soon have something like a Home Rule organization established in India, on Irish lines, under the patronage of Irish and Radical members of Parliament'.[24] It was unfortunate that the tone of the British official response to the awakening of Indian politics was set by a viceroy so determined to view their development from such an Irish perspective. His farewell message to India came in his St Andrew's Day speech in Calcutta in 1888 when he chose to castigate Congress as a 'microscopic minority'. This, he confided in his last official letter to Cross, had made 'the Home Rule party in India very angry'.[25] It was a legacy which served no one well, though Dufferin might have been confirmed in his jaundiced view had he known that in 1888 Parnell was in contact with the Indian National Congress, advising them to use whatever reforms came their way to press for further Home Rule.[26]

'Microscopic minority' or not, it was with the Indian National Congress that the future lay. Frustrated by British disdain and unresponsiveness, especially during the Viceroyalty of Lord Curzon from 1899 to 1905, by 1907 Congress had changed its demand from one of participation in the government of the Raj to that of self-government within the Empire. Forced by the quickening pace of Indian politics, in 1909 the Liberal government instituted the Morley-Minto Reforms, allowing educated Indians some say in the councils of government. Soon after, the events of the First World War changed Indian politics beyond recognition. The sterling performance of Indian soldiers raised national self-esteem at a time when British prestige was being lowered by such disasters as Gallipoli and the fall of Kut. At the same time revolutionary events in Europe, not least the Easter Rising in 1916, showed Indians that great empires were vulnerable. Such was the pressure that in August 1917, the Secretary of State for India, Edwin Montagu, announced to Parliament that the aim of British policy was 'responsible government' within the Empire. In 1918, together with the Viceroy, Lord Chelmsford, Montagu announced a scheme of reform carefully constructed to carry India along that path. Giving Indians wide authority in provincial governments, Montagu's vision was of governed and governors working together towards dominion status in the not-too-distant future.[27] Not everyone shared his view. Chief among his critics was the fiery Irishman who had presided as Lieutenant-Governor of the Punjab since 1913, Sir Michael O'Dwyer.

O'Dwyer was a classic illustration of what had been a consistent theme in Indian affairs since the time of Laurence Sulivan: a close Irish involvement in the administration of the Raj. India had never ceased to be a source of attraction to ambitious young Irishmen of all denominations and throughout the nineteenth century their representation at every level of the administration continued to be high.[28] In his memoirs O'Dwyer pointed to the reason: with nine sons and five daughters to bring up on five hundred acres his father 'made clear to his sons that all we could expect was a good education for whatever profession we decided to adopt'. Hence, two brothers became Jesuit priests and two others served in India, one in the Indian Medical Service, 38 per cent of whose recruits in the 1870s were Irish.[29] O'Dwyer himself passed into the elite Indian Civil Service in 1885, the year the Indian National Congress was founded. Despite his Irish Catholic background, O'Dwyer was to be no sympathiser with Indian political aspirations. On the contrary, he later recorded that in 1882 he 'for the first time felt ashamed of being an Irishman' when learning of the Phoenix Park Murders. The following year, his father died as the result of intimidation by 'lawless elements', something which seems to have left O'Dwyer with an abiding contempt for 'terrorism and violent crime', whether in Ireland or in India.[30]

Between 1913 and 1919, O'Dwyer stood at a pivotal point in Indian affairs. From the time of the Lawrences, the Punjab had been the 'sword arm of India' and as as Lieutenant-Governor it fell to him to direct its war effort. On one level he seemed spectacularly successful. In the winter of 1914–15, he defeated the revolutionary Ghadr movement amongst sections of the Sikhs, while in the course of the war he recruited half a million Punjabis in the imperial cause. But by the end of the war he was increasingly seen as lacking in judgement. His recruiting methods were needlessly harsh, he had bitterly opposed Montagu's plans for political progress, and he was openly dismissive of Indian hopes for constitutional advance. There is little reason to doubt that 'the terrible events that had been going on in Ireland since the Easter Day rebellion in 1916' influenced his judgement.[31] By the spring of 1919 the Punjab bridled under O'Dwyer's rule. What ignited this dangerous situation was the introduction by the government of India of

[88]

the Rowlatt Bills, measures intended to give the authorities special powers to deal with any recurrence of armed revolutionary activity of the sort O'Dwyer had thwarted in the early stages of the war. These unpopular, and as it happened unnecessary, measures marked the entry into Indian politics of Mahatma Gandhi, who had previously made a name for himself defending the rights of Indians in South Africa. Gandhi declared a mass campaign of non-violent protest, based on the philosophy of satyagraha, but the nature of his message failed to register in the Punjab where widespread riots took place. This set the scene for the Amritsar Massacre of 13 April 1919 when Brigadier-General Reginald Dyer entered the enclosed Jallianwala Bagh and, fearing for the fate of his small force, opened fire without warning on an unarmed crowd, leaving at least 379 dead and 1,200 injured. Although O'Dwyer, then at the provincial capital of Lahore, was not directly responsible, he immediately sent approval of Dyer's action, an action which was to lead to his assassination by a young Sikh in London in 1940. The massacre was but the most serious incident in the cycle of repression which descended on the Punjab. The damage done to Indian goodwill was immeasurable, compounded by Dyer's subsequent public boast to the official committee of inquiry that the massacre had been a deliberate action on his part. The significance of his dismissal from the army in 1920 was not lost on those who feared for the future of the Union with Ireland where the Crown forces were fighting the Irish Republican Army. It came, therefore, as no surprise that when Dyer's fate was discussed in the House of Commons it was the Irish Unionist leader Sir Edward Carson, briefed by O'Dwyer, who rose in the general's defence. These events proved to be the most decisive in the history of India's freedom movement, for they led directly to Gandhi's assumption of leadership of the Indian National Congress and the growth of irresistible pressure on the Raj. O'Dwyer and the link with contemporary events in Ireland are essential to an understanding of them.[32]

In late June 1920, as the events of the previous year were being debated in London, another outbreak took place in the Punjab, but not this time by Indians. On 28 June, men of the Connaught Rangers stationed at Jullundur and Solon refused to obey orders and raised the green, white and gold flag of the Irish Republic over their cantonments. Given their remoteness from Ireland and the strength of the British army in India it was a quixotic gesture, which cost one of the leaders his life and others periods of imprisonment. Nor is it clear that it made any real contribution to Ireland's war of independence. But it did show that Britain could no longer count on the support of even the most 'loyal' of Irishmen. It was not coincidental that the Connaughts' defiance took place in the Punjab, the scene of so much recent bloodshed.

The regiment was, one of their leaders argued, repressing the people of India just as the British army was doing in Ireland. The point might have been lost on the average Indian for whom the Connaughts were no less racist in their attitudes than other soldiers of their time, but there is no doubt that the 'mutineers' were able to see a connection between the events in the two countries just as clearly as senior British military officers who feared for the integrity of the Empire.[33]

The establishment of the Irish Free State and her growing assertiveness in the affairs of the Empire in the 1920s confirmed that Indians could look forward to a similar evolution, but Ireland's road to independence had been accompanied by another important precedent, that of partition. Ulster Protestant opposition to the prospect of becoming a minority within a predominantly Roman Catholic Ireland whose values they did not share culminated in the Government of Ireland Act of 1920 which established Northern Ireland as a distinctive entity within the United Kingdom. While partition was inevitable at the time, it proved ultimately unstable, for one-third of Northern Ireland's population consisted of Catholics who would have preferred a united Ireland. In the 1920s and 1930s, however, the extent of that instability had yet to surface and for most observers the partition of Ireland set a precedent, useful or dangerous depending on one's point of view, for other divided societies within the Empire, not least India where a quarter of the population was Muslim.

In his perceptive report on the Indian political situation written in 1942, Sir Reginald Coupland acknowledged that 'the old-standing quarrel between Catholics and Protestants in Ulster has certain similar features with the Hindu-Muslim quarrel in India'.[34] What prompted Coupland was the knowledge that Indian independence had ceased to be a straightforward affair, for in March 1940 the Moslem League led by Muhammad Ali Jinnah had passed the Lahore Resolution demanding the partition of India on religious grounds. This is not the place to recount the transformation in Indian Muslim politics in the 1930s which led Jinnah and others to move from claiming guaranteed minority status within an independent India to asserting the right to separate nationhood under the banner of Pakistan, but broad similarities with Ireland were obvious. India's Muslims were strongly concentrated in two blocks, in the north-west and north-east of the sub-continent. Just as the leaders of Ulster Unionism were prepared to sacrifice their fellow loyalists in the rest of Ireland, Jinnah knew that millions of Muslims scattered throughout India could only join Pakistan by abandoning their homes – as he himself had to do in Bombay. 'Nor' as Coupland conceded, 'is the gulf between Protestant and Catholic Irish Christians so deep as between Indian Moslems and Hindus; nor does religion permeate the daily life of Irishmen as it permeates that of Indians'. The parallels were clear.[35]

The Irish precedent was not lost on the supporters of Pakistan nor on the Indian National Congress whose leaders were still fighting for a united India and fearful of creating 'Ulsters' on the sub-continent. In April 1941, in response to an attack by the leading Congressman Rajendra Prasad, Jinnah stated that: 'Even in the case of partition of joint families with which Babu Rajindra Prasad is so familiar, there is either an agreement or a decree, and then comes the question how best and equitably to divide the property. The latest example in history is that of Ireland. The constitution of North and South of Ireland was finally agreed upon after the principle and basis of division had been settled'.[36] In Jinnah's mind the Irish analogy could not have been more obvious:

> The Irish Nationalist Leader, Redman [sic], met Carson, Ulster leader, and told him, 'Look here, can't we come to some settlement? Why do you want to separate from Ireland? Mind you, there is not one-millionth part of the differences between the people of Ulster and Ireland'. What was Carson's reply? 'I do not want to be ruled by you'. My reply to Mr Gandhi is, 'I do not want to be ruled by you'.[37]

Those sympathetic to Indian unity knew this too. In 1942 Leonard Woolf of the Labour Book League wrote in the preface to his friend Mulk Raj Anand's *Letters on India* that Anand 'and the Congress Party are beginning to treat the Muslims and Mr Jinnah as Mr de Valera treated Ulster ... do you really want to turn Mr Jinnah into an Indian Lord Craigavon?'.[38] By 1945 such debate was becoming academic, for Jinnah commanded the allegiance of the mass of India's Muslims. After an attempt at a federal solution in 1946 had failed, it fell to the last Viceroy, Lord Mountbatten, to decide that the partition of India was inevitable. It was perhaps fitting that it was an Irishman, Field Marshal Sir Claude Auchinleck, last Commander-in-Chief of the Indian Army and then Supreme Commander of the armies of India and Pakistan, who did more than any single individual to prevent the outbreak of war between the two states when they immediately quarrelled over the fate of Kashmir.[39]

Ireland and India touched at many points. Irish participation in the administration of India was so extensive as to help justify the claim that it was an 'Irish' as well as a 'British' empire, offering advancement, and often fame, to young Irishmen of relatively humble background. The Lawrence brothers would have cut no social standing in contemporary British society; India offered John Lawrence the possibility of becoming Viceroy. Claude Auchinleck's widowed mother would have found it hard to sustain him in a 'smart' British infantry regiment of the early twentieth century; in India he could use his potential to become Commander-in-Chief. While such men did not question the fabric of British imperial control, they often brought a distinctive Irish perspective to it. At critical points this was the defensive mentality of an Irish Protestant community long conscious of its minority position in the country. There is ample evidence that the Lawrences saw themselves as steeled in the 'No Surrender' tradition of the siege of Derry, and Lord Dufferin had no difficulty in seeing the fledgling Indian National Congress through the prism of his experiences in contemporary Belfast politics. Sir Michael O'Dwyer's record shows that such fervent imperialism was not confined to Irish Protestants.

Ireland's contribution to the growth of Indian nationalism is less easy to assess, despite the evidence of interest on the part of people like Daniel O'Connell, Margaret Noble and Frank Hugh O'Donnell. Indians looked to Ireland as an example of opposition to imperial control and were grateful for expressions of Irish interest and support, but the first generation of Indian politicians knew they were treading a difficult path and were reluctant to associate themselves with what they saw as the extremism of Irish politics. It is safe not to read too much into the relationship. Where Ireland did set a clear example was partition. It is important to remember that in the period when the question of the division of India on religious lines arose, partition seemed to have provided a relatively painless way out of the Irish problem. Ireland may be seen as occupying a distinctive place in the growth of the British Empire in India and in the manner of its demise.

Notes

Anyone interested in this theme should also read Ganesh Devi, 'India and Ireland: literary relations', in Joseph McMinn, *The Internationalism of Irish Literature and Drama*, Gerrard's Cross, 1992, pp. 294–308. I am grateful to Professor Devi for the fruitful discussions we had when engaged in our respective projects. Extracts from the papers of the first Marquess of Dufferin and Ava appear with the permission of the Deputy Keeper of the Records, Public Record Office of Northern Ireland and the Marchioness of Dufferin and Ava.

1 Sulivan's career is best described in Lucy S. Sutherland's classic study, *The East India Company in Eighteenth-Century Politics*, Oxford, 1952, especially Ch. 3.
2 For Macartney's Irish background see Peter Roebuck (ed.), *Macartney of Lisanoure 1737–1806*, Belfast, 1983, ch. 1.
3 Macartney's stewardship at Madras is analysed in the author's chapter 'India 1780–1786', in Roebuck, *Macartney of Lisanoure*.
4 See H. Furber (ed.) *The Correspondence of Edmund Burke*, V, Cambridge 1965, pp. 206–12.

5 Frederick P. Gibbon, *The Lawrences of the Punjab*, London, 1908, pp. 174–5.

6 Sir Charles Aitchison, *Lord Lawrence*, Oxford, 1892, p. 201.

7 See Gibbon, *The Lawrences of the Punjab*, Chs 18 & 21.

8 *Ibid.*, p. 295.

9 Lionel J. Trotter, *The Life of John Nicholson*, London, 1897, p. 252.

10 A. T. Harrison (ed.), *The Graham Indian Mutiny Papers*, Belfast, 1980, p. 40.

11 *Ibid.*, p. 36.

12 Sir Richard Temple, *Lord Lawrence*, London, 1890, p. 36.

13 Frank Houghton, *Amy Carmichael of Dohnavur*, London, 1953, *passim*. I am grateful to Miss Margaret Wilkinson of Castlerock, County Londonderry and the Dohnavur Community for her reminiscences of Amy Carmichael and insights into the Community's work.

14 See Romain Rolland, *The Life of Vivekananda and the Universal Gospel*, Calcutta, 7th edn, 1970, pp. 92–3.

15 See S. R. Mehotra, *The Emergence of the Indian National Congress*, Delhi, 1971, pp. 327–31.

16 F. H. O'Donnell, *A History of the Irish Parliamentary Party*, II, London, 1910, pp. 423–45.

17 Mehrotra, *The Emergence of the Indian National Congress*, p. 330.

18 The best analysis of Dufferin's imperial career is A. T. Harrison, 'The First Marquess of Dufferin and Ava: Whig, Ulster landlord and imperial statesman', unpublished D.Phil. thesis, New University of Ulster, 1983.

19 For a discussion see Briton Martin Jnr, *New India 1885*, Berkeley, 1969.

20 Dufferin to Reay, 17 May 1885, Dufferin and Ava Papers, PRONI, Mic.22/46 (quoted in Harrison, 'The First Marquess of Dufferin and Ava', p. 600).

21 Dufferin to Kimberley, 3 February 1885, Dufferin and Ava Papers, PRONI, D.1071H/M1/4, *ibid.*, p. 586.

22 Dufferin to Maine, 9 May 1886, Dufferin and Ava Papers, Mic. 22/43, *ibid.*, p. 601.

23 Dufferin to Kimberley, 21 March 1886, Dufferin and Ava Papers, PRONI, D.1071H/M1/5, *ibid.*, p. 605.

24 Dufferin to Cross, 17 August 1888, Dufferin and Ava Papers, PRONI, D.1071H/M1/7, *ibid.*, pp. 208–09.

25 Dufferin to Cross, 3 December 1888, Dufferin and Ava Papers, PRONI, D.1071H/M1/7, *ibid.*, p. 618.

26 J. P. Loughlin, *Gladstone, Home Rule and the Ulster Question 1882–93*, Dublin, 1986, p. 213.

27 See Montagu's magisterial state paper, written by Sir William Marris, *Report on Indian Constitutional Reforms*, Cd. 9109, 1918.

28 See Donald Harman Akenson, *The Irish Diaspora: A Primer*, Toronto & Belfast, 1993, Ch. 6.

29 Sir Michael O'Dwyer, *India as I knew it 1885–1925*, London, 1925, p. 6; Akenson, *The Irish Diaspora*, p. 145.

30 O'Dwyer, *India as I knew it*, p. 7.

31 *Ibid.*, p. 9.

32 O'Dwyer's book is essential reading for anyone seeking to understand these events. As those close to events knew how partial an account it was, it went largely unchallenged at the time. So pronounced were his Irish characteristics, that he was known in India as 'The Gombeen Man'. The late Professor L. F. Rushbrook Williams, Director of Information, Government of India, provided useful insights into O'Dwyer.

33 Sam Pollock, *Mutiny for the Cause*, London, 1969.

34 Sir Reginald Coupland, *The Indian Problem, 1833–1935*, Oxford, 1942, p. 28.

35 *Ibid.*, p. 29.

36 Jamil-ud-din Ahmad, *Speeches and Writings of Mr Jinnah*, I, Lahore, 1968, p. 281.

37 *Ibid.*, p. 510.

38 Mulk Raj Anand, *Letters on India*, London, 1942, p. 9.

39 John Connell, *Auchinleck*, London, 1959, pp. 930–2.

CHAPTER FOUR

The Irish military tradition and the British Empire

Keith Jeffery

Bernard Shaw once expressed the opinion that 'all an Irishman's hopes and ambitions turn on his opportunities of getting out of Ireland'. It followed, therefore, that the best way of persuading him to enlist in the British army was *not* to appeal to his patriotism but to 'his discontent, his deadly boredom, his thwarted curiosity and desire for change and adventure'. 'To escape from Ireland', continued Shaw, the Irishman 'will go abroad to risk his life for France, for the Papal States, for secession in America, and even, if no better may be, for England.'[1] If what Shaw asserts is true, then it might be supposed that the British Empire, with its world-wide opportunities for adventure, would have exercised an irresistible pull on restless young Irishmen. But Shaw's typically provocative analysis is not sufficient explanation in itself. Much of the business of Irish recruitment in the service of the British Empire, like that of imperial defence itself, was quite prosaic. The notion both of the alleged martial qualities of the 'Irish race' and the Irish propensity to join British armed forces may fundamentally owe more to economic necessity than any romantic – or other – urge to leave home. Whatever the truth of the matter, it is indisputable that Irishmen have both emigrated and enlisted (the two options may not be entirely unrelated) in very substantial numbers since at least the eighteenth century.

In the early nineteenth century Ireland supplied a disproportionate share of the soldiers in the British army. In 1830, when Ireland's share of the United Kingdom population was 32 per cent, 42 per cent of the army were Irish-born. There were, indeed, at this time more Irishmen than Englishmen in the army. The figures for the European armies of the East India Company were even more impressive. Between 1825 and 1850, 48 per cent of all recruits for the Bengal army were Irish.[2] Throughout the century, however, and particularly after the Great Famine in the 1840s, the proportion of Irishmen steadily declined, in line with the Irish proportion of the United Kingdom population. Yet

Irishmen consistently supplied more than the Irish population's share of the army. In 1881, 21 per cent of the army, as against 15 per cent of the population, was Irish. At the turn of the century the figures were 13 and 11 per cent respectively. Between 1900 and the beginning of the First World War both figures continued to decline, but, for the first time, from 1910 onwards the proportion of Irish in the army fell below the Irish share of the population. In 1913 only 9 per cent of the army were Irish, compared with 10 per cent of the population. If we look at actual recruiting figures, a similar pattern emerges. In 1878, 20 per cent of all recruits for the army were Irish; in 1899, 12 per cent; and in the recruiting year 1912–13 (1 October–30 September), 10 per cent.

During the period from the Second South African War (1899–1902) to the World War of 1914–18 criticism by nationalists of Irish recruitment to the British forces gathered strength. For Irish nationalists the Second South African War – the Boer War – clearly represented the 'unacceptable face' of British imperialism. Far from the Empire operating as a civilising influence – a plausible enough interpretation for many British and Irish people throughout much of the nineteenth century – the violent British challenge to the Boer republics – white, Christian, already 'civilised' – seemed to represent no more than an uncontrollable imperial lust for power and conquest. The Nationalist MP John Dillon told Parliament that Ireland's reluctance to enlist during the war was principally due to 'our hatred of imperialism. While the war fever in this country has been passing over the land and has made the war popular here, it has had the opposite effect in Ireland.'[3]

Advanced nationalists had already been attracted by the situation in southern Africa. Apart from North America, it was, as Donal McCracken has observed, 'the only place in the English-speaking world where a white nationalist people were effectively standing up to the British empire'.[4] Arthur Griffith, who founded Sinn Fein in 1905, spent some time in the Transvaal during the late 1890s. There he found the anti-British atmosphere most refreshing, and it confirmed his belief that 'God Almighty had not made the earth for the sole use of the Anglo-Saxon race'.[5] At the time of the Jameson Raid nationalist Irishmen in Johannesburg formed an 'Irish Brigade' and, after the outbreak of war in October 1899, two Transvaal Irish Brigades emerged: one led by an Irish-American adventurer, Colonel John Blake, along with Major John MacBride; the other commanded by Arthur Lynch. Although a few recruits joined from Ireland (and some Chicago-Irish), essentially these units were drawn from the Irish community already in South Africa. Together they never numbered more than about 400 men, a striking contrast to the estimated 28,000 Irishmen who served against them in the British army.[6] But their symbolic significance was very great – Irish soldiers banding together to fight against the British Empire – and their activities were exploited fully in anti-English propaganda disseminated by Griffith and others back home in Ireland.

Opposition to the South African War significantly invigorated the Irish nationalist movement at a time when it was still suffering from the effects of the Parnellite split in 1890. The conflict, moreover, prompted the first seriously organised attempts by nationalists to dissuade Irishmen from joining the British forces. The Irish 'Transvaal Committee', formed in October 1899 to support the Boer republics in their struggle against the British Empire and to dissuade Irishmen from joining up, led the way. One of its members, Maud Gonne, drafted a pamphlet entitled *Enlisting in the English Army is Treason to Ireland*. Gonne, who came from a British army family (her father had been a colonel), was also one of the founders in October 1900 of a nationalist women's organisation, Inghinidhe na hEireann (Daughters of Ireland), which embarked on a vigorous anti-recruiting campaign. Leaflets describing the 'shame of Irish girls consorting with the soldiers of the enemy in their country' were distributed to soldiers and 'their women of blemished character' in the streets and pubs of Dublin. Gonne and her colleagues in the Inghinidhe were helped by a number of men, including Griffith and Tom Kettle, who, ironically, was to die in France in 1917 serving in the 16th (Irish) Division.[7]

In April 1900 Queen Victoria visited Ireland for the last time. Maud Gonne believed that the visit had specifically been organised to stimulate Irish recruitment which, it was asserted, had been badly hit by the general unpopularity of the war in Ireland and the anti-recruiting campaign. The Queen, asserted Gonne, had taken a 'shamrock into her withered hand' to dare ask Ireland for more recruits.[8] The same month the monarch had assented to the creation of a new regiment of foot guards – the Irish Guards – 'to commemorate the bravery shown by the Irish Regiments during the operations in South Africa in the years 1899–1900'.[9] This notable action – no new regiment had been formed for many years – was the culmination of a campaign mounted for some official recognition for the 'daring and devotion' of the Queen's Irish troops in South Africa. Field Marshal Lord Wolseley, the Irish-born Commander-in-Chief of the army, had argued that 'the Queen's appreciation of the gallant services rendered by her Irish soldiers will have a magical effect upon that sentimental and imaginative race all over the world'.[10]

Perhaps Wolseley had the 'imperial dimension' of Irish service in mind, and perhaps, too, he was anxious to stimulate recruitment in Ireland. The evidence regarding the impact on enlistments of nationalist opposition to the war and the anti-recruiting campaign is mixed.

The Transvaal Committee naturally claimed that their efforts had met with great success: witness the necessity for a royal visit to bolster 'loyal' morale. Enlistments for the part-time militia fell from 5,615 (14 per cent of the U.K. total) in 1899 to 3,737 (10 per cent) in 1901. But the numbers volunteering for the regular army held up quite well during the war years, especially in the Dublin area, where the anti-recruiting campaign was concentrated.[11] What we can say is that nationalist pressures only had a slight impact, if any at all, on recruitment. Yet the war in South Africa had provided an excellent opportunity for the Transvaal Committee to exploit a combination of Irish national sentiment, sympathy with the plight of the gallant Boer republics, anti-English feeling (such as it was), and antagonism towards the army as an occupation of last resort for Ireland's urban unemployed.

Between the end of the South African War and 1910 there was both a gradual, though not consistent, decline in Irish enlistments and an increase in anti-recruiting activity. Understandably nationalists linked the two facts. When it was put to the Secretary for War in 1906 that recruiting in Ireland had fallen because of the influence of Sinn Fein and the Gaelic League, he replied that it had merely been part of a general fall.[12] In the years immediately preceding 1914 the level of enlistment picked up. In addition, Dublin was a consistently better recruiting area than supposedly more 'loyal' Belfast for the decade before the First World War. In both 1905 and 1911 nearly three times the number of recruits joined in the Dublin area than in Belfast.[13] There is, however, no reason to suppose that political considerations were especially important in influencing the decision of individual Irishmen whether to join up or not, nor that specific shifts in the rate of recruitment can be ascribed to the activities of particular groups. As the Under-Secretary for War told the Commons in 1914 when trying to explain variations in the statistics: 'there are many obscure causes which affect recruiting, and it is not always possible to identify with certainty the precise cause of any particular upward or downward movement'.[14] Economic factors were certainly important, and Joseph V. O'Brien has suggested that they were more significant than political influences, and that they also help to explain the apparent anomaly between Dublin and Belfast. 'Idle hands and empty stomachs', he writes, 'are a powerful antidote to patriotic idealism ... and there were more of these in Dublin than in any other part of the country'.[15]

The First World War, however, marked a significant watershed in Irish recruitment to the British army. During the war years political factors do seem at last to have affected recruitment very significantly indeed. But at first Ireland responded nearly as willingly to the call to arms as the rest of the United Kingdom. Reporting on recruitment during the first three months of the war (to 4 November 1914), Lord Midleton told the House of Lords in January 1915 that Scotland had produced the best returns of 237 recruits for every 10,000 population. In England, industrial and urban areas had provided more men than purely agricultural areas. Lancashire, for example, had 178 men per 10,000, while London and the home counties had returned 170. The figure for Ulster, Dublin, Wicklow, Carlow and Kildare was 127. By contrast, that for the west of England was 88, East Anglia, 80, but the agricultural districts of southern Ireland produced only 32.[16]

Throughout the United Kingdom there was a massive drop in enlistment after the first rush of recruits, which eventually prompted the government to introduce conscription for England, Scotland and Wales in March 1916. Although its imposition was threatened, especially in 1918, conscription was never applied to Ireland. Over the whole period of the conflict, therefore, Ireland proved to be a significantly poor recruiting area. After 1918 national and imperial rates of recruitment were officially calculated. Evidently reflecting the consistent application of compulsion, the 'percentage of the male population represented by enlistments' in England, Wales and Scotland was 24, 22 and 24 respectively. For Ireland, however, the figure was just 6 per cent. In partial explanation of this the compilers of the statistics warned 'it must be remembered that the male population of Ireland is composed chiefly of young men up to 18 years of age and of men over 50, as a large proportion of the remainder emigrate to the United States and Colonies'.[17]

Patrick Callan has argued that it is more useful to compare Ireland's recruiting record to that of the dominions, rather than Great Britain, but even here Ireland's showing was pretty poor. For Australia, Canada, New Zealand and South Africa the percentage of the white male population who joined up was calculated. The highest rate (not unexpectedly) was attained in New Zealand (19 per cent) which adopted conscription in May 1916. In August the following year it was introduced in Canada, which returned a figure of 13 per cent. But Australia, where two referendums rejected compulsory service, returned the same percentage, and South Africa, with a substantial non-British population and which had suffered an anti-war rebellion in 1914, still managed to return a figure of 11 per cent, nearly twice that of Ireland.[18]

Clearly, Ireland was different from the rest of the white empire. Even taking into account the apparently peculiar structure of the Irish male population, the Irish response over the whole war was low. Yet the extent to which political considerations directly affected the Irish willingness to enlist remains debatable. The recruiting statistics for Ireland itself do not completely match the acknowledged wartime changes in

[98]

Irish public opinion, especially among Irish nationalists. At the beginning of the hostilities the great majority of nationalists, as represented
by John Redmond's Irish Parliamentary Party, had placed themselves
behind the war effort, as had the Ulster Unionists, who since at least
the spring of 1914 had been threatening armed opposition to the British
government's Home Rule proposals. The more extreme, separatist,
nationalists, however, had resolutely come out against the British, and,
following the traditional axiom of 'England's extremity' being 'Ireland's opportunity', had launched the spectacular though immediately
unsuccessful Rising of Easter 1916. In Dublin, where the violence and
disruption was concentrated, the civil population were initially very
much opposed to the Rising, but feeling began to change with the crude
and heavy-handed British response to the challenge. The prolonged
series of executions of the rebel leaders which followed the suppression
of the Rising is frequently taken as the point at which nationalist opinion in Ireland began to swing strongly behind the separatist movement.
These events, coupled with the arrest and detention of many advanced
nationalists during 1916, undoubtedly had an impact on Irish opinions,
but so too did a progressive disenchantment with the war itself, and the
growing feeling that the continued prosecution of England's – or the
Empire's – war had little specific to offer Ireland. Such feelings found
practical expression in 1918 when a renewed threat of conscription
prompted the emergence of a broad coalition of Home Rule nationalists, Sinn Fein and the Catholic Church in opposition to the measure.
By the end of the war Irish nationalism had been so radicalised that the
old Nationalist Party was destroyed and the republican separatists of
Sinn Fein swept the board in Ireland in the 1918 United Kingdom general election. Meanwhile Irish Unionists, especially in the north of the
country, became more fervently loyal to the Union with Great Britain.
The sacrifices of the 36th (Ulster) Division at, for example, the battle of
the Somme in 1916, had, it was felt, sealed the Union with blood; a
comparable blood sacrifice to that made by the republicans of the 1916
Rising.

The pattern of Irish recruitment, however, does not quite match this
account. During the first eighteen months of the war (to the end of
February 1916), when voluntary enlistment applied throughout the
United Kingdom, Irish recruitment fell off quite dramatically, but in
almost exactly the same proportions as in England, Scotland and
Wales. Patrick Callan has calculated a six-monthly recruiting index for
the whole war. If the first six-month period – the peak period for voluntary enlistments – is 100, the second is 50 and the third 40. Despite the
fact that the recruiting response for Ireland as a whole was rather less
than for the rest of the state, the rate of decline was very similar. The

British index figures for the first three periods of the six months standing at 100, 50 and 39.[19] From February 1916 (before the Easter Rising) there was a further sharp drop in Irish recruiting, with only half as many men enlisting between February and August 1916 as had done so during the previous six months. After this the Irish returns dip still further, the lowest point being reached during February–August 1917, with a recruiting index of 11. Thereafter recruiting picked up slightly in the next two six-month periods (indexes of 13 and 12, respectively), and then quite markedly in the last three-and-a-half months of the war, from August to 11 November 1918. More men joined up during this short period than had done so during February–August 1916. Partly this was in response to a special recruiting campaign in 1918, which if successful was to be a possible substitute for conscription.

The striking success of the 1918 recruiting campaign casts some doubt on there being any unequivocally direct correlation between recruitment and political opinion. Army officials in Ireland certainly believed that social and economic factors were more important than political atmosphere.[20] Even more basic factors constrained recruitment. In the spring of 1918 one observer reported that 'without in any way discounting the very live National Feeling in Ireland today, the fear of conscription is the ordinary elementary fear of the average healthy human being of being tortured and killed'.[21] In 1918, moreover, Irishmen were encouraged to enlist in non-combatant branches of the armed services based at home. The army, too, seems to have been held in low regard, an attitude which had perhaps grown up particularly since the 1916 Rising, but also one which displayed a healthily pragmatic appreciation of the risks accompanying enlistment. In 1918 56 per cent of the recruits went to the Royal Air Force – attracted, among other things, by the labouring and technical opportunities offered – with only 36 per cent to the army, and the rest to the Royal Navy.[22]

There is no way of telling for certain whether the pattern of voluntary recruitment in Great Britain would have followed that of Ireland had conscription *not* been introduced, but the available evidence suggests that the Irish experience after February 1916 may not have been wholly unrepresentative of the voluntary spirit of service throughout the United Kingdom. The progressive (though not consistently so) unwillingness of Irishmen to serve Britain and, by extension, the Empire may say as much about contemporary attitudes to the war throughout the British Isles as it does about political circumstances in Ireland. It would be unwise to argue that the growth of separatist nationalism, and the concomitant alienation of much Irish political opinion from the British link, had *no* effect on recruitment, but that effect may have been less than has hitherto generally been supposed.

The figures for recruitment to the British army after the end of the Great War are, if anything, yet more ambiguous. During the period of hostilities from January 1919 until the truce in July 1921, significant numbers of Irishmen left the British army, while, at the other end of the cycle of military service, as many men from Ireland joined up as had done so in the past. In 1913, 9 per cent of the army was Irish-born. In 1920 and 1921 (the next years for which there are statistics) the proportion was 8 per cent; it fell to 5.5 per cent in 1922, and hovered about the 5 per cent mark throughout the inter-war years, until it rose slightly towards 6 per cent in the late 1930s. Recruitment held up quite well in the immediate post-war period. In 1919–20 and 1920–21, 9 per cent of all recruits were Irish, roughly in proportion to the Irish share of the United Kingdom population – as had been the case immediately before the First World War.[23]

When looked at in Irish regional terms, there was no dramatic polarisation of opinion – as expressed in the willingness to join the British army – between 'nationalist' and 'Unionist' Ireland. The office with the worst recruiting record[24] in Ireland in 1919–21 was Galway, but the second worst was Omagh in Ulster. Dublin still recruited better than Belfast. In 1919–20, unexpectedly, far and away the best recruiting office in Ireland was Clonmel, which drew recruits from the counties of Tipperary, Waterford, Kilkenny and Wexford. Here an astonishing 1,052 men enlisted, a figure equivalent to about one man in every 30 between the ages of 15 and 24. Even in 1920–21 recruitment in Clonmel remained above average, and was only bettered by Dublin and Armagh. During 1919–21 recruiting was marginally (but no more than that) better in northern districts as a whole than southern, but there is no *recruiting* evidence to suggest that the prevailing violent conflict in Ireland had any great impact. Despite the circumstances, for British army recruiting officers in Ireland at the time, the period 1919–21 seems by and large to have been 'business as usual'.

In December 1921, however, the situation did change markedly. After the signing of the Anglo-Irish Treaty, recruitment was suspended for all the Irish infantry regiments,[25] and in February 1922 all the recruiting offices in what became the Irish Free State were closed down – a preliminary to the disbandment of the five southern Irish infantry regiments of the line.[26] There was an immediate and dramatic effect on the numbers of Irishmen joining up. In 1921–22, the last year for which figures are available, only 3 per cent of all recruits were Irish. Nevertheless, considering the overall proportion of Irishmen in the army in subsequent years, it is reasonable to suppose that Irish recruitment from throughout the island recovered somewhat in the later 1920s and 1930s.

While the specifically 'southern' Irish infantry regiments were disbanded after the treaty, the new Irish Free State remained an important source of army recruits. The surviving Irish regiments, especially the Irish Guards, continued to accept recruits from independent Ireland after 1922. In 1926–27, for example, 27 per cent of the recruits for the Royal Inniskilling Fusiliers came from the twenty-six counties, and ten years later over one-third of the Royal Irish Fusiliers were 'Free Staters'. During the Second World War, although the Free State remained neutral, no impediment was placed on Irish men and women enlisting in the British services. In 1946 the Dominions Office calculated that over 43,000 people 'born in Eire' had joined up during the war. Over the same period about 38,000 people volunteered from Northern Ireland.[27]

After 1945 the army continued to regard recruitment from independent Ireland as important. In 1947 when the regular army was being reorganised in brigades, the colonels of the three Northern Ireland infantry regiments objected to any brigade title, such as 'Ulster' or 'Northern Ireland', which might identify their units solely with Northern Ireland and thus discourage men from Eire, who at the time comprised half of all their recruits, from joining up. The Northern Ireland government for their part objected to any purely 'Irish' title. In the end they compromised on the 'North Irish Brigade'. In 1949, after Ireland formally became a republic and left the British Commonwealth, the three British service ministries agreed that this should in no way affect the position of recruits from the new Irish Republic, who should 'continue to be treated in exactly the same way as UK citizens'.[28]

The Irish Republic remained a significant source of recruits, at least for the Irish infantry regiments. In the late 1950s, for example, one quarter of the officers of the Royal Irish Fusiliers, and over 40 per cent of the other ranks, had home addresses in the Republic. Family tradition has certainly sustained enlistment from Ireland, but also for those Irishmen who simply desired to pursue a military career, the British army (still in the 1950s and 60s with world-wide imperial responsibilities) offered more exciting opportunities than the Irish army. It was also true that the pay and working conditions in the British forces were rather better than those available in Ireland. Britain's shrinking overseas military commitments, improvements in Irish army pay and conditions, and, since the 1960s, Irish service with the United Nations, have all served to erode the particular attractions of service in the British forces. The lure of extensive imperial service is no longer available as an encouragement for Irish recruitment, yet the attraction of joining a comparatively large army remains.

Why did the army want to enlist Irishmen in particular? The first response to this question is that the British military authorities may not actually have had any bias towards the Irish *per se*, simply that there were more Irishmen available than, say, English or Scots. Surveying the nationality of the mid-Victorian army, H. J. Hanham did not think that 'there was anything special about Ireland that made the Irish particularly keen to enlist'. He concluded that Irish recruiting 'followed very much the same trend as English recruiting. Ireland was simply like good recruiting districts in England, where men were encouraged to enlist by want of alternative employment'.[29] Surveying a rather longer period, Peter Karsten decided that the 'green redcoats' of Ireland 'entered upon their army careers essentially in search of economic security and status'.[30] Alan Ramsay Skelly has asserted that in the first half of the nineteenth century 'massive unemployment and social disruption on a scale rarely experienced in the rest of the country rendered Ireland fertile for recruitment'. The drop in Irish enlistments thereafter merely paralleled the catastrophic fall in the Irish population and the development of large-scale emigration following the Great Famine of the late 1840s. Skelly remarks that the fall in the Irish population by some 32 per cent between 1851 and 1901 'had gone a long way to drying up the reservoir of recruits'.[31] But the continued relative poverty of Ireland meant that the supply of potential soldiers never entirely evaporated.

In the late nineteenth century emigration and recruitment varied in inverse proportion. There was, for example, a slump in emigration from Ireland between 1875 and 1880 and a peak in recruitment.[32] It may be, therefore, as Peter Karsten has observed, that 'when emigration opportunities look bad (due to recession in the British, Australian and North American economies) the queen's shilling looked good'.[33] An anecdote told by Sergeant A. V. Palmer in 1890 tends to confirm the economic motivation. An Irish recruit in his unit had complained of the inadequacy of the army diet. 'Then you didn't enlist from want?', the sergeant asked. 'Oh, no, Sergeant', he replied, 'I had lashin's o' that before I joined the Army.'[34] Even in the twentieth century comparatively high unemployment rates in Ireland continued to act as a stimulant to recruitment.

A second reason why the British army might particularly seek out Irish recruits is the supposed warlike qualities of the Irish themselves. In February 1916 John Redmond (himself rather an unmartial figure) asserted that 'the Irish people, like their racial kinsmen the French, are one of the peoples who have been endowed in a distinguished degree with a genuine military spirit, a natural genius and gift for war which produces born soldiers and commanders.'[35] Here we have the Irish presented as a 'martial race', perhaps not precisely in the British-Indian sense, but certainly a people who can be depended on to provide good fighting men. W. B. Yeats exemplified the adventurous, devil-may-care Irish volunteer in his poem 'An Irish airman foresees his death', written during the Great War:

> Nor law, nor duty bade me fight,
> Nor public men, nor cheering crowds.
> A lonely impulse of delight
> Drove to this tumult in the clouds.[36]

But there is not much hard evidence to test the hypothesis of the 'fighting Irish' one way or the other, merely plenty of anecdote and allegation. The sum of this is that the Irish are wild, fierce and impetuous soldiers, generally better in attack than defence, and with potential problems of discipline which could be overcome if they are 'carefully handled'. There is only one systematic, scholarly investigation of this phenomenon: a study of Irish soldiers in the First World War by Terence Denman. During the war, Charles à Court Repington declared that the Irish were 'the finest missile troops in the British army'; narrating an attack by the 16th (Irish) Division, the British official history of the war described the Irish troops as 'impetuous' and 'eager', whose 'ardour could not be restrained'. Reflecting on discipline, Major Sir Francis Vane, who served with the Munster Fusiliers, noted that 'a kindly familiarity which might injure discipline in a British [sic] regiment, will never be presumed upon by the Irish'. He compared the easygoing relationships between the officers and men in his regiment to those found in Australian or Canadian units. Terence Denman observes 'that during the First World War troops from Australia, New Zealand and Canada were often regarded in much the same way as Catholic Irish soldiers: as "shock troops" with a reputation for unruliness and indiscipline'. Denman also draws a parallel with attitudes towards France's black colonial troops: celebrated for their wild impulsiveness, but also 'criticised for their alleged lack of discipline and cohesion in battle; and patronised for their supposed limited intellectual capacity and their childlike qualities'. The generalisations, moreover, which were made about Catholic Irish troops: 'recklessness, negligence, credulity – too easily complemented claims that the Irish were incapable of organising their political life in a responsible way.' While conceding that 'it would be surprising ... if there were not particular characteristics which distinguished Catholic Irish soldiers', Denman's careful conclusion is that in matters of discipline and effectiveness, whether in attack or defence, they were not markedly different from other units of the British army.[37] Indeed, it may be the case that the attitudes with which the Irish troops were regarded did as much to define their behaviour as any innate 'racial' characteristics.

[104]

The nature of Irish recruitment to the British army can be viewed within three broad models of imperial military service: metropolitan, where the process is most similar to recruitment in other parts of the United Kingdom; dominion, where the Irish experience accords more closely to that of Canada, Australia, New Zealand or South Africa; and colonial, where Irish soldiers are scarcely better than mercenaries, employed to do the Empire's dirty work.

The metropolitan interpretation may be as much a result of the historiography as anything else. Most of the accounts of Irish military service under the British Crown have been written by ex-British soldiers themselves. Regimental histories, and official histories of the various wars in which Irish units have been involved, are an obvious example of this. Reviewing a recent volume devoted to 'the history of the Irish soldier', written by a British brigadier, an Irish writer observed that 'the Free State army and then the army of the Republic are briefly described without, one suspects, any real degree of enthusiasm'. The reviewer went on to remark somewhat tartly that 'the real Irish soldier for the brigadier is the one who has the crown above the harp'.[38] The official British position, following the abolition of the separate Irish military establishment under the Act of Union (1800), that Ireland was no different from any other part of the United Kingdom, was more or less adhered to during the nineteenth century. The 'Cardwell' reorganisation in the 1870s, which linked infantry battalions in pairs and attached them to specific localities, treated Irish regiments just the same as all the others. The reform, indeed, consolidated the Irish contribution to the British army and concentrated Irish recruits in specifically Irish units more fully than hitherto.[39] In military terms, Ireland was a domestic station, though the post of General-Officer-Commanding-in-Chief (GOC) of the Irish Command had some 'colonial' characteristics. While the GOC reported to the War Office in London, he was also chief military adviser to the Irish government (technically the Lord Lieutenant, as representative of the Crown, was at the head of the armed forces in Ireland), and the GOC was habitually appointed to the Irish Privy Council. The Irish Command, however, was one of seven Home Commands in the British Isles (as they emerged after 1900). It was, too, a very prestigious posting, and the not-very-onerous Dublin job was frequently used as a convenient resting-place for distinguished senior generals approaching, or even having passed, the summit of their careers.[40]

Irish units (including some cavalry regiments, which were less preponderantly 'Irish' than the infantry battalions) served throughout the United Kingdom and the Empire. Occasionally, though, there were worries about Irish soldiers serving in Ireland itself. Despite (or perhaps because of) being an Anglo-Irish Protestant, Lord Wolseley (GOC Ireland, 1890–95) doubted the reliability of Irish troops. The political controversy accompanying Gladstone's second Irish Home Rule Bill prompted him to favour the removal of all the Irish regiments from Ireland 'until Mr Gladstone dies or is turned out of office'.[41] In March 1895, after Gladstone had resigned, but while the Liberals were still in office, Wolseley, 'influenced by the conviction based upon my knowledge of Ireland and Irish ways', argued 'that you draw the teeth from the elements of possible internal disturbance whenever you remove from Ireland all regular Irish regiments, all the Army Reserve and all the Militia Regiments', except some Northern Protestant units.[42] On the other hand, Sir Neville Lyttelton (GOC Ireland, 1908–12) expressed his opinion in 1909 that there were now no grounds for mistrusting Irish troops and that 'the principle that Irish soldiers can safely be trusted while employed in Ireland' had also been accepted by the Army Council.[43]

When put to the test, this British faith in the reliability of Irish soldiers was vindicated since locally-raised troops, for example, served loyally against the nationalist insurgents during the Rising of Easter 1916. On the Western Front a German attempt to exploit the events in Dublin fell flat. In May 1916 a placard was put up opposite the trenches of the 8th Munster Fusiliers reading 'Irishmen! Heavy uproar in Ireland. English guns are firing at your wifes [sic] and children!'. According to the regimental history, the battalion replied to this by singing 'God Save the King', and one night a party crossed no-man's land and captured the notice which was later presented to King George V.[44] Nevertheless, during the 1919–21 hostilities, Irish units were not deployed in Ireland, a pattern incidentally repeated in the more recent Northern Ireland 'Troubles' from 1969 until the decision in the mid-1980s, when it was decided once again to station regular Irish units in the province.[45]

The clearest example of the metropolitan recruitment mode exists in officer enlistment. Here Ireland was even more over-represented than in the army as a whole. Throughout the second half of the nineteenth century about 17.5 per cent of all officers were Irish.[46] Almost entirely drawn from the Anglo-Irish Protestant landowning class, these men were natural Unionists, whose Irishness was perhaps more cultural (though rarely Gaelic) than anything else. Certainly there was a distinguished succession of Irish officers in the British army, which perhaps reached its highest point during the Second World War, with such men as Montgomery, Alexander, Alanbrooke, Dill and Auchinleck,[47] but their Irishness as celebrated in popular memory can be overstated. Consider, for example, a typical piece of doggerel from the time of the Great War:

Sir John French from Galway,
Good old Roberts too,
Kitchener from Kerry,
All Irish through and through.
There was a man named Wellington
Who fought at Waterloo;
So never let yourself forget
That you are Irish too.[48]

Although both French and Roberts were themselves proud of their Irish background, Kitchener was only coincidentally Irish, born on a farm recently purchased by his wholly English parents. Wellington is credited, no doubt apocryphally, with some hesitation regarding his Irishness. When taxed with the fact, he is reputed to have declared that 'being born in a stable doesn't necessarily mean that one is a horse'.[49] To a very great extent many of the Anglo-Irish officer class could regard themselves as Irish, British and even 'English' simultaneously. Born in Ireland, frequently educated in England, and serving the British Empire, these men carried a bewildering range of cultural national baggage with them throughout their careers.

Field Marshal Sir Henry Wilson is a classic example. Born in County Longford in southern Ireland of Ulster Protestant stock, he was educated at an English public school (Marlborough) and served in a fashionable English infantry regiment (the Rifle Brigade). Through his life he remained in his own eyes and in those of others an Irishman, but this was by no means a restrictive or exclusive national identification. There is an element of national confusion (at least as national identity is understood in the late twentieth century), for example, in a speech Wilson gave at the unveiling of a war memorial at Queen's University, Belfast, in January 1922. 'Scattered hither and thither over this dear country of theirs, of Ulster, and that dear land of theirs, England, were memorials of those ... who were not professional soldiers, the names of men who thought it was their duty to come forward to help their country when their country was in danger'.[50] After Wilson had been assassinated in June 1922 on his doorstep in London – by Irish nationalists claiming a national justification[51] – the tributes were equally unclear as to the Field Marshal's nationality. Lord Carson noted 'the loss of Ireland's greatest son and one of the Empire's greatest citizens; he died for Ulster's liberty'.[52] At a memorial service at the British army headquarters in Constantinople, Sir Tim Harington, an old friend of Wilson, and another general with Irish forebears, asserted that 'he died for Ireland ... England has lost a great patriot ... [Sir Henry] would have given his life cheerfully if he thought that England, the British Empire, and his beloved Ireland would gain.'[53]

Although most of the Irish generals in the British army were 'Anglo-Irish' and, no doubt, held broadly Unionist political views, there were one or two notable exceptions. Sir William Butler, a Tipperary-born Catholic, enjoyed a distinguished and archetypically 'imperial' career in the British army, serving in Canada, India, Burma, Egypt and the Sudan, West Africa and South Africa. In Ireland, however, he was a committed Home Ruler and a great admirer of Parnell. 'Though he was a member of an alien army,' declared one observer after Butler's death, 'and so, in a sense, an alien to the governed people of Ireland, he never lost the instincts of nationality that he drank in with his mother's milk.'[54] In May 1920 General Sir Edward Bulfin, a middle-class Dublin Catholic, was offered the job of Chief of Police and Head of Secret Intelligence in Ireland on the strength of his local knowledge and his successful handling of nationalist disorder in Egypt in the spring of 1919. But he declined the offer on the grounds 'that as a Catholic and an Irishman it would be distasteful to him to do any work ... which was not of a purely military character'.[55] Clearly in Bulfin's case, imperial military expertise against nationalists did not carry over into Ireland. Another Catholic Irish general was the brilliant but ill-stared Eric Dorman-Smith ('Chink'), admired by Auchinleck and hated by Montgomery, who after the end of the Second World War changed his name to O'Dorman Gowan and committed himself to the Irish republican cause, even to the extent of offering himself and his estate in County Cavan to the IRA for training purposes.[56]

In an ornamental fashion, as it were, or in a 'theatrical' sense (borrowing one of Walter Bagehot's terms for the less efficient parts of the British constitution[57]), connections between Ireland and the Empire are demonstrated by some of the titles taken by these Irish generals on their elevation to the peerage. Viscount Gough 'of Goojerat (Punjab) and Limerick' and Earl Roberts 'of Kandahar, Pretoria and Waterford', reflect imperial expansion, while Viscount French 'of Ypres and High Lake' (County Roscommon) illustrates a different aspect of Irish soldiering in the service of the Empire. A later set of titles, those of Harold Alexander, represents an unusually wide range of experience. Earl Alexander's subsidiary titles were 'Viscount Alexander of Tunis and Errigal (County Londonderry); and 'Baron Rideau of Ottawa and Castle Derg' (County Tyrone). The curious feature of all these titles (or is it so odd?) is the complete absence of any explicitly *English* dimension.

The second, 'dominion', model of service developed alongside the emergence of constitutional Irish nationalist agitation and the growing demand for Home Rule during the nineteenth century. Although the Irish Parliamentary Party before 1914 demanded (and, in the still-born

1914 Home Rule Act, gained) only a measure of devolution *within* the United Kingdom, many nationalists found common cause with the British colonies of settlement which progressively achieved responsible self-government in the late nineteenth and early twentieth centuries. Irish nationalist MPs, for example, made 'pointed references in the debates on the Commonwealth of Australia and South Africa Bills, to the liberties still denied to Irishmen but to be extended to Australians and South Africans'.[58]

The notion that the self-governing dominions 'completed their nationhood in the war'[59] found an echo in the Irish experience, at least as expressed by John Redmond at the time. In the first place Redmond argued that there was a contractual relationship between Ireland's contribution to the war effort and Britain's responsibility to apply Home Rule, the operation of which had been suspended for the duration of hostilities. Nationalist Ireland, he maintained, must make a clear and unequivocal contribution to the war effort. If this were done and the war was won, it would then be 'absolutely inconceivable' that England could 'deny the charter which Ireland has won by generations of long, peaceful and constitutional effort'.[60] In 1916 Redmond wrote that 'at long last, after centuries of misunderstanding, the democracy of Great Britain had finally and irrevocably decided to trust Ireland with self-government'. This 'profound change ... in the relations of Ireland to the Empire' being so, he 'called upon Ireland to prove that this concession of liberty would have the same effect in our country as it has had in every other portion of the Empire, and that henceforth Ireland would be a strength instead of a weakness'[61] – ironic enough words in the light of the Easter Rising. 'For the first time in the history of the Wars of England', declared Redmond, 'there is a huge Irish army in the field.'[62] It was a 'national army',[63] in its own way expressing Irish nationhood.

On St Patrick's Day 1917 Redmond wrote that Irishmen 'Unionist and Nationalist, Catholic and Protestant' had 'combined for a common purpose: to fight the good fight for liberty and civilisation, and, in a special way, for the future liberty and honour of their own country'.[64] But this constitutional and gradualist nationalist vision, which in any case owed much to wishful thinking about the allegedly unifying impact of Catholic and Protestant war service, was under sharp attack from the purer and more intransigent national vision promulgated by the men of 1916 and their successors. The idea that the cause of Ireland was being advanced in France, or Gallipoli, or Salonika, was steadily superseded by the more immediately plausible (and for the most part physically safer) notion that Ireland's interests were best served by action at home.

The rise of militant Irish nationalism had an effect on military

recruitment in the wider empire. Politicians in Canada and Australia
had intermittently taken an interest in the campaign for Irish Home
Rule. As early as 1882 the Canadian legislature passed a resolution in
favour of Irish self-government. In 1905, and again in 1914, the Australians followed suit.[65] In Australia, however, the Irish issue had become
especially salient during the Great War because opposition to conscription, which the government attempted to introduce in the autumn of
1916, was particularly concentrated among the country's substantial
Irish community. In December 1916, following the defeat of a referendum on compulsory military service, the Australian Prime Minister,
W. M. Hughes, telegraphed Lloyd George to say that he could not
attend the forthcoming Imperial Conference in London due to the difficult political position at home. 'As things are', he wired, 'recruiting is
practically at a standstill and considerable section more or less openly
hostile to war.' The Irish population of Australia, which, he said, comprised about 25 per cent of the total and 'not less than eighty per cent of
those in the Labour movement' was overwhelmingly 'at present hostile
to policy necessary to effective prosecution of war.' 'Defeat of referendum', he continued, 'mainly due to Irish opposition which was very
bitter.' Hughes argued that Irish matters were 'thus seen to have far
reaching effects and direct bearing upon prosecution of war in Britain
itself as well as Australia and [it is] seriously prejudicing ... imperial
developments'. The 'Irish Question', he asserted, 'is now [an] imperial
Question and ought to be so treated. In my opinion it must be settled
without delay.' The effect in Australia of an Irish settlement, he added,
'would be profound. We could get reinforcements ... [and] prosecute [a]
vigorous war policy.'[66]

Lloyd George was sympathetic to Hughes's difficulties but replied
'that it is not possible for me to settle Irish Question just as I please.
The consent and co-operation of the Irish Parties is essential.' He urged
the Australian to 'put pressure on Irish leaders to accept any settlement
which would not involve compelling Ulster by force of arms to accept
Home Rule. It must also be based upon whole-hearted Irish assistance
in winning the war.'[67] During 1917 Hughes again wanted Lloyd George
to appreciate the importance of the Irish issue in Australia. 'An unsettled
Ireland', he stated bluntly, 'seriously weakens Empire in field and in
eyes of neutrals ... Present position in Ireland now rendered acute
makes neutrals regard our cry that we are fighting for rights small
nations as hypocritical. Effect of present position in Ireland upon manpower most serious throughout Empire.'[68] Hughes was rather overstat-
ing the case here; in New Zealand, for example, albeit with a rather
smaller Irish community, there was much less excitement. Indeed, one
immediate response to the Easter Rising was a call for yet greater

efforts in the prosecution of the war. A New Zealand Irish meeting at Dunedin, called to protest *against* the Rising, passed a resolution calling 'on every one of our fellow countrymen of an age and fit who have not yet enrolled to offer their services at once to their country'.[69] But in Australia the political conflict was particularly bitter, and in December 1917 conscription was rejected in a second referendum.

Reflecting on the impact of the Great War on the dominions – the 'catalyst of war' – Nicholas Mansergh noted that 'the challenge and the sacrifices of war sharpened their sense of separate identities and strengthened their feelings of nationality'.[70] At a high political level the creation of the Imperial War Cabinet in 1917, for example, helped to advance dominion independence. This was 'the high road of prime ministerial consultation'. But, as Desmond Morton has observed, 'there was also a low road of practical military collaboration along which the military forces of the dominions found their way to greater autonomy'.[71] It was this road, perhaps, to which John Redmond aspired for the Irish divisions of Kitchener's 'New Armies'. But Kitchener himself was opposed to the establishment of specifically Irish formations for precisely the reason that they might conduce to the development of military autonomy within the British army, which while possibly stimulating, say, Irish recruitment, would weaken the collective imperial war effort.[72] Redmond's vision of an Irish 'national army' serving in the Great War had, in any case, become wholly unrealistic by about the last year of the war. The identification of Ireland with other 'small nations' for whose freedom the war was being fought ('Irishmen! Remember Belgium!', instructed one 1914 recruiting pamphlet[73]) cut little ice with the separatists, who saw Irish service in the British forces as merely confirming Ireland's continuing subjugation to the British Empire.

The dominion model of recruitment, which combined loyalty to the Empire with the assertion of Irish nationality, did not survive the Great War, even though four-fifths of Ireland actually became a dominion after 1922. Although Lloyd George insisted in July 1921 that continued recruitment in Ireland be included in any Anglo-Irish settlement, the stipulation was quietly forgotten and did not appear in the treaty signed the following December.[74] In the post-war years the only survivals of the Redmondite identification of service in the British forces with service for Ireland occurred at the dedication of Great War memorials in the Irish Free State. The monument at Castlebellingham, County Louth, bids by-standers 'pray for those ... who died for Ireland in the Great International War, 1914–1918'. The Cork memorial, significantly erected by a nationalist ex-servicemen's association, commemorated 'comrades who fell in the Great War fighting for the freedom of small nations'.[75]

Unveiling a memorial at Kells, County Meath, in April 1924, Major-General Sir Oliver Nugent waxed quite lyrical on the imperial ramifications of service during the war. 'Memorials such as these', he said, 'are not commemorations of the men themselves only. They commemorate the period which saw the uniting of the Nations of British and Irish birth into one great Commonwealth ... Every man who served his country during that period is a rivet in the fabric of the Empire.'[76] In Northern Ireland, of course, there was less hesitation about celebrating the imperial dimension. At a meeting in Cookstown, County Tyrone, in October 1925, the Northern Ireland organiser of the British Legion, Captain Creighton, noted that 'in this part of the Empire' there had been no conscription. 'Every man', he said, 'volunteered, not only for their own land, but for a far greater, the British Empire.'[77]

The third, 'colonial', model of recruitment sees Irish military service as representing no more than the conventional exploitation of colonial human resources by the imperial power. One study of Irish soldiers in the British army from the 1790s to the 1920s explicitly posed the question: 'What are the consequences of an imperial power recruiting members of a subject colony for the ranks of its military forces?'.[78] Cynthia Enloe's stimulating survey, *Ethnic Soldiers*, firmly places Ireland in the colonial context. She places consideration of Ireland in a chapter on 'martial races'. 'Joining the conqueror's army', she maintains, might be seen as a form of 'ethnic political adaptation'. In times of communal civil war, such as has occurred in Ireland, 'enlisting now becomes an act of political allegiance, and a statement of communal allegiance'.[79]

The colonial interpretation was espoused, for example, by the separatist nationalists who formed the Transvaal Committee in 1899, who also argued that joining the British forces served to consolidate the British hold on Ireland. 'Irishmen,' read one anti-recruiting hand-bill, 'will you keep your country enslaved and under the heels of England by joining the English army, navy or police forces?'[80] The anti-enlistment campaign continued after the end of the South African War. In October 1905 two Dublin men, one wittily calling himself 'Tommy Atkins', were prosecuted for distributing copies of an 'offensive poster' in the city which proclaimed:

> Let us fight the battle for Ireland here on her own sod. Don't be deluded by the false promises of the recruiting sergeant. Regiments of the British Army with Irish names ... are only Irish in their title. The man who joins them is an anti-Irishman. They are part of the English garrison holding Ireland in subjection.[81]

When the First World War broke out and John Redmond offered the services of the Irish Volunteers (the nationalist paramilitary organisation) to the British war effort, the advanced, separatist, wing broke away. The issue between them and Redmond was 'clear and simple'. It was 'whether the Irish Volunteers are pledged to the cause of Ireland, or all Ireland, and of Ireland only, or are likewise bound to serve the Imperial Government in defence of the British Empire'. The republicans, moreover, repudiated 'the claim of any man to offer up the blood and lives of the sons of Irishmen and Irish women to the services of the British Empire while no National government which could speak and act for the people of Ireland is allowed to exist'.[82] Redmond's response was that since Home Rule was on the statute-book (albeit not yet operational) Irishmen could with a clear conscience serve the Empire's cause – which was as he believed, after all, a just one.

The threat that conscription might be imposed on Ireland in 1918 served to confirm for the separatists (and others) the colonial nature of the Anglo-Irish relationship and that Britain as an imperial power sought merely to exploit Ireland's manpower resources. A wide spectrum of nationalist opinion argued that Ireland *per se* had been given no opportunity to decide for itself on the question of compulsory service. In April 1918 a conference, including nationalists from Redmond's party, affirmed that 'the passing of the Conscription Bill by the British House of Commons must be regarded as a declaration of war on the Irish nation. The alternative to accepting it as such is to surrender our liberties and to acknowledge ourselves slaves.' The Catholic hierarchy, considering that an attempt was being made 'to force conscription upon Ireland against the will of the Irish nation and in defiance of the protests of its leaders', concluded that 'conscription forced in this way ... is an oppressive and inhuman law, which the Irish people have a right to resist by all means that are consonant with the law of God'.[83] The conscription issue galvanised opposition to the war and greatly boosted the political fortunes of Sinn Fein. Conscription, recalled a republican, 'was the dynamic that set the struggle alight ... It tore the last barriers against full hearted support for the national movement. It was a bigger mistake even than the executions.'[84]

One factor the colonial model of recruitment shares with the metropolitan is the economic stimulus to enlistment. In economic terms the colonial exploitation of the country might so depress employment and wages that an individual might be left with no alternative but that of joining up. Writing in 1915, James Connolly, the socialist revolutionary leader of the Irish Citizen Army (which took part in the 1916 Rising), who had himself served in the King's Liverpool Regiment, addressed the question of 'economic conscription'. 'Fighting at the front to-day', he argued, 'there are many thousands whose whole soul revolts against what they are doing, but who must nevertheless continue fighting and murdering because they were deprived of a living at home, and compelled to enlist that those dear to them might not starve.' Connolly asserted that only freedom for Ireland would provide economic and social freedom for Irish people. 'We do not believe', he wrote, 'that the existence of the British Empire is compatible with either the freedom or the security of the Irish working class. That freedom and security can only come as a result of complete absence of foreign domination.'[85] In another essay, Connolly specifically and ironically linked Ireland's situation with the Empire. 'Irish soldiers in the English Army', he declared, 'are fighting in Flanders to win for Belgium, we are told, all those things which the British Empire, now as in the past, denies to Ireland.' [86]

In addition to economic necessity, another characteristic of colonial recruitment is a concern on the part of the imperial power with the political reliability of the recruits. We have already noted Lord Wolseley's worry about the stationing of Irish soldiers in Ireland, but, on the whole, Irish soldiers in the British army remained consistently loyal. The problem of subversion, or at least attempted subversion, did occasionally arise. In the 1860s the Fenians, led by John Devoy, had attempted, with very little success, to seduce Irishmen from their 'allegiance to a foreign power'. 'Red-coated Fenians', Devoy had claimed, 'would form a fine backbone for an insurgent Irish army.'[87] During the Great War Sir Roger Casement attempted in Germany to raise an 'Irish Brigade' from Irish prisoners-of-war. But only about fifty men responded to the call and Casement himself believed that their motives stemmed not so much from Irish patriotism as a desire for better treatment. 'They are mercenaries pure and simple,' he thought, 'and even had I the means to bribe them, I should not attempt to do so'.[88]

There was, however, an imperial angle to the raising of the Irish Brigade. When Casement secured permission to attempt to raise the formation, he drew up an agreement with the German authorities that it would be formed 'solely to achieve the independence of Ireland'. A clause was included in the document, however, that if the German navy were unable to transport the men to Ireland, it was agreed that they might be used to help the Egyptians gain their freedom. Casement believed that 'short of directly fighting to free Ireland from British rule, a blow struck at the British invaders of Egypt, to aid Egyptian national freedom, is a blow struck for a kindred cause to that of Ireland'. In the event, the brigade, such as it was, did nothing for either Ireland or Egypt. In any case, John Devoy in the United States and the Clan na Gael leadership, who were funding Casement's stay in Germany, did not think much of the scheme. 'We in America', wrote Devoy, 'strongly object to any such proposal, and our friends in Dublin are unalterably opposed to it.'[89]

The 'Troubles' in Ireland immediately following the end of the Great War had some impact on the Irish regiments of the British army, though this should be put in the context of the whole British army being in a poor state during these post-war years.[90] Early in 1920 Charles Bonham-Carter took over command of the 2nd Royal Dublin Fusiliers, then stationed at Constantinople. He recollected that there were two distinct types of men in the battalion: re-enlisted war veterans, the great majority of whom were 'good fellows'; and post-war recruits which 'included with youngsters a number of the worst sort of corner-boys from Dublin'. Certainly it seems to have been a generally poor battalion. 'I don't think I shall ever be able to make the battalion a sober one', wrote Bonham-Carter in February 1920. During the time the Fusiliers were at Constantinople (January–November 1920) there were three trials for murder and 'many courts-martial'. When the unit was posted to India in November 1920, Bonham-Carter was permitted to send home some two hundred 'undesirable' soldiers and 'from that time on', he wrote, 'the conduct of the men could scarcely have been better. Some of the bad discipline may have been due to the troublous times through which Ireland was passing at that time'. Helpfully, however, the Catholic chaplain warned Bonham-Carter 'from time to time of men who were followers of Sinn Fein, but it was not possible to combat their influence completely. Afterwards in India, although one or two men arrived with a draft with the intention of making trouble, they had no influence.'[91]

There were difficulties closer to home as well. In May 1920, Harold Burgess, a left-wing activist, manager of Sylvia Pankhurst's communist newspaper the *Workers' Dreadnought*, was arrested and charged with attempting to cause disaffection amongst the Irish Guards at Caterham. He had, reported the Special Branch, 'supplied certain Guardsmen with copies of the pamphlet "Soviets for the British" for distribution amongst their comrades and gave them money'.[92] There is some evidence of nationalist feeling affecting Irish units. In the summer of 1920 Sir Henry Wilson, then Chief of the Imperial General Staff, was asked by General Percy Radcliffe in Warsaw if he could withdraw the 1st Battalion Royal Irish Regiment from Allenstein, where it was serving as part of the Allied force supervising a League of Nations plebiscite in East Prussia. The battalion, wrote Radcliffe, 'are full of Sinn Fein and cannot be relied on nor is their conduct doing any good to our prestige'.[93]

The battalion was removed to the Army of the Rhine whose GOC, General Sir Thomas Morland, complained about it in February 1921. The following month Morland learned that he was to receive two more Irish battalions – since Irish units were not used in Ireland, they were disproportionately represented in the armies of occupation. Morland complained to Wilson. 'The Communists', he wrote, 'are always trying to get at the Irish – and one Irish battalion in the garrison is enough.' But his wish was not to be granted. In May 1921 Lloyd George agreed to supply British units to help supervise the League of Nations plebiscite in Silesia. The Cabinet decided to send mostly Irish troops since 'under existing conditions [they] were not suitable for service in the United Kingdom'. Wilson assured Morland (under whose command they would come) that he would only send 'good' battalions. And, indeed, in September the Munster Fusiliers struck Morland 'as a particularly smart and well-ordered battalion'.[94]

Two months later a potentially serious situation arose in the Irish Guards. Over the weekend of 19–20 November two machine guns were taken from the Guards Barracks at Windsor. On 22 November a sergeant of the Irish Guards and three civilians (all members of the Irish Self-Determination League) were arrested and the stolen arms recovered. The police reported that the case was 'satisfactory in the sense that the evidence does not indicate anything in the nature of organised conspiracy in the ranks of the Guards'. The sergeant in question, it seemed, owed his downfall to 'the twin failings of drink and bad company'. The Special Branch, however, felt that there was 'no doubt' that there was a conspiracy in Great Britain 'to corrupt members of His Majesty's Forces, particularly those of Irish nationality'.[95] In addition, since the Anglo-Irish Treaty negotiations were at a critical juncture, the colonel of the guards battalion was strictly instructed to suppress all the facts of the case.[96]

The most striking problem of the period was the Connaught Rangers mutiny in the Punjab in June 1920. Between 28 June and 2 July 1920 three hundred or so men of the 1st Battalion Connaught Rangers mutinied, giving as their reason that they were 'in sympathy with their country' and that they 'would do no more work until the British troops had been removed from Ireland'.[97] Although a combination of causes, including 'the unrest in Ireland', 'very poor discipline', 'want of satisfactory occupation and activity', and 'the hot weather',[98] appear to have contributed to the mutiny, the initial reaction in India blamed the outbreak on the current Irish situation. The mutiny, Delhi told London on 2 July, was 'a protest against the situation in Ireland where they [the mutineers] consider their friends are being oppressed'. This immediately threw suspicion on to the other Irish regiments stationed in India. The Indian high command at once took steps to censor the mails of all Irish units, 'in order to ascertain the character of the correspondence that may be proceeding from Ireland and in order to determine whether the Irish regiments are in communication with each other in India for the purpose of combining against authority'.[99] Within a fortnight, however, Delhi reported that the situation regarding the Connaught Rangers was now satisfactory and censorship was not after all to be imposed.[100]

The investigation of the other Irish regiments stationed in India which followed the mutiny threw up some interesting information. The units included two Irish cavalry regiments: the 8th (King's Royal Irish) Hussars and the 5th (Royal Irish) Lancers. It was reported that the Hussars were about half Catholic and half Church of England and 'most of the Irishmen in them enlisted to escape from Sinn Fein'. Only about 30 per cent of the Lancers were Irish, mostly from the North and presumably, therefore, reliable. The commander of the 2nd Royal Irish Regiment reported that 'there was not a more contented unit in India' (an evident contrast with the 1st Battalion on the Rhine).[101] The mutiny was taken more seriously in other quarters. In July a Paris newspaper, the *Tribuna*, published a letter from the Hungarian communist Bela Kun to Lenin. 'Henceforth', he wrote, 'the focus of the world's revolution will be in India, where Irish soldiers will provide the Indians with abundance of arms and ammunition.'[102]

The courts-martial which followed the mutiny convicted sixty-one men and imposed fourteen sentences of death. Just one, that of Private James Daly, was confirmed. In London this worried Lord Lytton, the Under-Secretary for India. While he agreed that mutiny should be dealt with severely, he observed that there had been political considerations behind the offence. He argued perceptively that if the relations between England and Ireland were happily adjusted in the future, there would be the possibility of an amnesty, which might apply to the mutineers. He urged the Viceroy, therefore, to consider carefully whether the execution should proceed. But the Indian military authorities were adamant. 'The interests of Ireland', telegraphed the Viceroy, 'have not only to be appraised, but also the possibility of maintaining in the future discipline in the Indian Army. The Commander-in-Chief considers that the example of mutiny set up in this case by a British Regiment cannot fail to re-act with disastrous results on the Indian Army if condonation is practised.'[103] Thus, the interests of India (where mutiny was understandably a sensitive issue), the army and the Empire overrode those of Ireland and Anglo-Irish relations. James Daly was shot at dawn on 2 November 1920.

The Connaught Rangers mutineers became celebrated as Irish patriots in the years that followed. Popular verses and ballads were written about the mutiny. There was indeed an amnesty and the prisoners were all released by early 1923. In the late 1930s the Irish government granted pensions to the surviving mutineers, and to James Daly's aged father. The enabling legislation, the Connaught Rangers (Pensions) Bill, was not entirely unopposed. One member of the Dail, Frank MacDermott, who had served in the Irish Guards during the war and who sat as an Independent, was anxious to place on the record his view of the men's actions: 'They went into the British Army of their own free will, took the oath of allegiance of their own free will, took upon themselves the obligation of maintaining the splendid traditions of the Connaught Rangers, and yet in spite of that they mutinied while in the service of the Crown'.[104] Such criticism was very much a minority view. Yet MacDermott lit upon an interesting circumstance in terms of the conditions under which the men involved in the mutiny joined the British army. In effect they seem to have enlisted, even in the aftermath of the Great War, within the metropolitan mode of recruitment. More than anything else, they were simply young men seeking employment, and there is no suggestion that any political ramification entered their minds. But the changing political environment in Ireland during the 1919–21 hostilities meant that by 1920 they had practically become colonial troops, perhaps even mercenaries, certainly with loosening and conflicting ties of loyalty and patriotic sentiment.

The relations between Ireland, Great Britain and the Empire-Commonwealth, as they developed during the late nineteenth and twentieth centuries, do not make for any straightforward categorisation. As we have seen, the military relationship – which, dealing as it does with matters of life and death, is one of considerable importance – displays characteristics of both imperial unity and separatism, affection and enmity, service and subversion. The history and pattern of recruitment demonstrates that for Irishmen (and it was almost entirely a male preserve) the British army and Empire presented a series of challenges accompanied by both benefits and costs. On the positive side, the army provided employment, and for those so disposed, no doubt, a measure of excitement and adventure. As to the costs, apart from the physical risks of soldiering – it is, after all, a potentially very dangerous occupation – on a political level these became increasingly apparent with the progressive growing apart of nationalist Ireland from the rest of the United Kingdom. So much so that no Irish recruit to the British army today can scarcely be unaware, however dimly, of the political dimension of his action in 'taking the queen's shilling'. Yet Irishmen, from North and South, still join the British army.[105] The inherent attractions of serving what remains of the British Empire still find some response, it seems, in the martial Irish breast.[106]

Notes

1 Preface to *O'Flaherty V.C.* (1917), in Bernard Shaw, *Selected One-Act Plays*, Harmondsworth, 1972, p. 68.
2 The main secondary sources for recruitment to the army are: H. J. Hanham, 'Religion and nationality in the mid-Victorian army', in M. R. D. Foot (ed.), *War and Society*, London, 1973, pp. 159–81; Alan Ramsay Skelly, *The Victorian Army at Home*, London, 1977; E. M. Spiers, 'Army organisation and society in the nineteenth century', in Thomas Bartlett & Keith Jeffery (eds), *A Military History of Ireland*, Cambridge, forthcoming; Patrick Callan, 'Recruiting for the British army in Ireland during the First World War', unpublished Ph.D. thesis, University College, Dublin, 1984.
3 *Hansard*, 14 May 1901, H.C. Deb. 4s, col. 80.
4 Donal P. McCracken, 'Irish settlement and identity in South Africa before 1910', *Irish Historical Studies*, XXVIII (1992–93), p. 146. See also McCracken, *The Irish Pro-Boers, 1877–1902*, Johannesburg, 1989.
5 Quoted in Calton Younger, *Arthur Griffith*, Dublin, 1981, p. 10.
6 McCracken, 'Irish settlement', pp. 147–8. During the fighting at Surpise Hill in December 1899, one Boer 'is said to have remarked to a British Rifleman, "Don't prod me, I'm an Irishman." "So am I, ye ——," replied the Rifleman, as he skewered him.' (from the *Morning Post*, March 1900, reprinted in the *Rifle Brigade Chronicle for 1900*, p. 169). The British soldiers were under the command of an Anglo-Irish officer, Captain John Gough, brother of Hubert Gough of 'Curragh incident' (1914) fame.
7 Callan, 'Recruiting for the British army', Ch. 1, pp. 8–9; Margaret Ward, *Unmanageable Revolutionaries: Women and Irish Nationalism*, London, 1983, pp. 50, 53–4; Terence Denman, '"The red livery of shame": the campaign against army recruitment in Ireland, 1899–1914', *Irish Historical Studies*, XXIX (1994–5), pp. 208–33.
8 Maud Gonne MacBride, *A Servant of the Queen*, London, 1974 edn, p. 293; Nancy Cardoza, *Maud Gonne: Lucky Eyes and a High Heart*, London, 1979, pp. 185–6.
9 Peter Verney, *The Micks: the Story of the Irish Guards*, pbk edn, London, 1973, p. 4.
10 *Ibid.*, pp. 2–3.
11 See Joseph V. O'Brien, *'Dear Dirty Dublin': a City in Distress, 1899–1916*, Berkeley, 1982, p. 245.
12 *Hansard*, 22 February 1906, H.C. Deb. 4s, col. 491.
13 O'Brien, *'Dear Dirty Dublin'*, p. 245.
14 *Hansard*, 23 April 1914, H.C. Deb. 5s, col. 1126.
15 O'Brien, *'Dear Dirty Dublin'*, pp. 243–4.
16 *Hansard*, 8 January 1915, H.L. 5s, col. 351–2; see also Peter Simkins, *Kitchener's Army: the Raising of the New Armies*, Manchester, 1988, p. 112.
17 'Statistical abstract of information regarding the armies at home and abroad, 1914–20', United Kingdom Public Record Office (PRO), WO 161/82.
18 *Ibid.*; Patrick Callan, 'British recruitment in Ireland, 1914–1918', *Revue Internationale d'Histoire Militaire*, LXIII (1985), p. 48.
19 Patrick Callan, 'Recruiting for the British army in Ireland during the First World War', *Irish Sword*, XVII (1987), pp. 42–3.
20 *Ibid.*
21 Quoted in Richard Holmes, *The Little Field Marshal: Sir John French*, London, 1918, p. 326.
22 Callan, 'British recruitment', p. 48.
23 Figures calculated from the *General Annual Report of the British army for the year ending 30 September … 1920* (1922, cmd. 1610), *1921* (1923, cmd. 1941), *1922* (1924, cmd. 2114), *1923* (1924, cmd. 2272), *1924* (925, cmd. 2342), *1930* (1931, cmd. 3800), … *for year ending 31 December 1938* (1939 cmd. 5950).
24 Using the statistics published in the *General Annual Report* and the Irish census figures, a 'recruiting index' for each recruiting district in Ireland was worked out by calculating the number of recruits per 1,000 males aged 15–24 inclusive (from which cohort not less that 95 per cent of all recruits were drawn), and, in order to iron out

the varying annual demand for troops, presenting the figures in relation to an annual national average for enlistments of 100. The eight recruiting offices were: Armagh (covering Counties Armagh, Monaghan, Cavan, Louth); Belfast (Antrim, Down); Clonmel (Tipperary, Waterford, Kilkenny, Wexford); Cork (Cork, Kerry, Limerick, Clare); Dublin (Dublin, Kildare, Wicklow, Carlow); Galway (Galway, Roscommon, Mayo, Sligo, Leitrim); Mullingar (Longford, Meath, Westmeath, King's County (Offaly) Queen's County (Leix)); and Omagh (Donegal, Londonderry, Tyrone, Fermanagh). The results for the recruiting years (ending 30 September) 1912–13, 1919–20 and 1920–21 are as follows:

	1912–13	1919–20	1920–21
Armagh	67	115	153
Belfast	92	105	103
Clonmel	106	190	115
Cork	99	98	103
Dublin	235	116	134
Galway	30	50	37
Mullingar	109	94	85
Omagh	20	63	85

25 See enclosure in Sir Wilfrid Spender to Sir Henry Wilson, 22 December 1921, Imperial War Museum (IWM), Wilson Papers HHW 2/63/8 (quotations from the Wilson Papers are by permission of the Trustees of the Imperial War Museum).

26 The Royal Irish Regiment; Connaught Rangers; Leinster Regiment; Royal Munster Fusiliers; and Royal Dublin Fusiliers.

27 See Keith Jeffery, 'The British army and Northern Ireland since 1922', in Bartlett & Jeffery, Military History of Ireland.

28 Ibid.; and see papers in PRO WO 32/13259.

29 Hanham, 'Religion and nationality', p. 162.

30 Peter Karsten, 'Irish soldiers in the British army, 1792–1922: suborned or subordinate', Journal of Social History, XVII (1983–84), p. 54.

31 Skelly, Victorian Army at Home, pp. 284–5.

32 D. N. Haire, 'The British army in Ireland, 1868–90', unpublished M.Litt. thesis, Trinity College, Dublin, 1973, p. 359.

33 Karsten, 'Irish soldiers', p. 39.

34 Arthur V. Palmer, 'A private soldier on the private soldier's wrongs', Nineteenth Century, XXVIII (July–December 1890), p. 328 (quoted in Haire, 'The British army', pp. 275–6).

35 Redmond, 'Introduction', to Michael MacDonagh, The Irish at the Front, London, 1916, p. 3.

36 The Collected Poems of W. B. Yeats, London, 2nd edn, 1950, p. 152.

37 Terence Denman, 'The Catholic Irish soldier in the First World War: the "racial environment"', Irish Historical Studies, XXVII (1990–91), pp. 352–65.

38 'K. M.' (Kevin Myers), review of A. E. C. Bredin, A History of the Irish Soldier, Belfast, 1987, in The Irish Sword, XVIII (1991), p. 164.

39 Spiers, 'Army organisation'.

40 Elizabeth A. Muenger, The British Military Dilemma in Ireland: Occupation Politics, 1886–1914, Lawrence, Kansas, & Dublin, 1991, pp. 72–3.

41 Spiers, 'Army organisation'.

42 Muenger, British Military Dilemma, p. 146.

43 Ibid.

44 Stouppe McCance, History of the Royal Munster Fusiliers, II, from 1861 to 1922 (Disbandment), Aldershot, 1927, p. 197.

45 Jeffery, 'The British army and Northern Ireland'.

46 Spiers, 'Army organisation'; see also E. M. Spiers, The Late Victorian Army 1868–1902, Manchester, 1992, pp. 96–8.

47 See Richard Doherty, *Irish Generals*, Belfast, 1993, for an uncritical celebration of these men, and others.
48 Communicated to the author by Mrs Davies of Larne, County Antrim.
49 This remark has also been ascribed to Lord Kitchener.
50 *Belfast News-Letter*, 20 January 1922.
51 See Peter Hart, 'Michael Collins and the assassination of Sir Henry Wilson', *Irish Historical Studies*, XXVIII (1992–93), pp. 150–70. Ironically, both assassins had served in the British army during the Great War.
52 'Lord Carson's message to Ulster', *Morning Post*, 26 June 1922.
53 As reported in *The Orient News* ('an independent British Daily Organ in the Near East'), 26 June 1922 (copy in Harington MSS, City of Liverpool Museum). For Harington's family background, see his autobiography, *Tim Harington Looks Back*, London, 1940.
54 Eulogy by the Ven. Archdeacon Ryan P.P. to Tipperary Executive Council (June 1910), quoted in Edward McCourt, *Remember Butler: the Story of Sir William Butler*, London, 1967, pp. 259–60.
55 Winston Churchill to Lord Stamfordham (private secretary to King George V), 13 May 1920, in Martin Gilbert, *Winston Churchill*, IV, companion part 2 (Documents July 1919–March 1921), London, 1977, p. 1096; Keith Jeffery, *The British Army and the Crisis of Empire*, Manchester, 1984, pp. 82, 112.
56 See Lavinia Greacen, *Chink: a Biography*, London, 1989.
57 Walter Bagehot, *The English Constitution* (ed. R. H. S. Crossman), London, 1963, pp. 61, 64.
58 Nicholas Mansergh, *The Commonwealth Experience*, London, 1969, p. 196.
59 Sir Charles Lucas, *The Story of Empire*, London, 1924, p. 254.
60 Quoted in Terence Denman, 'The 10th (Irish) Division 1914–15: a study in military and political interaction', *The Irish Sword*, XVII (1987), p. 20.
61 Redmond, 'Introduction', to MacDonagh, *The Irish on the Somme*, London, 1917, pp. v–vi.
62 *Ibid.*, p. vii.
63 MacDonagh, *The Irish at the Front*, p. 6.
64 'Appreciation' by Redmond in Bryan Cooper, *The Tenth (Irish) Division in Gallipoli*, London, 1918, p. xiii.
65 Memo, 'The Dominions and Ireland', n.d. (c. 1919), House of Lords Record Office, Lloyd George Papers, F/180/1/3.
66 Hughes to Lloyd George, 29 December 1916, *ibid.*, F/32/4/14.
67 Lloyd George to Hughes, 18 January 1917, *ibid.*, F/32/4/22.
68 Hughes to [?Keith Murdoch] (for Lloyd George), 12 March 1917, *ibid.*, F/28/2/1.
69 Richard P. Davis, *Irish Issues in New Zealand Politics, 1868–1922*, Dunedin, 1974, p. 132.
70 Mansergh, *Commonwealth Experience*, p. 166.
71 Desmond Morton, '"Junior but sovereign allies": the transformation of the Canadian Expeditionary Force, 1914–1918', *Journal of Imperial and Commonwealth History*, VIII (1979), p. 56.
72 See Terence Denman, *Ireland's Unknown Soldiers: the 16th (Irish) Division in the Great War*, Dublin, 1992, pp. 20–6; and Tom Johnstone, *Orange, Green and Khaki: the Story of the Irish Regiments in the Great War, 1914–18*, Dublin, 1992, pp. 9–16.
73 In the possession of the author.
74 Jeffery, 'The British army and Ireland'.
75 Irish war memorials are discussed in Keith Jeffery, 'The Great War in modern Irish memory', in T. G. Fraser & Keith Jeffery (eds), *Men, Women and War* (Historical Studies XVIII), Dublin, 1993, pp. 144–52; and Jeffrey, 'Irish culture and the Great War', *Bullán: an Irish Studies Journal*, I (1994), pp. 88–90.
76 Text of address, 27 April 1924, Public Record Office of Northern Ireland (PRONI), Nugent Papers, D.3835/E/7/23.
77 *Mid-Ulster Mail*, c. 6 October 1925, PRONI LA 28/10AB/1.
78 Peter Karsten, 'Green Redcoats. The Irish in the British army from the 1790s to the

1920s: who were they and what did they become?', unpublished paper. The question quoted does not appear in the revised published version of the paper, cited in n. 30 above.

79 Cynthia H. Enloe, *Ethnic Soldiers: State Security in a Divided Society*, Harmondsworth, 1980, pp. 47, 195.
80 O'Brien, *'Dear, Dirty Dublin'*, p. 243.
81 Callan, 'Recruiting for the British Army', Ch. 1, p. 12.
82 F. X. Martin (ed.), *The Irish Volunteers*, Dublin, 1963, pp. 168, 154.
83 Arthur Mitchell & Padraig Ó Snodaigh (eds), *Irish Political Documents 1916–49*, Blackrock, County Dublin, p. 42.
84 John Harrington's words, in Uinseann MacEoin, *Survivors*, Dublin, 2nd edn, 1987, p. 495. The executions were those of the 1916 leaders.
85 James Connolly, *A Socialist and War, 1914–1916* (ed. P. J. Musgrove), London, 1941, pp. 102, 104.
86 *Ibid.*, p. 113.
87 A. J. Semple, 'The Fenian infiltration of the British army', *Journal of the Society for Army Historical Research*, LII (1974), pp. 133, 146.
88 Brian Inglis, *Roger Casement*, London, pbk edn, 1974, p. 302.
89 *Ibid.*, pp. 301, 309–10.
90 Keith Jeffery, *The British Army and the Crisis of Empire 1918–22*, Manchester, 1984, pp. 16–17.
91 Charles Bonham-Carter, typescript autobiography, Ch. 10; and letter to Joan (sister), 7 February 1920 (Churchill College, Cambridge, Bonham-Carter Papers BHCT 9/2, 2/2).
92 Home Office Weekly Report on Revolutionary Organisations in the United Kingdom, no. 55, 20 May 1920, PRO CAB 24/106 C.P. 1328.
93 Radcliffe to Wilson, 26 July 1920, IWM HHW 2/20B/7. See also Sir Richard Haking (GOC Allied Troops in East Prussia) to Wilson, 16 July 1920, IWM HHW 2/48A/26.
94 Morland to Wilson, 26 February, 26 May & 5 September 1921, IWM HHW 2/55/13, 35 & 46; Cabinet minutes, 24 May 1921, PRO CAB 23/25/40(21).
95 Home Office Weekly Reports nos 132 & 133, PRO CAB 14/131, C.P. 3509 & 3526; Gen. W. Horwood (Commissioner of the Metropolitan Police) to Lloyd George, 29 November 1921, Lloyd George Papers F/28/1/7.
96 Diary of Sir Henry Wilson (Imperial War Museum), 7 & 8 December 1921.
97 The best study of the mutiny is Anthony Babington, *The Devil to Pay: the Mutiny of the Connaught Rangers, India, July 1920*, London, 1991. The book was superbly researched by Julian Putkowski.
98 Causes listed by one of the members of the subsequent court-martial. *Ibid.*, p. 86.
99 Viceroy to Secretary of State for India, 2 July 1920, India Office Records (IOR) Chelmsford Papers Mss. Eur. E.264, vol. 13, pp. 8–9.
100 Viceroy to Secretary of State, 15 July 1920, IOR L/MIL/7/13314.
101 *Ibid.*
102 Press report from Paris, 20 July 1920, *ibid.*
103 Minute by Lytton, 28 October 1920; Viceroy to Secretary of State, 31 October 1920, *ibid.*
104 Babington, *The Devil to Pay*, p. 160. A significant number of the mutineers had actually enlisted after the end of the First World War.
105 In 1989, for example, about 20 per cent of the 2nd Battalion Royal Irish Rangers came from the Irish Republic (*Irish Times*, 22 July 1989).
106 Earlier versions of this essay were presented to the 'Guardians of Empire' conference, School of Oriental and African Studies, University of London, 1–2 July 1993, and to the Cambridge University Irish Studies Seminar, 17 May 1994. I am very grateful to the participants at these occasions for their advice and criticism, especially David Killingray, Brendan Bradshaw, David Dumville, Peter Gray and Brendan Simms

CHAPTER FIVE

Irish Unionists and the Empire, 1880–1920: classes and masses

Alvin Jackson

> Approach the map and scan the varied space,
> Far-flung indeed, with half the world between,
> The spots renowned in England's hist'ry trace,
> Where deeds of Cook and Clive and Wolfe are seen.
>
> Here scattered red, in continent and island
> The home of races white and black and tan
> Her flag of freedom waves on vale and highland –
> The greatest Empire since the world began![1]

So wrote the Belfast schoolmaster and poet, James Logan, in 1925. Logan's soliloquy on the splendours of Empire, together with his other verse, found little favour even with tame literary lions such as Stephen Gwynn; but his work won a rather more appreciative audience among the patriarchs of the Unionist movement – among men such as Sir John Ross, the last Lord Chancellor of Ireland, or Lord Ernest Hamilton, the loyalist ideologue and historian.[2] Logan, therefore, offers few insights into the Irish literary establishment, but he is a more certain guide to the taste of popular lower-middle-class Unionism in Ulster, and the literary and political enthusiasms of the Unionist command. More specifically, he offers an insight into these enthusiasms as they were re-emerging in the mid-1920s. Logan illustrates a particular jingoistic cast of mind at a particular moment in its development; as a popular versifier he illustrates one of the ways in which an imperial fervour might be communicated. He therefore serves to introduce the central themes of this essay: the varied nature of Unionist attitudes towards the Empire, the ways in which these attitudes might be formed, and the chronology of their development.

Logan's celebration of Empire won favour among leading Unionists, and indeed it might have been expected that an uncomplicated jingoism would win a ready response in this quarter. Unionists were enthusiastic celebrants of Empire, and the political beneficiaries of popular imperialism, but these propositions need further qualification and elaboration. Irish Unionist intellectuals and propagandists showed little interest in Empire; Irish Unionist parliamentarians, even the most voluble, contributed little to debate on the Empire. Unionist leaders who were, under certain conditions, keen to celebrate the imperial dimension to their political faith, more frequently demonstrated that their true political priorities had little to do with the future security of the Empire.

Thoughtful politicians from all the parties recognised that the question of Irish legislative autonomy formed part of a broader, and more complex, debate on imperial government. Thoughtful politicians perceived that the bond between England and Ireland had, or might be seen as having, imperial parallels in the Union of South Africa or the Commonwealth of Australia or the Federation of Canada. Home Rulers of a particular, perhaps pragmatic disposition – men like John Redmond or Erskine Childers – argued that Home Rule would convert Irish disaffection into an enthusiastic imperial commitment; certain pragmatic imperialists – notably Cecil Rhodes – clung to the same conviction. Throughout the Empire, it seemed that self-government propagated imperial swans out of anglophobic, nationalist ducklings – creating imperial statesmen out of a Boer like Smuts or a Quebecois like Wilfrid Laurier. English Unionists of all kinds countered these arguments. L. S. Amery brilliantly dissected the arguments of Childers's *The Framework of Home Rule* (1911).[3] An intellectually less subtle propagandist, Pembroke Wicks, Carson's private secretary, cribbed several of Amery's arguments in questioning the relevance of the Australian and Canadian constitutional analogy to Irish conditions; he cribbed from Amery in exploring the parallels between the government of the United Kingdom and that of both South Africa and New Zealand.[4] Other Unionist polemicists – such as Philip Cambray, secretary of Walter Long's Union Defence League – trod similar constitutional paths.[5] Liberals and nationalists – J. H. Morgan, Henry Harrison, W. A. S. Armour – enthusiastically challenged their Unionist foes for possession of the imperial grail.[6]

What is missing in this intellectual ferment are Irish Unionists. Irish Unionist ideologues on the whole did not make any serious contribution to these debates on Ireland and the Empire. Indeed the only Irish Unionist to broach the subject at some length, T. W. Russell, did so as part of the rite of passage towards Home Rule.[7] Why did orthodox Unionists shy from this intellectual exchange? Several responses may be considered. It is possible that what has been often identified as the anti-intellectual culture of Unionism may have disarmed interested loyalists. It is equally possible, however, that Unionists with any real interest in imperial questions were few in number.

If Unionist popular culture in the Home Rule era was anti-intellectual, then there were able Unionists who argued their case in almost
every permutation – except that of Empire. English Unionist intellectuals were interested in abstract constitutional questions; Irish Unionist intellectuals and polemicists were interested in some of the more
parochial and tangible questions associated with Home Rule. A. W.
Samuels, a distinguished Unionist lawyer, devoted cursory attention to
the Australian and South African analogies in his *Home Rule: What is
it?* (1911), but displayed rather greater enthusiasm and volubility in
reviewing the financial aspects of the Home Rule debate.[8] J. H. M.
Campbell, another graduate from the Trinity law school, devoted his
very considerable abilities to a rigorous clause-by-clause dissection of
the Home Rule Bill.[9] Peter Kerr-Smiley, Unionist MP for North Antrim
and a Cambridge graduate, declared conventionally that 'Home Rule
means disaster both to Ireland and to the great British Empire', but he
did not explore the imperial aspects of his concern in his otherwise
comprehensive *The Peril of Home Rule* (1911).[10] In the most popular
Unionist manual of the third Home Rule Bill era, S. Rosenbaum's
Against Home Rule (1912), Irish loyalists contributed essays on Irish
history, the judicial and religious questions, Irish finance and poor law
reform; but it was an English Unionist, L. S. Amery, who wrote on
Empire.[11] Irish Unionist leaders and intellectuals wrote extensively to
the newspapers often on particular, local aspects of the Home Rule
threat; but it was an English Unionist, F. S. Oliver, who used his letters
to *The Times* in order to review the case for a federalist settlement.[12]

Irish Unionists were therefore intellectually combative, but within
a particular zone of the polemical battlefield. They left the more direct
defence and exploration of Empire to others. Were they therefore
unmoved by Empire? They were sentimentally and superficially committed, but – as will be argued – it often took a more personal connection to transform uncritical sentiment into a more pro-active imperial
faith. In 1886 and in 1893, during debate on the first and second Home
Rule Bills, Unionists occasionally cast their concerns in an imperial
mould, but it is hard to escape the impression that this was done more
with a view to influencing English parliamentary opinion than out of
simple conviction. Certainly few Irish Unionists showed the slightest
concern when imperial issues were debated on their own, as opposed to
Irish, terms. Significantly, it was an Englishman sitting for a Belfast
constituency, H. O. Arnold-Forster, who demonstrated the most disinterested faith in Empire, in the particular form of an abiding commitment to naval and imperial defence issues.[13]

If Irish Unionist intellectuals were only rarely enthused by Empire,
then what of the attitudes of other social and political leaders and

opinion formers within the movement? The Empire and the commercial opportunities created by imperial expansion affected and interested much of the Belfast commercial elite, a class which exercised
very great influence over the strategic direction of Ulster Unionism.
The shipping and freight industries were, as Peter Gibbon has observed,
particular focuses of an imperial Unionism; and the representatives of
these industries, in turn, feature very largely at the most senior level of
the movement.[14] The shipbuilding firms Harland and Wolff and Work-
man Clark benefited directly from the growth of imperial trade and the
concomitant expansion in the Royal Navy. Both firms were major suppliers of naval vessels during the First World War, when the Chairman
of Harland, W. J. Pirrie, served as Controller General of Merchant Shipping. Harland and Wolff had enjoyed a modest amount of Admiralty
business since 1868, nine years after the creation of the firm, when the
gunboat HMS Lynx was launched; in 1886, in the aftermath of the
expedition to relieve General Gordon, two 'Bramble'–class gunboats
were commissioned for the Royal Navy.[15] After 1891–92 Harland and
Wolff had also built up a substantial holding in the African Steamship
Company, a business which was well placed to benefit from the European 'scramble for Africa'.[16]

The captains of these great shipbuilding empires contributed both
business expertise and a breadth of vision to the leadership of Unionism. Edward Harland, G. W. Wolff, and George Clark all served as
Unionist MPs for Belfast constituencies. Harland was Unionist Mayor
of Belfast in 1885–86, at the time of the first Home Rule Bill, and was
therefore one of the most conspicuous opponents of the measure. His
junior partner, Pirrie, publicly declared that, in the event of Home
Rule, the firm would relocate on the River Clyde, although in reality
there were secret contingency plans to move to Liverpool. Pirrie, too,
served as Unionist Lord Mayor of Belfast (though in the rather more
propitious years, for the opponents of Home Rule, of 1896–97).[17]

Yet, just as with Irish Protestant and Unionist intellectuals, so the
imperialist enthusiasms of these commercial and industrial magnates
should not be exaggerated. It is undoubtedly true that Unionism
attracted the majority of Ireland's business leaders; it is equally true
that Belfast industry and commerce were export-oriented, looking for
markets beyond the Irish shores. Yet, just as with the intellectuals, so
the unquestionable strength of Unionism among the business classes
did not always imply a marked eagerness for Empire. A residual laissez-
faire liberalism continued to influence, in particular, the Presbyterian
business and farming communities, even though these men and
women might nominally have been Unionist. Throughout the Edwardian
era official Unionists were being challenged by Liberal Independents,

recruited from and recruiting support from the Presbyterian middle classes. Sometimes, as with R. G. Glendinning, the Belfast linen magnate and Liberal MP for North Antrim, these men were old-style Gladstonians, who had survived the party political deluge of 1886.[18] Sometimes, as with the Russellites, the Liberal followers of T. W. Russell, these were simultaneously class-based politicians and instinctive Unionists – men whose particular class convictions overpowered their Unionism in determining party allegiance. Russell, one of the most ferocious defenders of the Union in the 1880s, shifted gradually towards Liberalism after 1900, carrying some Presbyterian middle class support with him. Russell's followers embraced a spectrum of opinion on the Empire, ranging from absolute apathy, or 'little England' convictions, through to advanced imperialist ideologues such as Arnold White, author of the celebrated *Efficiency and Empire* (1901).[19] Sometimes the business interests of these liberals overreached both the confines of the British Empire and the need to placate the Unionist elders of the Belfast commercial elite. This was most obviously true of W. J. Pirrie who, despite his posturing in 1886, could afford to break with the party of Empire in 1905–6 in order to join the Liberals. The once ferocious proponent of Empire was, by the mid-Edwardian era, financing Liberal parliamentary candidates; the one time Unionist Lord Mayor of Belfast, the recipient of an Irish Privy Counsellorship from the patriarch of Empire, Lord Salisbury, was among the first Liberals ennobled after the election victory of 1906.[20]

However, three Liberals, even three prominent and influential Liberals, did not in themselves represent an anti-Unionist backlash; these three particular Liberals, who thought carefully about Empire, and who effectively served the interests of Empire, did not represent an anti-imperial movement. These three men, though conspicuous, could not claim to speak for middle-class Protestants in Belfast and Ulster. What the convictions of these men *do* indicate, however, is that the imperialism of the Belfast commercial elite should not be taken for granted. Belfast business benefited from the profits of Empire, but Belfast businessmen were followers, and often tardy followers of popular imperialist feeling: they were not the originators or the enthusiastic proponents of such sentiment. These men were often, at heart, laissez-faire liberals for whom expensive interventionist imperial endeavours were highly unwelcome. These were men who, if they profited from Empire, were often unwilling to pay for its propagation and advancement. The Belfast city fathers often took a tight-fisted approach to the celebration of imperial anniversaries: there was little official expenditure for Victoria's Golden Jubilee, and although it was claimed that 'for all practical purposes the Jubilee Day must be regarded as a holiday universally

[127]

observed' by no means all of the workforce were given time off work either in 1887, or at the time of the Diamond Jubilee, in 1897.[21] The Empire Day movement, founded by the Earl of Meath in 1902, seems only to have taken a significant hold over Belfast by 1908-9, even though large claims were being made for the success of Meath's campaign elsewhere as early as 1905.[22] At the time of the Empire's greatest achievement, the Armistice of November 1918, the workforce at Harland and Wolff had, in the absence of any official celebrations, to take an unofficial holiday of one week.[23]

Most Belfast businessmen were Unionist, and many profited from Empire; but here again one should be wary of any hazy or inexact correlation between the profits of Empire, imperialist sentiment, and Unionism.[24] Belfast business was of course diverse, and it did not simply depend upon the stimulus of Empire. The retail side of Belfast business was, almost by definition, dependent upon local, rather than imperial markets: retailers like the chemist Sir James Haslett were well-represented within the Unionist command.[25] Not all manufacturers or wholesalers depended upon the imperial connection: some, like the father of Lord Craigavon, James Craig senior, a whiskey distiller, looked first to local, Irish suppliers and purchasers, rather than to the Empire.[26] Some manufacturers or industrialists, on the other hand, transcended the imperial connection. Harland and Wolff benefited from imperial trade, but in a sense the firm outgrew the Empire: Harland and Wolff in fact illustrates usefully the complex nature of the connection between the Unionist business community and Empire. The company had strong bonds with Britain, yet depended originally upon German capital. They benefited from defence contracts, yet only as a microscopic element of their business: between July 1859 and August 1914 – the heyday of Empire, and the first fifty-five years of the company's activity – only six out of around 450 ships built were commissioned by the Admiralty; four of these were small vessels, each weighing under 900 tons.[27] Indeed so little official business was brought to Belfast that in 1900 one of the ablest Ulster Unionist MPs, W. G. Ellison-Macartney, a junior minister at the Admiralty, was nearly driven from office on account of his disinterested administration.[28] Although the shipyard built vessels for 'imperial' lines, such as Union-Castle, Bibby, Dominion and Shaw Savill, during the Edwardian climacteric of the company its profits came largely from supplying the transatlantic trade rather than more directly from the Empire. Only during the First World War did Harland and Wolff, like so much of British industry, become tied to an imperial cause: only after the First World War, in the last years of his life, did W. J. Pirrie renounce the Liberal and 'little England' cause, and return to the embrace of Unionism and Empire.[29]

A similar complex relationship bound the Irish gentry class to the Empire: with landed gentlemen, as with businessmen, no crude hypothesis will adequately illustrate the difficult nature of the imperial commitment. At a glance, however, the links between this class and Empire were great and enduring: the Irish gentry supplied administrators to the colonies, officers to the British army, and investment capital for colonial industry. Frederick Temple Hamilton-Temple-Blackwood, first Marquis of Dufferin and Ava, was the most spectacularly successful of the many Irish gentlemen who aspired to rule the late Victorian Empire. His recently refurbished statue in the centre of Belfast proclaims the *cursus honorum* of his proconsular career: Canada, Constantinople, Moscow, India, Paris, Rome.[30] A former Gladstonian, he returned to Ireland in 1896 as the patriarch of Liberal Unionism. But the north of Ireland exported other loyalist gentlemen to the colonies. The Earl of Ranfurly, patron of the Ulster Loyalist Union, and mentor of Fred Crawford, the gun-runner, governed New Zealand between 1897 and 1904.[31] William Ellison-Macartney, whose imperial vision and impartial administration of the Admiralty had found little favour in Ulster, located his reward not in Belfast but at the Royal Mint, and later as Governor of Tasmania and of Western Australia. Earlier Conservative Unionists had graduated, like Ellison-Macartney, from Irish constituencies to gubernatorial careers: the Earl of Mayo, a former MP for County Kildare and for Coleraine Borough, served as Viceroy of India between 1867 and 1872; Sir William Gregory sat as an MP for Dublin and for County Galway before holding the Governorship of Ceylon (1871–77).[32]

Some of the impulses which propelled Irish gentlemen into the colonial service also drove them into the army. Chief amongst these pressures was, perhaps, relative poverty.[33] Straitened finances, rather than an expensive commitment to the Empire, dictated the career paths of many landed Unionists. Ellison-Macartney, a minor landowner in Tyrone, was probably driven to the Mint and to Australia through want of money; Dufferin was certainly pressed for cash throughout his life, relying on official salaries, and falling easy prey to the quick-fix promises of the crooked financier, Whitaker Wright.[34] William Johnston, the Orange MP for South Belfast and a County Down landowner, sought relief from his creditors through a colonial governorship; Lord Arthur Hill, his patron, and a younger son of the fourth Marquis of Downshire, pursued a similar course. Both men were near-bankrupt – Johnston through the mismanagement of his patrimony, Hill through having been swindled by a thieving solicitor.[35] For both men personal finances appear to have exercised a greater influence than any imperial vision: both sought a dignified escape from local poverty and humiliation.

At a less elevated, and military, sphere, the same logic applied. Throughout the Empire the sons of the Irish gentry served as officers of the Queen-Empress. Irish landed families provided heroes and generals in plenty to the late Victorian and Edwardian army: Roberts, Wolseley, White of Ladysmith, French, Gough – all could claim an Irish birthplace or direct Irish descent and all were the offspring of Irish landed families. Distinguished sailors were also recruited from the Big Houses: Earl Beatty was the son of a minor County Wexford gentleman who in 1892 owned 1,330 acres and collected a rent of £800.[36] A mixture of motives drove men such as these: some, such as Wolseley, do indeed appear to have had a sense of imperial mission and a commitment to British supremacy; others like French or Beatty appear to have been more frankly careerist. But the initial impetus behind many Irish military careers was undoubtedly financial. The army, especially colonial service in the army, offered the prospects of promotion and of heroic achievement; above all it offered a cheap dignity, conferring status on bargain basement terms.[37] Living as a gentleman – responding to local expectations of extravagance – was an altogether more daunting financial prospect.

Money, convention and patriotism combined to propel Irish gentlemen into the army. It would be misleading to write off national sentiment as a contributory motive; but it would be equally unrealistic to seek any widespread philosophical commitment to Empire amongst the Irish officer class. Young Irishmen appear to have joined the Victorian army primarily because the lifestyle was simultaneously appealing and affordable; a sentimental and hazy feeling for the outward symbols of Empire – flag, crown – may have played a role, but surely a secondary role. Moreover, the roll-call of Irish generals notwithstanding, there are grounds for suggesting that the Irish gentry's position within the British army – perhaps even its commitment to the army – was declining at precisely the moment when the Empire reached its apogee. Elizabeth Muenger has persuasively questioned the extent to which the late Victorian and Edwardian officer corps was an Anglo-Irish monopoly.[38] Alternative opportunities, the incursions made by the status-hungry middle classes, the professionalisation of the army – all may have helped to diminish the role of the young Irish squire.

Recruitment to the army may have depended more upon youthful energy and recklessness and domestic economy than upon any worthwhile imperial zeal; yet it is arguable that the army bestowed, if it did not exploit, an active imperialism. An abstract and hazy imperialism often only became a passion for the social and political leaders of Unionism through some personal involvement, military or otherwise. In this respect South Africa and the Boer War seem to have had a peculiarly great, and yet unrecognised significance. Certainly earlier imperial exploits had enthused and energised Irish loyalists: those Irish regiments which recruited primarily in the north of Ireland (83rd, 86th, 87th, 89th) had fought in the Crimea, through the Indian Mutiny and, later, in Egypt. The north of Ireland supplied one of the central figures of Victorian imperial romance, John Nicholson, the hero of the siege of Delhi; the north of Ireland also supplied one of the greatest of Victorian proconsuls, Lord Dufferin, during whose viceregal reign Upper Burmah was added to the Indian Empire. Both Nicholson and Dufferin were commemorated by statues in, respectively, Lisburn and Belfast; both men won the attention of respectful biographers.[39] But isolated individuals such as these, or the exploits of Irish regiments, did not by themselves create an imperial fervour or even any profound imperial vision. It was rather the war in South Africa which altered the vision, certainly of the leadership caste within Unionism, providing otherwise blinkered businessmen and professionals with an awareness of Empire, and with a more vivid appreciation of the relationship between Irish loyalism and the imperial movement.

The energising effects of the Boer War on Irish nationalism are only now winning an adequate assessment.[40] On the other hand, the profound impact made by South Africa on the Unionist leadership has still rarely been identified, let alone explained. But for contemporary Unionists the war, and its effects, were inescapable. More Irish people, and therefore more Irish loyalists, were engaged in the war than in any earlier purely imperial conflict. New battalions were added to existing northern Irish regiments; a new Irish regiment was created in the shape of the Irish Guards (this with the blessing of the Queen-Empress); new, northern companies of the Imperial Yeomanry were raised. Conscription was of course never introduced, but, given the scale of military involvement, the popular impact of the Boer War in Ireland was immense. More Irish generals were engaged in the war than in any other conflict of the late nineteenth century: Roberts, French, White. These men were uniformly of Irish loyalist ancestry, and one – Sir George White, the hero of Ladysmith – was from the Unionist heartland of County Antrim. In addition, Irish Unionists perceived closer parallels between Ireland and South Africa than between Ireland and any other imperial conflict; more than in any other imperial conflict Irish Unionists saw lessons for themselves arising from the campaign against the Boers.

Irish Unionist leaders had a more intimate connection with this war than perhaps with any other modern campaign, excepting only the First World War. This was partly – though only partly – because their community was actively engaged by the conflict. But Unionist leaders had themselves a personal stake in South Africa. Edward Saunderson, who before the late 1890s had only the most hazy and uncritical devotion to the Empire, saw, refracted through the tensions in South Africa, an imperial dimension to the small town loyalism of his own North Armagh constituency. Visiting South Africa in the winter of 1897–98, Saunderson discovered parallels between the loyal Uitlander minority in the Transvaal and the hostile Boer majority; he perceived parallels between the role of the National League in Ireland and that of the Boer Afrikaner Bond within Cape Colony. Joseph Chamberlain, hitherto regarded with ambivalence, emerged in Saunderson's rhetoric as a national apostle, equalled only in jingoistic purity by Cecil Rhodes.[41] These convictions, and this rhetoric, were intensified after the outbreak of hostilities in October 1899. Saunderson had long since retired as a colonel of militia, and none of his sons fought in the war, but Saunderson's personal connection with this territory was strong, forged during his lengthy visit and through his association with the British South Africa Company. He had visited South Africa as a guest of the Company, and more specifically as a guest of its Chairman, the second Duke of Abercorn. Abercorn, a Tyrone landowner and the grey eminence of the 1892 Ulster Unionist Convention, was a long-standing ally of Saunderson, both in 1886 and in 1893 fighting for the Union, and throughout the 1890s in defending the economic interests of Irish landed proprietors.

For other, younger, Irish Unionists the Boer War was a personal and imperial watershed. Several of the new middle-class stars of Edwardian Unionism shared experiences of the war; and there is some circumstantial evidence to suggest that the most hawkish Unionists of the 1912–14 era were linked and made more militant by their war service. James Craig, the architect of Ulster Unionist resistance in 1912–14, served in South Africa as a captain in the Royal Irish Rifles: he was wounded at Lindley in May 1900, was (briefly) imprisoned by the Boers, and on release was gazetted as Deputy Assistant Director of the Imperial Military Railways. The repercussions were, as his biographer, St John Ervine, pointed out, long-lasting: 'South Africa had taught him more than he yet realised. Its lessons were in his head, but were not yet fully perceived. The first and chief of these was a profound belief in the value of unity tempered by variety: the British Empire had become a reality to him; it was no longer an abstraction'.[42] South Africa provided Craig with logistical experience which in turn served him well in 1912; it provided, as Ervine observed, a real appreciation of Empire; and it recruited him to a freemasonry of military-minded Irish Unionists who emerged from their wartime experiences with a revivified imperial zeal and aggression.

Craig's lieutenants in 1912 were often South African veterans. The gun-runner and imperial visionary, Fred Crawford, had fought as an artillery captain in 1900–1; Crawford's fellow-conspirator, Colonel T. V. P. McCammon, was a veteran of the war.[43] The leading Orangeman and influential hawk, R. H. Wallace, had commanded the 5th Royal Irish Rifles in South Africa.[44] Several Irish Unionist MPs had fought in the war: Peter Kerr-Smiley, MP for North Antrim (1910–22) had served with the 21st Lancers; Robert McCalmont, MP for East Antrim (1913–19), had served with the Irish Guards; the Marquess of Hamilton, MP for Londonderry City (1900–13), had served with the Life Guards. Among the Liberal Unionists, Lord Dufferin had lost his eldest son, the Earl of Ava, killed in action with the 12th Lancers in 1900.[45]

It would be misleading to place too great a weight of interpretation upon the war experiences of each and all of these men. It is only where family papers and memoirs survive, as with Craig, Crawford and Wallace, that it is possible to chart with certainty the personal impact of the conflict.[46] Nevertheless, the importance of the Boer War as a source of inspiration and unity among leading militants is beyond question; and the importance of the war even for those Unionist leaders who were not veterans is also beyond question. Carson's interest in Empire was profound, though of a somewhat late flowering. As a vigorous and ambitious lawyer in the 1880s and 1890s Carson's political vision did not extend far beyond the courts and the defence of the propertied interest. Yet his legal work brought an entanglement in the politics of southern Africa and a vicarious interest in the British campaign against the Boers. In July 1896 Carson, led by Sir Edward Clarke, acted to defend the architects of the Jameson Raid against a state prosecution under the terms of the Foreign Enlistment Act. Clarke's ponderous defence of L. S. Jameson and his four lieutenants produced much polished speechifying but not their acquittal. Yet Carson himself was successful in a number of subsidiary cases, and thereby earned the devotion of Jameson's patron and mentor, Cecil Rhodes. Rhodes expressed his thanks more tangibly through the gift of land in Rhodesia to Carson's son, Harry. Harry subsequently fought in Rhodes's cavalry regiment against the Boers.[47]

In 1896 Carson had unsuccessfully defended a British patriot and anti-Boer, Jameson; and in 1903 he successfully prosecuted an Irish patriot and pro-Boer, Colonel Lynch.[48] These were more than usually important cases, for they attracted very considerable public attention: they were consequently cases which made a deep impression upon Carson himself. Fighting the Boers in the courts, while his son fought the Boers on the veldt, Carson was bound to South Africa and to an imperial vision. His Unionism had hitherto been based upon a defence

[133]

of property right and the maintenance of law and order. After the Lynch case Carson's interest in Empire blossomed. There were of course other influences over this intellectual evolution. South Africa was important, but Carson's increasing prominence within British national politics meant that his repertoire of political interests was gradually expanding. The Ulster Unionist campaign against the third Home Rule Bill, and Carson's leadership of this campaign, were not distinguished by any strong imperial slant; but the First World War reactivated his concern for Empire. His criticism of the British abandonment of Serbia in 1915 and his assault on Asquith in December 1916 were justified in imperial terms. He acted as patron to the ultra-Unionist British Empire Union after 1918. At the very end of his life, in the early 1930s, he embraced a diehard stand on the self-government of India, influenced by what he still regarded as the disastrous British retreat from Ireland through the Treaty of 1921.[49]

But, whether in regard to South Africa or India, Carson's political priorities were indisputable. The Empire and imperial concerns were viewed from the perspective of Ireland. India mattered only in so far as Carson foresaw the British government cajoling and betraying its friends there as it had done so brutally in Ireland. South Africa mattered only in so far as the war involved loyal Irishmen such as the soldiers of the Royal Dublin Fusiliers, and disloyal Irishmen such as Arthur Lynch; South Africa mattered because it involved his own son. South Africa did not create a resounding imperial commitment in Carson, because the only unshakeable commitment in Carson's career was to the Irish people and, in particular, to Irish loyalty. But the South African war did mark the beginning, for Carson, of a more intimate acquaintance with the Empire, and of a greater readiness to acknowledge its political relevance.

What are the connections between the tortured imperialism of the Unionist elite and popular jingoism in late Victorian Ulster? One, negative, relationship will be at once evident. The qualms and hesitation of Unionist leaders in approaching the Empire precluded the possibility of any ideological hegemony. Unionist leaders did not generate any comprehensive imperialist ideology; Unionist leaders did not therefore create or even clearly direct the popular imperialism of Irish Protestants. A qualified imperialism certainly helped to unify Protestant society, but if any cultural imposition was involved, then this originated outside Irish Unionism, and indeed outside Ireland itself. This is an important point, and will be addressed more fully later in the chapter. For the moment it is sufficient to observe that, just as outside events and issues enforced or dampened the imperial fervour of the Unionist elite, so outside events determined the condition of popular imperialism in Ulster. In particular, just as the Boer War constituted an imperial epiphany for an influential section of the Unionist leadership, so the War – and indeed the events of 1897–1902 generally – energised the whole imperial movement in Ireland.

This broaches the question of chronology: when did popular imperialism develop in the north of Ireland? Before the 1890s there is little evidence of any popularly-held imperial faith. The traditional focuses of demotic loyalism – the 12 July demonstrations, royal visits – were not, before the late 1890s, in any sense imperial festivals. The Orange commemorations of the mid and late 1880s were celebrated with a ferocious determination; royal events such as the visit of the Prince and Princess of Wales to Belfast in 1886, or Victoria's Golden Jubilee in 1887, provoked demonstrations of loyalty to the Crown, but little overt celebration of Empire.[50] It was only at the end of Victoria's reign, when, increasingly, royal festivals were given an imperial meaning, and when the empire itself faced a crisis of the first order, that popular imperial feeling took root. In other words, imperialism followed the creation of Unionism in Ireland, rather than the reverse. The spread of popular images of Empire, and the popular celebration of Empire undoubtedly helped to consolidate Unionist feeling in Ireland; but popular Unionism also predated popular imperialism, and provided the foundations for its growth.

The Diamond Jubilee of 1897 and the Boer War of 1899–1902 were turning points in the popularisation of Empire in Ulster and Ireland. The Golden Jubilee of 1887 had contained no significant imperial element, and the 1880s had on the whole brought no significant crisis of Empire. Through the pressure of Joseph Chamberlain the Diamond Jubilee was a much more costly imperial jamboree than its predecessor, with the invited presence of colonial prime ministers, colonial troops, and with lavish honours for colonial politicians.[51] Chamberlain, almost single-handedly, turned a royal and national celebration into an imperial and international celebration: accompanying the royal events of the Jubilee was a counterpoint of imperial politicking, dinners for colonial leaders, conferences and excursions to provincial cities, including Belfast. This served to highlight the Jubilee's imperial significance, and journalists on newspapers such as the *Belfast News-Letter* responded to the prompt. 'Taking the Imperial aspect of the reign', the *News-Letter* rhapsodised on 23 June 1897, 'the progress has been simply wonderful ... during the Queen's reign the Empire has been extended to embrace almost every variety of race, and to include every variety of climate.'[52] The *News-Letter* and other Irish Unionist papers elaborated the imperial theme with much greater care and imagination than in 1887. Attention was paid to celebrations of the Jubilee in far-off colonies, with the *News-Letter* devoting considerable space on 12 August 1897 to a report of the festivities in West Africa ('one of the greatest events that have occurred at Lagos ...').[53] Imperialist journalism, combined with the manifold imperial imagery which the Diamond Jubilee generated, undoubtedly stimulated Unionist jingoism.

The impact of the Diamond Jubilee was heightened and sustained by an unprecedented sequence of royal festivals in the period up to August 1902. The news of Victoria's death on 22 January 1901 resonated throughout her territories and was treated, not merely as a national calamity, but as the loss of the presiding genius of the Empire: her funeral, held on 2 February, was a sombre, imperial occasion which was captured on film, and replayed to hushed audiences in Belfast and throughout the United Kingdom.[54] Edward VII's coronation, which dominated the Irish Unionist press throughout the summer of 1902, had a more protracted impact than might have been imagined, since the King developed appendicitis and his enthronement had to be postponed from June to August. When held, the coronation revived the imperial grandiloquence of the Diamond Jubilee. Like the Jubilee and other imperial festivals the coronation was lavishly reported, filmed and otherwise marketed.[55] Like the Jubilee, the coronation helped to underpin imperialist sentiment among Irish Unionists.

Some attention has been paid to the impact of the Boer War on the Unionist elite. The war, in association with the royal and imperial celebrations of 1897–1902, propagated a mass audience for the imperial message. It gave many Irishmen, enrolled in the militia, or yeomanry, their first direct contact with the Empire. It gave many Irish women, from the Marchioness of Dufferin and Ava in her palazzo at Clandeboye to charwomen in the slums of Belfast, their first bitter taste of bereavement, their first blood-sacrifice to the cause of Empire: thousands of Irish soldiers died in the Boer War, including Lady Dufferin's eldest son, the Earl of Ava. The Boer War gave rise to the first significant crop of public war memorials, including those commemorating the dead of the Royal Irish Fusiliers (in the Mall, Armagh City), and those of the Royal Irish Rifles (at the City Hall, Belfast). The Boer War provided popular imperial heroes like Roberts, Baden-Powell, and – especially appealing for an Ulster audience – White of Ladysmith. The war stimulated a triumphalist journalism, bringing through the medium of the penny press an imperial cause to a mass readership. The war provided imagery and messages for advertising, commercial packaging, and entertainment. Involving 28,000 Irishmen, bringing glorious victories after grim defeat, generating pervasive slogans and images, the war bound Unionist Ireland to the Empire as never before. Unsurprisingly, a Unionist intellectual like St John Ervine (who was born in 1888) believed that his generation had been formed between the shock of the Boer War and the horror of the trenches.[56]

After the peace of Vereeniging popular imperialist fervour in the north of Ireland appears to have diminished. Until 1914 there were no great military conflicts to stimulate and focus patriotic and imperial feeling. There were certainly minor colonial enterprises, but even the most significant of these (such as the Natal uprising of 1906) made little impression upon the Irish public: only very rarely were Irish soldiers involved, and then only in small numbers (this in contradistinction to the heavy Irish involvement in the 1880s and 1890s in Egypt and India). Until 1910–11 there was no great royal occasion to serve, as in 1897 or 1902, as a pageant of Empire. Imperialist ceremonial in Edwardian Belfast was supplied only through the celebration of Empire Day; and even this festival only seems to have found general favour by 1908–9, despite small-scale, localised enthusiasm after its inauguration in 1904. Empire Day in 1910 coincided with the period of mourning for Edward VII, and was therefore a muted affair.

Between 1911 and 1914 there was a renewed upsurge in the public expression of imperialist feeling. The opportunities for this were created by a combination of circumstances: the coincidence in May–July 1911 of several imperial festivals, namely Empire Day, the Imperial Conference, the coronation of George V and his visit to Ireland. All this meant that for several weeks the public in the north of Ireland was cocooned by imperial sentiment: imperial news in the daily newspapers, imperial images in the illustrated weeklies, and on advertising hoardings, imperial bric-a-brac and souvenirs in the shops. A delegation of colonial dignitaries visited Belfast in early June 1911; and although George V did not include Belfast or the north in his Irish itinerary, film of both his coronation and his Dublin visit was being played to Belfast audiences by mid-July.[57] Indeed, only really by 1911 was the Belfast cinema beginning to rival the music hall as a means of reflecting and subtly directing popular taste. A lavish new cinema, the Belfast Picture Palace, was opened by Unionist civic dignitaries in June 1911, and, certainly for the first weeks of its existence, fed its patrons a steady diet of royal and imperial images, from George V at Kingstown Harbour through to the coronation naval review at Spithead.[58]

It would be wrong, however, to see such royal and imperial imagery simply as a cultural imposition. On the contrary, the receptiveness of the Unionist public in 1911 for such visual and verbal stimuli was high, for the challenge of Home Rule had again re-emerged and political attitudes which had been defined long before the era of popular jingoism were exhumed and revivified. Popular imperialism re-emerged in 1911–14 because, in the context of Home Rule and the threatened dismemberment of the United Kingdom, Empire had a renewed if still secondary importance as an adjunct to Unionism. The growth and diversification of Unionism in 1912–14 involved the annexation and exploitation of the imperial movement. Empire Day, which had been hitherto, at least in theory, a secular and non-partisan occasion, was increasingly redefined as a celebration of Protestantism and Unionism. The most conspicuous aspects of the Empire Day celebrations were taken over by organised Unionism and by the Protestant churches or Protestant youth movements. Between 1912 and 1914 the Unionist club movement was the chief celebrant of Empire Day in Belfast and in eastern Ulster; in these years and after the principal focus of the annual Empire festival was the religious service held on each Empire Sunday by the main Protestant denominations.[59] In 1915, in the last of the popular Empire Day celebrations before the revival of the mid-1920s, the central event was a great fair and charity drive for the funds of the UVF hospital.[60] Once again the subservience of the Empire movement to the institutions of Unionism is apparent. The Ulster Volunteer Force (UVF) Hospital was created by the Ulster Unionist Council in 1914 for the benefit of Unionist casualties of war; by 1917 it was sited at James Craig's home, Craigavon, in the eastern suburbs of Belfast. Though now, in 1915, it catered for the needs of the 36th (Ulster) Division, regardless of politics or religion, the hospital retained the name and imprint of its UVF founders.

Unionism and imperialism were intertwined, and to some extent interdependent. But, though the challenge of Home Rule and of the Great War evoked an apparently more exuberant imperial mood in Ulster, it will be already apparent that the relationship between Union and Empire in these years was by no means straightforward. Royal and imperial festivals in 1911 certainly provoked a superficially more imperialist Unionism; and the celebration of Empire Day was, between 1911 and 1915, simultaneously elaborated by Unionists and for the first time explicitly controlled by them. But, equally, inherent in the Home Rule crisis and in the Great War were influences militating against an ebullient imperial Unionism. On Empire Day Unionist politicians and clergy spoke lovingly of Empire; Unionism in general tapped into the jingoistic popular culture which had spread into the north of Ireland from Britain. But the Unionism which exploited Empire was simultaneously more localised in terms of organisational balance and leadership, and political vision, than ever before; the Unionism which exploited Empire simultaneously defied the imperial Parliament and the imperial government.[61] Unionists supported Empire, even though the Empire supported Home Rule; many colonial politicians supported John Redmond and the Irish Parliamentary Party.[62]

Unionists exploited Empire, yet would not surrender their Irish cause in the interests of a wider, imperial vision. During the First World War calls were frequently made to Ulster Unionists to make political sacrifices for the Empire just as they had made a blood-sacrifice for Ulster at the Somme and elsewhere.[63] But Ulster was worth dying for, while the Empire scarcely merited the thought, let alone the reality, of political sacrifice.

The war, therefore, did not bring any upsurge of Unionist jingoism. There was no Mafeking to focus imperial pride (the Somme quickly assumed a largely local colouring and significance); there was no Roberts or White to serve as a popular deity (the generals of the First World War tended to be reviled rather than revered). Although Empire Day became an official holiday in 1916, its celebration remained, until 1924, a low-key affair. There was of course no place for vacuous celebrations when the daily newspapers were dominated by casualty lists, by vignettes of the last moments of heroic officers, or grim personal details concerning local men who had been killed in action. As the war developed, even these records gave way to a stark roll-call of the dead and injured. The commemoration of the armistice was for the most part subdued, with little of the triumphalist imperialism associated with the victories of the Boer War: the City of Belfast Peace Day Reception was, as the official title suggests, a welcome rather than a triumph, and a celebration of peace rather than of imperial ascendancy. The numerous composite battalions who took part in the reception – battalions made up from the battered fragments of other units – hinted at the carnage which had gone before.[64]

The war, therefore, did not fuel Unionist imperialism in any uncomplicated fashion; indeed, paradoxically, the war contributed to Unionist localism. For the war made possible the partition of Ireland, and the diversion of Unionist energies away from the imperial Parliament and the imperial heartland and into the local Home Rule assembly based in Belfast. Until the mid-1920s the Irish Troubles dominated press and popular attention. Elections for the Northern Irish Parliament were held on Empire Day 1921, but it was the condition of Ireland rather than of the Empire which determined votes. The diminution of violence after 1922–23, combined with the British Empire Exhibition of 1924, stimulated the rebirth of the Empire Day festival and of popular imperial celebration.[65] Yet the Unionist public were turning to the Empire while the Empire was turning from Britain: the public who had scarcely noticed the colonies when they were approaching their greatest extent revived the celebration of Empire in order to soften the impact of its loss. By the 1930s popular imperialism remained in place in Northern Ireland, a political culture divorced from both the condition of the Empire and, indeed, Northern Ireland itself. Popular imperialism remained a sentimental relic of an attitude of mind that had never been. In the grim and rapidly changing Belfast of the 1930s popular imperialism offered a culture of consolation: an explanation for the carnage of 1914–18, and a nostalgic retreat to a more distant age of full employment, national pride and colonial promise. The celebration of Empire in the 1920s and 1930s bore no relation to the political aspirations of Unionist politicians or the social aspirations of the Unionist public; but it offered an exotic distraction, and a colourful stimulus to the imagination which could not be supplied by impoverished, threatened Ulster.

A final comment should be devoted to the means by which a popular imperialism was sustained in the north of Ireland.[66] Here, as in Britain, royal and imperial images and messages percolated into almost every aspect of daily life: education, work, recreation, religion, consumerism. In Ireland, as in Britain, the interrelationship between the jingoistic popular culture and the propagation of popular political attitudes was complex. A number of points may be emphasised here. As has been suggested, it cannot be assumed that an imperial popular culture directly created imperial attitudes: businessmen, copy-writers and journalists were surely as much *responding* to popular tastes and prejudices as *creating* them. And in fact the growth of imperialist imagery followed long after both the development of Irish involvement in the British Empire and the evolution of patriotic Unionist attitudes and institutions.

Another aspect of this bond between imperialist popular culture and Unionist political attitudes demands attention. The origins of imperialist advertising and packaging, imperialist novels and journalism, imperialist souvenirs and bric-a-brac lay almost exclusively outside Ireland. Northern Protestant businessmen do not appear to have favoured the theme of Empire in their advertising and marketing; northern Protestant writers of the period – St John Ervine, Forrest Reid, Alexander Irvine, even highly popular writers like Lynn Doyle – did not produce the militaristic or imperialist romances of a Henty or a Le Queux. The production of imperialist tat – coronation mugs and medals and other pottery or metal souvenirs – was handled, not in the north of Ireland, but in England or in Germany. The coronation mugs presented by the Belfast Corporation to school children in 1911 were manufactured in England; Unionist commemorative ware of 1912–14 might be made in Germany. Paradoxically, northern Protestant manufacturers – the great linen houses, Beleek china works, manufacturing jewellers like Sharman Neill – were much more influenced by the Gaelic rather than the imperial revival.

This leads to a further point. Imperial dogma and imagery seeped into the north of Ireland from England but this was offset by the impact of Celtic revivalism in the visual arts and in literature. Irish plays as well as imperial dramas were staged in the Belfast theatres, and there is no evidence to suggest any sectarian segregation of the audience depending on theme. In August 1902, at the time of the coronation of Edward VII, the Alhambra Theatre, Belfast, offered 'a special engagement of the American biomotograph showing all the latest films, including the coronation pictures'; while the Theatre Royal staged 'the great Irish drama "Emigration"'.[67] In May 1903, the year of Edward VII's visit to Ireland, the Empire Theatre, Belfast, featured G. H. Chirurgin, 'The white-eyed Kaffir', while the Theatre Royal staged an Irish drama of the 1898 Rising, 'The Old Land'.[68] In July 1911, shortly after the coronation of George V, the Alexandra Theatre offered the musical comedy 'My Irish Molly', while the Picture Palace was showing images of the coronation procession and the naval review.[69] The work of Yeats and Synge and the other stars of the literary revival had, by 1910, made no observable popular impact in Belfast; but more frothy, less demanding works by nineteenth-century Irish dramatists like Dion Boucicault evidently enjoyed general approval.

Irishness as well as Empire invaded leisure time. Celtic revivalism was a dominant inspiration for most forms of northern manufacture. Celtic ornament adorned the work of porcelain and linen manufacturers and jewellers. Harps, round towers, and wolfhounds were woven into damask linen tablecloths; Celtic styles were adapted for jewellery. Beleek porcelain borrowed heavily from the themes and motifs of the revival. Unionist people and Unionist institutions were dependent upon Celtic revivalism for cultural self-definition and artistic stimulus. The Unionist Convention of 1892 generated imagery which combined British and Irish cultural references: delegates to the Convention were greeted by Union flags and Irish language mottos; the souvenir medals produced for the Convention united the Irish harp, Celtic ornament, and the British lion. Even during the prelude to the third Home Rule Bill crisis, in July 1911, the Unionist-controlled Belfast Corporation chose to present its loyal address in a magnificent casket based on the design of an Irish reliquary, and heavily adorned with Celtic ornament and Irish language tags.[70]

Celtic revivalism did not create Irish nationalists; neither did imperialist imagery create Irish Unionists or jingoists. It is probably true that the impact of revivalism was greatest in the luxury trades and therefore only felt by the middle classes of Ulster: imperialist popular culture was by definition demotic and vulgar and tawdry and effective. But revivalism was unquestionably a cultural influence on Unionists,

[141]

even if this dependence is not generally recognised, or if it does not conform to expectations. The cultural roots of Unionism defy glib assessment.

Having entered these caveats and qualifications, it remains true that imperial imagery was important in the north of Ireland. Unionist children read stories of colonial derring-do in the work of Henty or in the *Boy's Own Paper*.[71] Unionist children were taught respect for the Empire at school, where the classroom was often dominated by the most potent image associated with imperialist popular culture: the pink-splashed map of the world. Children were given a holiday on Empire Day, and taught to salute the flag: the socially exclusive Belfast school, Campbell College, held a flag-raising ceremony for its boys from 1909 at which homilies were delivered on the glories and responsibilities of Empire.[72] At Sunday School children would be given books or pamphlets telling of Irish missionary endeavour throughout the Empire and beyond: Irish Presbyterians were especially active in this respect, in India and farther east in China.[73] Children's voluntary and recreational associations – the Boys' Brigade, the Boy Scouts – reflected the military cult which was associated with popular imperialism in the years before the First World War. Such organisations regularly participated in the celebration of Empire Day and occasionally engaged the interest of leading Unionists (like Fred Crawford).[74]

For adults the challenge of Empire was equally inescapable. The advertising and packaging of household goods bore royal and imperial images: in 1911 readers of the *News-Letter* were urged to buy Huntley and Palmer's 'Royal Sovereign' biscuits, baked with a royal crown etched out in apricot jam; or they might acquire the Ensignette camera ('the camera that fits a waistcoat pocket'), advertised using the Royal Navy ensign.[75] Other naval allusions were broached by the Belfast tobacco company, Gallaher, in their popular 'Senior Service' brand of cigarette. Visitors to the Belfast department store, Robinson and Cleaver's, in June 1911, could buy coronation medals bearing the image of the King-Emperor at the price of 3d (large) or 1d (small), both 'having the appearance of old gold'.[76]

Moving from the advertising hoardings and the shops, Belfast Unionists could pursue the celebration of Empire in many forms of leisure activity. The part-time soldiers of the yeomanry or militia drilled and fought mock battles in defence of Empire. Women could spend their recreation in local organisations such as the Daughters of Empire or in Empire Choirs which sprang up every year before 24 May: one Empire Day celebration in 1915, even boasted the Ladies' Drill Class of St Mark's Parish Church, Ballysillan.[77] Empire stalked the stage of Belfast theatres, and the screens of the picture houses: in April 1911 the Kelvin

Picture Palace featured 'Lieutenant Rose and the Stolen Code' while in June the Royal Hippodrome played host to the 'Eight Empire Girls'. In the previous year the Hippodrome had spanned the spectrum of imperial emotions by combining in one programme 'the great military comedy, "Private Potts"' (which involved the elaborate escapades of a British soldier in an Indian harem) with film of the funeral of Edward VII, accompanied by Chopin's 'Marche Funebre'.[78]

Protestantism and Empire were coupled as effectively for adults as for children. On each Empire Day Protestant ministers preached, linking the spread of the Empire to the values of Protestantism, and warning of the fate of nations which abandoned a true Christian commitment (through an inversion of Gibbon the fall of Rome on one occasion was ascribed to a lapse in Christian practice).[79] The achievements of Irish Protestant missionaries were trumpeted to Ulster congregations. The central purpose of Empire was often defined in terms of Christian missionary endeavour.

These imperial influences were uneven in intensity, peaking in 1902, and to a lesser extent in 1911 and after 1923–24. These influences did not generally originate with the political and business leaders of Unionism: they did not create Unionism, and were mitigated by other cultural influences within the north of Ireland; they were certainly mitigated by the increasingly local emphasis within Unionism itself. It is possible to argue that Unionism created imperialism in Ireland rather than vice versa : it is obviously true that Unionist ideas and institutions predated and conditioned popular imperialism.

Accepting all of this, it remains clear that Unionist people at this time were bombarded at every stage of their lives and in every sphere of their activity with the image of Empire. This is important, but not primarily because such images created an imperial vision (they undoubtedly *focused* popular Unionism and imperialism). Despite this ideological onslaught, the north of Ireland produced no truly imperial political leader or polemicist and the popular awareness of Empire appears to have remained superficial and sentimental. More interesting than any tenuous argument for cultural hegemony is the evidence illustrating the way in which Unionist people responded to this imperial cannonade. Popular imperial sympathy appears to have peaked in association with royal festivals and in the aftermath of national crises such as the Boer War or the Great War or the Troubles of the early 1920s. Popular imperialism in Ulster, therefore, had little to do with the objective condition of the Empire, and a great deal to do with popular political morale; popular imperialism in Ulster reflected more directly the relationship between Unionism and the British Crown and the relationship between Unionism and the rest of Irish politics.[80]

Popular imperialism was a culture of consolation, rather than a culture of triumphalism. Irish imperialism, as embodied within Unionism, remained more Irish than imperialist, more firmly located in Irish mists than within the Empire upon which the sun never set.

James Logan had eulogised the British Empire against the backdrop of creeping imperial disintegration. Writing in 1924–25 in the comfortable seclusion of the southern suburbs of Belfast, he could accept the rhetoric of the Wembley Empire Exhibition at face value, and turn a blind eye to the conflict which had left Northern Ireland politically vulnerable and the Irish Free State clinging tenuously to the imperial connection. A prominent celebrant of Ulster and the Union, Logan loved the Empire – but not much. He devoted two poems to imperial themes in a collection of fifty verses otherwise dominated by local concerns.[81] This localism – this attention to local, Belfast and Ulster, character, identity and dialect – pervades Logan's most conspicuous work from the 1920s, *Ulster in the X-Rays* (1923). Elsewhere Logan, the sentimental and reflective Ulsterman, wrote on subjects close to his professional life as a schoolmaster: *The Brighter Side of School Life*, and, rather undermining the jaunty claims of this title, *School and Examination Book-Keeping*.[82]

Logan spoke for northern Unionists, and he accurately charted the dimensions of their concern for Empire. Like Logan the leaders of Unionism were only intermittently captivated by Empire; like Logan the Unionist social and political elite were, after the Edwardian era, increasingly local in their perspectives and enthusiasms. Just as Logan's imperial rhapsodising seems to have been stimulated by the British Empire Exhibition, so the imperialism of Unionist leaders often depended on outside influences: the Jubilee of 1897, the Boer War of 1899–1902, the coronations of 1902 and 1911. Bereft of outside influences, however, this imperial fervour seems to have waned. The general tendency within Ulster Unionism in these years was towards localisation, and this was interrupted, but not reversed, by the great festivals of Empire.

For Logan, as for most Unionists, the Boer War had a significance: when he came to celebrate the Ulster military tradition, Logan thought first of Sir George White and his heroic defence of Ladysmith.[83] The war altered the political perspectives of the Ulster Unionist public and its leadership. More than any earlier colonial conflict the war involved ordinary civilian Irish people: it taxed the resources of the professional army, stimulated a comprehensive propaganda, and provided an imperial vision to those who had hitherto been untouched by Empire. In combination with the royal festivals of 1897 and 1902, the Boer War supplied the foundations of both elite and popular imperialism in

Edwardian Ulster. Moreover, the War supplied military and administrative experience to the Unionist command, and reinforced the network of hawkish loyalists who dominated Unionism in the crucial years before 1914.

Logan wrote about Empire and other, Irish, topics. At an individual level, therefore, he represented the complicated range of ideological influences bearing in upon the Unionist public. He celebrated Ulster and the Empire, but he wrote as an Irishman; he wrote sentimentally of the Empire, but he dwelt much more thoughtfully on the relationship between Ulster and Ireland. Imperial images and rhetoric pervaded the lives of the Unionist public, but these images did not predominate, and in most cases they did not originate from within Ireland. Imperial propaganda was undoubtedly significant for Edwardian Unionists, but only as part of a much more complex ideological environment. Irishness, whether on stage, in print, or in art, was as important a cultural reference-point as Empire within the lives of northern Unionists. In fact, Ireland and the Empire were bound, for many Unionists, by an inverse relationship: Logan's imperialism, like the popular imperialism of Unionists generally, seems to have been partly a response to political and cultural challenge or disappointment within Ireland. Unionists clung to Empire as a form of spiritual comfort when Catholic nationalism seemed to be ascendant – in 1911–14, or in the tortured early years of the Northern Irish state. Imperialism was one strategy by which Ulster Unionists reconciled themselves to the redefinition of Irishness.

James Logan died in 1943, having remained silent on the theme of Empire for twenty years: he died when the British Empire in Asia had all but collapsed, and when his own 'Imperial Province' was edging towards a sectarian abyss. The Empire now represented neither a political nor a spiritual resource, and the strength and confidence of Unionists like Logan were proportionately weakened. Logan spent his last years cocooned in the polite suburbs of south Belfast where both imperialism and revolutionary nationalism had always been distant abstractions, and where life was scarcely touched by decolonisation or insurgency. He died, confused by the new forces in Irish life, and disappointed by the fallibility of once certain political creeds.

Notes

1 James Logan, *Verses: Grave and Gladsome*, London, 1925, p. 72.
2 *Ibid.*, pp. 7, 9.
3 L. S. Amery, 'Home Rule and the colonial analogy', in S. Rosenbaum (ed.), *Against Home Rule: the Case for the Union*, London, 1912, pp. 128–52.
4 Pembroke Wicks, *The Truth about Home Rule*, Boston, 1913, p. 130.

5 Philip Cambray, *Irish Affairs and the Home Rule Question*, London, 1911, pp. 66–84.

6 J. H. Morgan, *The New Irish Constitution*, London, 1912; Henry Harrison, *Ulster and the British Empire: Help or Hindrance?*, London, 1939; W. A. S. Armour, *Facing the Irish Question*, London, 1935.

7 T. W. Russell, *Ireland and the Empire: a Review*, London, 1901.

8 A. W. Samuels, *Home Rule Finance: an Examination of the Financial Bearings of the Government of Ireland Bill*, London, 1912.

9 J. H. M. Campbell, *A Guide to the Home Rule Bill*, London, 1912.

10 Peter Kerr-Smiley, *The Peril of Home Rule*, London, 1911, preface.

11 Amery, 'Home Rule and the colonial analogy'.

12 'Pacificus', *Federalism and Home Rule*, London, 1910.

13 Alvin Jackson, *The Ulster Party: Irish Unionists in the House of Commons, 1884–1911*, Oxford, 1989, p. 98.

14 Peter Gibbon, *The Origins of Ulster Unionism*, Manchester, 1975, p. 143.

15 Michael Moss & John R. Hume, *Shipbuilders to the World: 125 Years of Harland and Wolff, Belfast (1861–1986)*, Belfast, 1986, p. 56.

16 *Ibid.*, p. 69.

17 *Ibid.*, p. 55.

18 J. R. B. McMinn, 'Liberalism in north Antrim, 1900–14', *Irish Historical Studies*, XXIII (1982–83), p. 24.

19 See Arnold White, *Efficiency and Empire* (ed. G. R. Searle), Brighton, 1973, introduction. See also G. R. Searle, *The Quest for National Efficiency: a Study in British Politics and Political Thought, 1899–1914*, London, 1971.

20 Austen Morgan, *Labour and Partition: the Belfast Working Class, 1905–23*, London, 1991, pp. 45, 52.

21 *Belfast News-Letter* (hereafter *BNL*), 22 June 1887.

22 *Ibid.*, 24 May 1905.

23 Moss and Hume, *Harland and Wolff*, p. 205.

24 As opposed to the arguments forwarded in Gibbon, *Ulster Unionism*.

25 Jackson, *The Ulster Party*, p. 59.

26 St John Ervine, *Craigavon: Ulsterman*, London, 1949, pp. 22–4.

27 Calculated from the list of ships constructed by the firm in Moss and Hume, *Harland and Wolff*, pp. 506–19.

28 Edward Saunderson to Ellison-Macartney, 1 October 1900, Public Record Office of Northern Ireland, W. G. Ellison-Macartney Papers, D.3649/20/51.

29 Moss and Hume, *Harland and Wolff*, pp. 225–6.

30 See the biographies by C. E. D. Black, *The Marquis of Dufferin and Ava*, London, 1903; A. C. Lyall, *The Life of the Marquis of Dufferin & Ava*, 2 vols, London, 1905.

31 F. H. Crawford, *Guns for Ulster*, Belfast, 1947, pp. 10–15.

32 Brian M. Walker (ed.), *Parliamentary Election Results in Ireland, 1801–1922*, Dublin, 1978, pp. 271, 283.

33 Elizabeth A. Muenger, *The British Military Dilemma in Ireland: Occupation Politics, 1886–1914*, Dublin, 1991, p. 17.

34 Black, *Dufferin*, pp. 378–81.

35 Aiken McClelland, *William Johnston of Ballykilbeg*, Lurgan, 1990.

36 Stephen Roskill, *Admiral of the Fleet Earl Beatty*, London, 1981, p. 20.

37 Muenger, *British Military Dilemma*, p. 17.

38 *Ibid.*, pp. 18–19.

39 See note 30. There is a biography of Nicholson by Lionel James Trotter, *The Life of John Nicholson, Soldier and Administrator*, London, 1897. See also Hiram Morgan, 'Empire building: an uncomfortable Irish heritage', *Linen Hall Review*, X, no. 2 (Autumn 1993), p. 10.

40 Donal McCracken, 'Irish settlement and identity in South Africa before 1910', *Irish Historical Studies*, XXVIII (1992–93), p. 149. As McCracken observes, Roy Foster's *Modern Ireland, 1600–1972*, London, 1988, 'is the first general Irish history textbook to identify the important impact of the Anglo-Boer War on Irish politics'.

41 Alvin Jackson, *Colonel Edward Saunderson: Land and Loyalty in Victorian Ireland*, Oxford, 1995, p. 133.
42 Ervine, *Craigavon*, p. 69. See also McCracken, 'Irish settlement and identity', p. 149.
43 A. T. Q. Stewart, *The Ulster Crisis: Resistance to Home Rule, 1912–14*, London, 2nd ed, 1979, pp. 90, 134.
44 See the biographical essay in Cecil Kilpatrick (ed.), *The Formation of the Orange Order, 1795–1798: the Edited Papers of Colonel William Blacker and Colonel Robert H. Wallace*, Belfast, 1994, pp. 21–2. See also Stewart, *Ulster Crisis*, p. 69.
45 Lord Ava's brother also fought in South Africa: R. A. Hanna, 'The Career of Lord Basil Blackwood in South Africa, 1899–1907', unpublished M.A. thesis, Queen's University, Belfast, 1981, p. 55.
46 The papers of all these men are in the Public Record Office of Northern Ireland.
47 H. M. Hyde, *Carson: the Life of Sir Edward Carson, Baron Carson of Duncairn*, London, 1953, pp. 153, 156–7.
48 *Ibid.*, pp. 176–7.
49 *Ibid.*, pp. 491–2. See also Alvin Jackson, *Sir Edward Carson*, Dublin, 1993.
50 *BNL*, 22 June 1887.
51 Jeffrey Lant, *Insubstantial Pageant: Ceremony and Confusion at Queen Victoria's Court*, London, 1979, pp. 219–20.
52 *BNL*, 23 June 1897.
53 *Ibid.*, 12 August 1897.
54 Lant, *Insubstantial Pageant*, pp. 247–56.
55 *BNL*, 11 August 1902, 19 September 1902.
56 St John Ervine, 'A Testament of Middle Age' in F. J. Harvey (ed.), *Essays of 1930–1*, London, 1931. I am grateful to Dr Patrick Maume for this reference.
57 *BNL*, 3 July 1911, 14 July 1911.
58 *Ibid.*, 20 June 1911. For a general discussion of film and empire see Jeffrey Richards, 'Boy's Own Empire: feature films and imperialism in the 1930s' in John MacKenzie (ed.), *Imperialism and Popular Culture*, Manchester, 1986, pp. 140–64.
59 *BNL*, 25 May 1912, 27 May 1912, 26 May 1913, 25 May 1914. For a general discussion of Empire Day see J. A. Mangan, '"The grit of our forefathers": invented traditions, propaganda and imperialism' in MacKenzie (ed.), *Imperialism and Popular Culture*, pp. 130–3.
60 *BLN*, 22 May 1915.
61 Jackson, *Ulster Party*, pp. 322–26.
62 Denis Gwynn, *The Life of John Redmond*, London, 1932, p. 203; McCracken, 'Irish settlement and identity', pp. 146–7.
63 For a summary see Jackson, *Carson*, pp. 52–7.
64 See the souvenir programme: *Official Order of March: City of Belfast Peace Day Demonstration, 2 August 1919*, Belfast, 1919. A copy of this is in the Linen Hall Library, Belfast.
65 Morgan, 'Empire-Building', p. 10.
66 This section owes much to John MacKenzie, *Propaganda and Empire: The Manipulation of British Public Opinion, 1880–1960*, Manchester, 1984.
67 *BNL*, 19 August 1902.
68 *Ibid.*, 19 May 1903.
69 *Ibid.*, 3 July 1911.
70 *Ibid.*, 11 July 1911.
71 For a general discussion of this literature see: J. S. Bratton, 'Of England, home and duty: the image of England in Victorian and Edwardian juvenile fiction' in MacKenzie (ed.), *Imperialism and Popular Culture*, pp. 73–93.
72 *BLN*, 25 May 1909.
73 See for example the work of R. H. Boyd (*Couriers of the Dawn*, Belfast, 1938, and *Waymakers in Manchuria: the Story of the Irish Presbyterian Missionaries to Manchuria*, Belfast, 1940). See also Finlay Holmes, *Our Irish Presbyterian Heritage*, Belfast, 1985, pp. 160–1.
74 *BNL*, 4 May 1911 (report of a Boys' Brigade battalion inspection by F. H. Crawford).

75 *Ibid.*, 26 May 1911, 8 June 1911.
76 *Ibid.*, 14 June 1911.
77 *Ibid.*, 26 May 1915.
78 *Ibid.*, 24 June 1910.
79 *Ibid.*, 27 May 1912, 25 May 1913.
80 Compare Richards, 'Boys Own Empire', p. 161.
81 James Logan, 'Britain's Empire' and 'The Ulster Folk' in *Verses*.
82 See the entry for Logan in *Who's Who in Northern Ireland*, Belfast, 1938.
83 James Logan, *Ulster in the X-rays*, London, 1923, p. 127.

CHAPTER SIX

Empire Day in Ireland 1896–1962

David H. Hume

It was the advent of Queen Victoria's Golden Jubilee which prompted the fifty-five year old twelfth Earl of Meath to write to *The Times* of London in December 1896: 'A special effort should be made during the coming year to include the teaching of loyalty and patriotism in our system of national education. If sentiment be steadied by knowledge, we need not fear lest patriotism should degenerate into jingoism. The latter is the offspring of ignorance, the former of reason.' Lord Meath then advocated that the managers of all the schools throughout the United Kingdom of Great Britain and Ireland should ensure that

the outward emblems of the united Empire – a portrait of the Sovereign and the Union Jack, be supplied to every department. While the former retains a permanent position in the school room, let the latter hang week by week over the class which has distinguished itself the most during the past seven days. Finally, let the anniversary of the accession of the Queen be made a universal school holiday, the scholars meeting in the morning in the school-house to sing the National Anthem and to salute the flag.[1]

Not much more was heard of this for the next six years, apart from some echoes in Canada.[2] It was the unexpectedly high cost of the Anglo-Boer War, in casualties and reputation of the army, which prompted Lord Meath to write in 1902: 'What is the future of the British Empire? We have just escaped by the skin of our teeth from a highly perilous position. During the recent war we had to send out men who could neither ride, shoot nor scout', and he concluded, 'every healthy British lad should be so trained in his youth that, if the occasion ever arose, he could without delay take an active and efficient part in the defence of his country'.[3] Meath then took the opportunity provided by the meeting of the Empire Prime Ministers for the Coronation Colonial Conference in London that year, to raise the question of Empire Day with the British Colonial Secretary, Joseph Chamberlain.

Meath initially received little encouragement from the government, although Chamberlain did suggest that he should 'bring the matter to the notice of the representatives now in this country, or of any of the other Colonies concerned'.[4] This Meath did, and on 24 May 1903 (the anniversary of Queen Victoria's birthday) Empire Day was celebrated in no fewer than nine countries of the Empire, including Canada and India, and by 1910 Australia and South Africa had joined in the celebrations.[5] Clearly, Meath's proposal had tapped a rich vein of popular imperial sentiment at the heart of the nations of the Empire.

Not unnaturally, considering his upbringing, Lord Meath's social and political attitudes reflected the Conservative and Unionist views of the day. Born into the aristocracy of Anglo-Irish landlords, he was educated at Eton and in Germany. While he loved Ireland and cared about his estate at Killruddery, County Wicklow,[6] he was to all intents and purposes indistinguishable from most other members of the British aristocracy, and lived in Chertsey, near London, before inheriting his title. Meath began his career in public life as a clerk in the British Foreign Office, but was soon appointed to the Diplomatic Corps, serving in Berlin, the Hague and Paris during the 1860s. While in Germany, he encountered what he considered to be Teutonic arrogance and contempt for the English, perhaps his first experience that another nation could feel equally passionately for its destiny.[7] His career was unexpectedly cut short in 1874 when his wife's parents[8] objected to his taking up a posting to Athens, and Meath resigned from the Foreign Service. He and Lady Meath immediately decided to take up what they described as 'social and philanthropic work',[9] which they pursued with great energy and vigour, travelling widely across the world. For the last thirty years of his life Meath devoted much of his energies to the ideals which he believed the British Empire should represent.[10]

Lord Meath wanted to use Empire Day to promote the training of youth in their responsibilities towards the Empire, about which he felt they were largely ignorant. Since he believed that 'in youth, the mind is more open to receive the impression either of noble and elevating ideas and sentiments, or the reverse',[11] he devised a simple and memorable message: 'One King, One Flag, One Navy' as the motto of the movement, and 'Unity, Responsibility, Duty, Sympathy and Self-Sacrifice' as its watchwords.[12] In an effort to keep the work free from party politics, Meath ran the administration and finances (about £5,000 a year) of the Empire Day movement himself for the first ten years from 1903, although the two words 'Protestant Unionist' in his Who's Who entry left no doubts as to where his loyalties lay in Irish politics.

The worsening political situation in Europe in the first decade of the century, in particular British fears of German expansionism, saw the media in general and *The Times* of London in particular, begin to take Empire Day seriously. By the advent of the First World War, *The Times* was regularly producing a special supplement of up to twelve pages on 24 May each year, covering a great variety of subjects connected to the Empire. The recruitment crisis of 1916 saw the British government's first official endorsement of Empire Day, and from then on it was celebrated every year in schools and churches throughout the United Kingdom and the dominions until the early 1960s.

'The Irish are perhaps the most delightful, the most witty and the best mannered people on the face of the earth, if only the subjects of land tenure, religion and politics may be eliminated in conversation or in dealings with them',[13] wrote Lord Meath in what was a typical view of the Irish people by a more-or-less absentee Protestant landlord; a view no doubt sincerely held but coloured by the outlook of the English establishment, among whom he had made his home. Such sentiments epitomised the attitudes of many, but not all, of the ascendancy class, in their determination not to be identified with those whom they looked down on as native Irish, while at the same time considering themselves to be wholly Irish. This ambivalence largely dated from the Act of Union of 1800, although it had its roots deep in previous centuries of dominance, and was the crux of the divide between the Irish who saw themselves as loyal to the British Crown, and the Irish who wished to create an independent nation.

There is no evidence that Lord Meath himself took part in the organisation of Empire Day in Ireland. The various Irish newspapers, however, gave the celebration attention, and their particular editorial viewpoint depended on their political attitude to the Empire. For example, the first mention of Empire Day in the *Irish News*, the Belfast nationalist paper, was not until 1924, while the Conservative Unionist *Belfast News-Letter*[14] printed a full and glowing account of the inaugural meeting of Empire Day held in London in 1904. Their editorial struck the right tone exactly, with this view of the Empire: 'Through all, the inherent genius and indomitable spirit of the race carried it triumphant and to us, the heirs, is bequeathed the priceless memory and heritage of the past'. After a paean of praise for the Empire's history, the editorial ends on a particular note emphasising the Unionist complexion of the paper:

> What strong reasons, therefore, we have to be loyal to the great Empire of which we are a part and of which we should be so proud. The Union Jack is our birthright; it is our very own. Kings may die, Governments may change, dynasties pass away, but the flag remains. Loyalty to the flag means loyalty to ourselves.[15]

[151]

Ironically, and no doubt unconsciously, this last sentence reflected a developing philosophy in the Irish nationalist party, which emerged in 1905 as Arthur Griffith's policy of 'Sinn Fein' (ourselves alone). Sir Charles Petrie, writing in 1960, comments on this use of the national flag by the Unionists: 'In England, Scotland and Wales, the Crown acted as a centripetal force, but in Ireland such was not the case, and the Union Jack was, as it still is, a party emblem'.[16]

The other influential daily newspaper in the north, the *Northern Whig*, had been a more Liberal Unionist paper since the early 1890s, while in Dublin, the *Irish Times* fulfilled a similar role, at least until the 1940s. The *Northern Whig* greeted Empire Day in 1904 with a note in 'Our London Letter' which merely reported the initial meeting (so graphically described above by the *News-Letter*): 'Lord Meath presided over a large gathering of local boys and girls at the St James's Hall in London'.[17] The *Irish Times* reported Empire Day being celebrated in the Meath Protestant Industrial School in Blackrock, County Louth, where the pupils were

> marched into the schoolroom, to have the flag explained to them, together with the history of the British Empire during the reign of Queen Victoria. Several patriotic poems were recited and a special song for the occasion was sung, after which the flag was ceremonially saluted, the National anthem sung and three cheers for His Majesty. In the afternoon the boys were granted a holiday.[18]

This was to be the pattern in many schools from then on, varied only by the particular views of the principal. As for the special songs, Rudyard Kipling wrote to Lord Meath in 1906 offering one of his poems for use in schools during Empire Day, to be set to suitable music, which Meath gladly accepted:

> Land of our Birth, our Faith, our Pride,
> For whose dear sake our fathers died.
> O! Motherland, we pledge to thee
> Head, heart and hand through the years to be.

was the last of eight verses in similar patriotic vein.[19]

Influential support for the concept of empire during this period also came from the Church of Ireland, which was the church of the Protestant ascendancy class, affiliated to the Anglican communion.[20] Its weekly magazine, the *Church of Ireland Gazette*, in a full-page article about Lord Meath's social work in 1904, summed up his Empire crusade: 'He reminds us of the strong and lofty Imperialism which seeks to realise in the British Empire righteousness, peace and joy, which are fundamental principles of the Kingdom of God'.[21] This was reflected by an editorial in the London *Daily Graphic*, reprinted in the *News-Letter*:

> At present the Empire Day movement is a purely secular feature, a holiday like any other ... but because Imperialists desire to blend the aspiration which the Empire creates with the highest ideals of national ethics, we sincerely hope that the churches of all denominations in the Empire perceive it to be at once their duty, and their privilege to give sympathetic consideration to Lord Meath's appeal.[22]

Over the decades which followed, many Protestant churches gave increasing support to Empire Day. Already in 1907, the *News-Letter* was reporting that over 50,000 schools throughout the United Kingdom would be taking part in the celebrations.[23] Clearly, the Church of Ireland's clergy considered they had a duty to be in the vanguard of promoting the Empire in this way. This is not altogether surprising, as they came from the caste which was brought up to believe in the British Empire's 'civilising mission', were educated at English schools or their equivalent in Ireland, and received their theological training at Trinity College, Dublin, at that time almost entirely Anglican.[24] The Irish Presbyterian Church, on the other hand, while being largely in favour of the Union and the Empire, did not appear to use their pulpits to promote Empire Day; if they had, it would almost certainly have been reported by the *News-Letter* and definitely by their church's weekly newspaper, the *Witness*.[25] However, the relationship of both churches with the state following partition is well described by David Kennedy, writing of the 1930s: 'In its relations with the Government of Northern Ireland the Church of Ireland had slipped easily into the position a State Church would have occupied'. He points out that the Archbishop of Armagh, Charles Frederick D'Arcy, was a personal friend of the Prime Minister, Sir James Craig, and had read prayers at the first session of the new Parliament, opened by King George V, and notes that other prelates made frequent appearances on public platforms. Kennedy then adds a significant point: 'But the role of an official Church was one which the Church of Ireland had to share with the Presbyterian Church, which also regarded itself as capable of filling in Northern Ireland a role similar to that of its sister Church in Scotland'.[26]

While it was the mystique of empire propaganda which dominated the reports of Empire Day in the newspapers during the first decade of the century, Lord Meath's strong moral and racial tone must also have appealed to many of the editors. Meath stressed that.it was not his intention to glorify the British race but to produce 'a Spartan-like, virile race, imbued with the determination to make themselves worthy of the responsibility which rests upon their shoulder'.[27] On Empire Day in 1907 the *News-Letter* quoted Lord Meath: 'I would not have laboured to promote the movement had it not contained an inner spiritual meaning, which was the subordination of selfish and class interests to those of the State and the community'. *The News-Letter*'s editorial added a political barb to Meath's high-mindedness, reflecting their view of the usefulness of Empire Day: 'It appeals to the imagination. The conception which the phrase Empire Day embodies dwarfs and shames all such petty provincialisms as an Independent Ireland. What sane patriot wishes his country to stagnate in isolation, cut off from the great tides of life which surge pulsing through the Empire?'[28]

In the years which followed, Lord Meath's writings continued to show a preoccupation with the indoctrination of youth. In an article in 1912 on 'How to Improve the Race', he asserted that 'the race can never be improved physically unless it can also be improved mentally and more especially morally'. Proper training could ensure that 'a race might gradually evolve which was worthy to bear the white man's burden and not be afraid, if God wills, to face the immense responsibility attached to the government of this wonderful British Empire'.[29] This was written at a time when the relationship between Great Britain and Ireland was plunged into the crisis created by the Home Rule Bill in the imperial Parliament in London. Unionists in Ireland and Britain feared that Home Rule would take Ireland out of the Empire; in Ulster, militia were being raised to provide a military backing for a provisional government, which Unionists planned to set up. This was being done quite legally, for the law allowed magistrates to authorise military operations in defence of the constitution. The force was not as yet armed, but as Mark Bence-Jones comments: 'The men who joined the Ulster Volunteers were young, fit and easy to train; above all, they were determined',[30] although this was probably not for the purpose Lord Meath had in mind. Not surprisingly, over the following years, the reports of Empire Day laid a greater emphasis on the struggle to resist Home Rule than on the training of youthful minds to love and revere the Empire.

Again, the leadership of the Church of Ireland was in the vanguard of support for the Union and the Empire. Preaching in his cathedral on Empire Sunday in 1912, the Bishop of Derry delivered a resounding peroration: 'There was no such conquering race in history, none so just, so merciful, so disinterested, in the kindliest and most potent Empire that ever the sun shone upon, the best and truest handmaid of the very Kingdom of God, that had yet been seen by mortals'.[31] The Bishop of Clogher, preaching at Clones, County Monaghan, chose Empire Day to preach against Home Rule: 'If Unionists only stood determinedly by the flag of the Union, used every lawful opposition to home rule and were not afraid to let everybody see the strength of their opposition, then with God's blessing, they would win in the end'.[32] The Unionists also had support from a powerful quarter, in the person of Andrew Bonar Law, at that time leader of the Conservative parliamentary opposition at Westminster and later Prime Minister.[33] On Easter Tuesday 1912, at a parade of 100,000 men at Balmoral on the outskirts of Belfast, and after prayers led by the Church of Ireland Primate and the Moderator of the Presbyterian Church in Ireland, Bonar Law evoked the emotive idiom of the siege of Derry in the seventeenth century: 'Once more you hold the pass for the Empire. You are a besieged city. The timid have left you; your Lundys have betrayed you; but you have closed your gates.'[34]

The political polarisation left no room for compromise. The Unionists felt they were correct in their analysis that the choice was either an Ireland within the Empire or an independent Irish republic, and since for Unionists this was a question of national identity, it was not subject to debate; to think otherwise was tantamount to treason. Both 1913 and 1914 saw a heightened emphasis on the political use of the Empire Day celebrations to defend the Union, with full pages in the *News-Letter* and the *Northern Whig* reporting events all across Ulster. The *Northern Whig*'s tone was epitomised by the comment that the celebrations were being carried out 'in a loyal and befitting manner', while the *News-Letter* thundered forth as before. Sir Robert Kennedy, Chairman of the Governors of the prestigious Belfast school, Campbell College, chose Empire Day in 1913 to suggest to the people of Holywood, County Down, that 'we should turn our backs upon present day politicians and demagogues. There is a stern duty to rally round the Throne and present an unbroken front to all the King's enemies.'[35]

In the same year, the *News-Letter* drew attention to the many churches which held services on Empire Sunday, where the preachers used the occasions both to impress on their congregations the lessons to be drawn from 'building up a great Empire', and to deliver some direct political warnings to the government. The Reverend W. S. Kerr, a prominent educationalist, addressing a packed audience in the Ulster Hall, Belfast, asserted: 'Ulstermen are taking part in the Empire celebrations under the shadow of a great apprehension of being thrust from the place within the Empire they have always known' and he was amazed 'at seeing the people who had consistently hated the Empire being petted as favourites, whilst every species of insult and rancour was levelled against ourselves'. He believed that 'if such treatment be persisted in, a deadly wound would be given to the heart of the Empire', and suggested that 'the insulted and estranged love Ulstermen might develop for England could be turned into hatred, by an insensate government, which would drive the Empire's children into actual hostility'.[36] Writing in an Empire Day editorial in 1914, against the setting of the illegal importation into Ulster of over £45,000 worth of German arms and ammunition earlier that year, the *News-Letter* delivered a broadside against the government's plans for Home Rule: 'To all Irishmen, we have good reason to believe, the late gallant gun-running made its powerful appeal. It furnished a much needed object lesson that there are still more powerful factors in our national life than the subtle craft of that revolutionary committee dignified by the name of Cabinet.' The editorial ended with what appeared to be a warning of civil war: 'Against such wiles, Ulster stands for King and country and Empire. If the Government attempts to coerce it, there will be bloodshed on an extensive scale.'[37]

In similar vein on Empire Sunday 1914, Charles Grierson, the Dean of St Anne's Cathedral, Belfast, in the course of a political polemic, summed up his position precisely: 'I believe Ulster will never submit as a conquered province. Men speak of Ireland as a Nation but an independent nation it is clearly the will of Providence she can never be.'[38] On the same day, the Reverend Dr Joseph L. Burton, Rural Dean of Down, preaching at an open air service at Belfast's Oval football ground attended by clergy from all the Protestant denominations, exhorted 3,500 men from the Ulster Volunteer Force: 'If they must fight, let them resolve not to strike the first blow, but when the fight did begin, let them be the last to leave it'.[39] The situation was a singular example of the conditional nature of the Ulster Unionists' loyalty to the United Kingdom government: when the political climate suited the Unionists, they fully supported the status quo, but when their position in Ireland appeared to be threatened, particularly by the Westminster government, they would rise up in anger, even to the point of threatening armed rebellion.

In marked contrast to the previous few years, the reports of the Empire Day celebrations in 1915 in the *News-Letter*, the *Northern Whig* and the *Irish Times* were as different as night from day. Gone were the full pages describing meetings, fetes, church services, marches and drilling, because there were none to report. The explanation was simple: the Home Rule Act was shelved by the British government for the duration of the First World War, so there was no immediate need for a Unionist campaign to defend the Union and the integrity of the Empire. By 1916, however, the very high casualties of the war, especially among the troops from Ulster, had a profound and lasting effect of a different nature. Over 5,500 men of the 36th (Ulster) Division, which had been specially created at Lord Kitchener's request, were killed or wounded in the first two days of the Battle of the Somme.[40]

Jonathan Bardon comments: 'On 12 July 1916 the Twelfth celebrations were abandoned as the province remembered the fallen in deep silence … Ulster's tightknit Protestant community would never forget the terrible sacrifice that had been made'.[41] That year saw the British government facing an increasing crisis on all the war fronts, which demanded an ever greater enlistment of troops. On 5 April Viscount Milner spoke up on behalf of Empire Day in the House of Lords, seconded by Lord Meath.[42] The government had decided that the time had come officially to recognise Empire Day, and on 24 May King George V sent a special message to the front lines, through the Commander-in-Chief, Sir Douglas Haig. Since the troops came from all the dominions, the King's message received world-wide publicity, putting Empire Day on a different footing from then on.

Political events in Ireland were once again moving rapidly. The 1916 Easter Rising in Dublin, seen from London as the height of treason in wartime, was vigorously suppressed. The execution of the leaders, however, had the opposite effect on the nationalist population to that hoped for by the British Cabinet. Together with the ill-advised attempt to conscript Irishmen in the spring of 1918, these two events united the majority of nationalists against the British presence in Ireland. The rapid rise of the electoral popularity of Sinn Fein and its success in the 1918 general election, saw the setting up of the republican Dail government in Dublin. This was not recognised by London, and armed hostilities between Irish insurgents and Crown forces began in January 1919, a conflict which later became known as the Anglo-Irish War. However, just a month after the outbreak of the 1916 Rising, the *Irish Times* reported that the Empire Day celebrations saw 'more flags flying from many government buildings in Dublin than usual'. The paper added that 'a green flag with a harp and crown was noticed over the home of the Provost of Trinity College'.[43]

In the immediate post-war period, Empire Day continued as before to provide newspaper editors and others with opportunities for reflections, particularly on the proposal in 1920 to establish Home Rule Parliaments in both Belfast and Dublin. This provoked the *News-Letter* to publish an editorial with a headline across the page: 'Conspiracy Against the Empire'. The 'Bolshevics of Russia' were included with 'Irish Americans and Germans everywhere' as people who 'hated Great Britain and would be only too pleased to see the destruction of the Empire'. In the same edition, a reprinted *Sunday Chronicle* article quoted an English peer, the Duke of Northumberland, asserting that 'the sole purpose of the Irish rebellion is the disruption of the Empire. It should not be forgotten that behind the anti-British conspiracy in all parts of the world is the influence of the Roman Catholic church.'[44]

'The Last Word' was the *News-Letter*'s appropriate headline for their 1921 Empire Day editorial. Empire Day coincided that year with polling day for the first Northern Ireland Parliament. Some 124 Sinn Fein representatives had already been returned unopposed to the Dublin Parliament, and the election was seen by the *News-Letter*'s editor as crucial:

> Ireland as a Republic would be the enemy of Great Britain of a deadly sort, since Ireland commands Great Britain's seas. Our loyalty to the Crown and Constitution and Empire means we shall have nothing but opposition to offer to any Parliament for the whole of Ireland. Loss of support in England for the Union means we must defend ourselves alone.[45]

This final sentence epitomised once again the deeply felt belief of an independently-minded people, who feared becoming a minority in what they believed would be a Catholic Ireland no longer connected to a Protestant England and Empire.

The *Irish Times* took a more detached view of the Empire Day celebrations. In 1920, their Lady Correspondent wrote a column on the social aspects of the events in Dublin's Phoenix Park, where there was 'an excellent programme of athletic sports, attended by the Chief Secretary and Lady Greenwood ... and the band of the 1st Battalion Lancashire Fusiliers played pleasing Irish airs'.[46] Another article described the 'picturesque ceremony of saluting the flag at Campbell College' at a ceremonial Officer Training Corps parade, which continued every Empire Day at that Belfast school until well into the 1960s. In 1924, in a more sombre tone, the *Irish Times* drew attention to a mass meeting of ten thousand children at Ormeau Park, Belfast, where the Governor, the Duke of Abercorn, spoke of Empire Day as 'a very sacred anniversary for all Britishers' and declared that his motto for them was: 'Courage to live for, and if necessary to die for, the Empire'.[47]

In 1922 the Anglo-Irish war spread north into Ulster, triggering what Jonathan Bardon calls 'a sectarian conflict there more vicious and lethal than all the northern riots of the previous century put together'.[48] Once again, the Unionists saw these events as a direct threat, not only to the Union but particularly to the Empire, and two speeches fully reported by the *News-Letter* highlighted this. The first was by the Northern Ireland Minister of Finance, Hugh Pollock. He was presenting his Budget on Empire Day, which coincided with the first anniversary of the creation of the new Northern Ireland Parliament. While discussing the financing of the special police, he interrupted his speech

> to raise it to the plane of Imperial sentiment, Imperial Honour and Imperial Duty ... we regard Ulster today as a key-stone of the arch of the

British Empire ... Ulster has been selected as the cock-pit of strife by those whose object is the Destruction of the Empire, rather than the mere acquisition of Ulster. Here in this province the whole principle of Empire is at stake: we the people of Ulster are the children of the Empire.[49]

The second reported speech on this theme was made in Belfast by Lord Hugh Cecil, Unionist MP for Oxford University since 1910. He was the principal speaker at an Empire Day demonstration chaired by the Lord Mayor of Belfast, and held in the Presbyterian Church Assembly Hall, under the auspices of the Ulster Branch of the British Empire Union and the National Citizens Union. In the course of a review of contemporary events, he cited Germany and Ireland as showing 'undisciplined excesses of patriotic nationalist sentiments, which were very far from being of service to mankind'. Cecil asserted that, in his view, the creation of a republic would not only threaten Ireland's allegiance to the British Empire, but was 'a challenge to civilised standards', since their policy had been 'created by murders and dominated by murderers. Who was there who was not a madman who would wish to become a member of such a community? They were divided from it by the rivers of blood that Sinn Fein had caused.' He declared that his object was to bring home to 'Roman Catholics all over the world the black shame that had overtaken their religion' because their church had given its support to the 'rebellion in Ireland'. He contrasted this with his belief that Protestants 'had the pure light of the Gospel of Peace ... they were enemies of no particular faith or particular party or any particular nation', and he assured his audience that 'crime can be beaten and *pax Britannica* re-established from one end of the Six Counties to the other'.[50]

Following the end of the Anglo-Irish hostilities, it took the span of only a year to see a complete change in the *News-Letter*'s approach to Empire Day; it was almost as if *pax Britannica* had indeed been re-established. In place of the bombast of the year before, their 1923 editorial wrote: 'Some thought Empire Day was to cultivate an aggressive Imperial spirit; it is not intended to stimulate pride but to quicken a sense of duty, and renewal of confidence in our race and faith in our future. There should never be any likelihood of anyone writing a history of the decline and fall of the British Empire.'[51] In 1924 there was sufficient stability in Northern Ireland for twelve thousand children to meet 'on parade' on Empire Day at the Oval football ground in Belfast, on which the *News-Letter* commented: 'Empire Day is spreading the right concept of pride in the Empire, inculcating a proper patriotism and loyalty to the Throne and the Flag. Our genius for colonization and the ruling of subject races is but a natural expression of our development along the path of civilization.'[52]

[159]

At the same time as this large gathering of young people was meeting in Belfast, *The Times* reported that an estimated hundred thousand people met in Wembley Stadium, London, for an impressive Empire Day religious ceremony, which included King George V in Field-Marshal's uniform, other members of the Royal Family, the Lord Mayor of London, and many dominion dignitaries. The Archbishop of Canterbury, in the course of an analysis of the actual political situation within the Empire, from a rather broader perspective than that of the *News-Letter*, asked his audience whether enough attention was being given to the progress of education and justice in Great Britain's overseas colonies in Africa and the Far East, adding: 'Or India? What pains have we taken or are taking to understand or appraise the aspirations, wise or foolish, workable or unworkable, which the spirit of nationalism within the Empire sets astir?'[53] The relevance of these comments was underlined by the *News-Letter* itself, which carried the news of Gandhi's campaign for independence, amid widespread unrest in India. Ten years later, the Bishop of Exeter, Lord William Cecil, elder brother of Lord Hugh, writing about Empire Day in his *Diocesan Gazette*, reflected the Archbishop's convictions: 'I must confess grave foreboding with regard to keeping that day. I feel that the boasting and jactitation about empire is calling upon us God's punishment for our disregard for the plain teaching of Holy Writ in such matters. It is because I wish to save the country that I oppose the vanity of Empire Day rejoicing.'[54]

The editors of the Northern Catholic nationalist paper, the *Irish News*, would have understood the sentiments of these English clerics. The paper had begun reporting the Empire Day celebrations from the mid-1920s, but they made no editorial comments unless there were political issues raised in which they had a particular interest. The first of these incidents coincided with the next major change which was to take place in the Empire Day celebrations: its use as a promoter of Empire trade. During 1927, the Empire Marketing Board launched a 'British Empire Week' to promote British goods, which the *Irish News* thought was an excellent idea, although they felt 'we should patronize Ireland before thinking of the Empire'. But a more controversial issue quickly arose: since the new Irish state was a member of the Commonwealth, the Irish flag was flown with the rest of the Commonwealth flags at the City Hall, the principal venue of the British Empire Week celebrations in Belfast. However, according to the *Irish News*, it was 'down by lunch time'. The conclusion the editor drew was that 'the Orange Order runs this country', and he continued

> The Catholic is a citizen; he is supposed to be on the level with other citizens ... Let him seek a position in the service of the government or the

Corporation and he will soon realise the essential difference between him and other citizens of the same kind. He may be on equal terms with the best in London, or Manchester, Glasgow, Melbourne or Montreal. Here he is hunted because he is a Catholic, and the Government have accepted this as easily and openly as they have the dictum with regard to the Free State Flag.[55]

During the 1930s, Empire Day continued to be reported, and was intermittently linked with topical concerns. In 1935, for example, the border issue moved a Mrs Harnett, who called herself a 'fanatical loyalist and Ulsterwoman', to tell an Empire Day meeting in the Ulster Hall, Belfast, that 'if she had troops, she'd use them to defend the border, at present undefended, which the IRA knew well enough'.[56] On a broader front, following the debate on the Statute of Westminster in 1931 which led to the virtual independence of the white dominions, the *News-Letter*'s Empire Day editorial warned: 'When we are changing the kind of grip which keeps us together, easy would it be to lose grip altogether; so the Commonwealth would fall away into a group of separate states foreign to each other. No greater calamity could befall the world, or the Dominions themselves.'[57] This conviction was later underlined by Stanley Baldwin, who chose Empire Day in 1937 to make his last speech before resigning as Prime Minister of Britain; emphasising the need for unity in the Empire, he posed the question 'And how are we going to keep it together?', and answered 'By the Crown. The Crown is the one tangible link that we all know, and it is the link which, we think, cannot be broken. If it were, which God forbid, would the Commonwealth hold together?'[58]

It was, of course, the outbreak of the Second World War in September 1939 which brought the nations of the Commonwealth together, rather than any supposed threat to the Crown's influence. Throughout the war, Empire Day celebrations were kept at a low key, although the various religious services and messages were given full publicity by the press as before. There were occasional outbursts on particular issues, such as that by the *Irish News* on Empire Day 1941, on the possibility of conscription being imposed in Northern Ireland, about which the editor made the point that 'no greater degradation of the ideal of Irish nationhood is imaginable than that any of her sons should be compelled to serve a foreign power'.[59] Although the Northern Ireland Cabinet was in favour of conscription generally, there was no way in which the London government felt it could be enforced against the wishes of the Catholic minority.[60] As if to underline this, in 1944 the *News-Letter* reported Northern Ireland's Prime Minister, Sir Basil Brooke, telling an Empire Day meeting in Belfast, on returning from a visit to the dominions: 'what struck him most was the strong sense of nationalism everywhere. In Ulster they were determined to remain part of the United Kingdom but they too had their own national outlook.'[61] Clearly, a sea-change had taken place in attitudes to the Empire, and the pragmatic editors of the *News-Letter* were not long in perceiving it.

In attempting to evaluate the impact of Empire Day on the concept of empire, there were many who no doubt felt that it was mere harmless propaganda for a good cause, but it would be a mistake to dismiss it in this way. It may not be easy to differentiate between social and political issues in a highly polarised community, but at least one clear social issue was raised by the celebrations of Empire Day, especially in the schools and churches of Northern Ireland. Since Empire Day was specifically aimed at the youth of the nation, and was usually linked with military type parades and sanctified by church services, the constant reiteration of the symbolism of 'loyalty, Crown, service and flag' in order deliberately to instil into young minds the idea that 'British is best', however subtly disguised by devotional ritual, must inevitably have contributed to a feeling of superiority towards the 'subject races', in the phrase made popular by Edwardian newspaper editors. A. H. Halsey, remembering the village classroom in Britain in the 1920s, wrote that 'they were steeped in officially sanctioned nationalism. The world map was red for the Empire and dull brown for the rest. The Greenwich meridian placed London at the centre of the world. Empire Day ritualised an established national supremacy.'[62] On the political issue, the identification by the Unionists with the perceived glories of a great Empire, combined with the aura of mystique which epitomised their attitude to the Crown, provided an emotional and psychological support for the realities of the Union. The editors of the *News-Letter* were clearly ready to use this emotional response to empire as a convenient weapon for political advantage, as and when the occasion demanded.

Probably one of the last examples of this latter use of the concept of empire and the Crown was the visit of the young, newly married Princess Elizabeth, and her husband Prince Philip, to Belfast on Empire Day in 1949. In a fully reported speech of thanks after receiving the Freedom of the City, the Princess's opening remarks reflected the welcome the royal couple had been given by the people in the city streets that morning:

> The warmth of an Irish welcome, the loyalty which the very name of Ulster recalls, removes any thought of separation and makes us feel as much at home in your midst as in any other part of the United Kingdom. We know this springs largely from the fact that the Crown is the focus of

our unity, comradeship and moral standards ... We are and cannot help being a Mother Country ... and yet the great self-governing countries which are our children have not forgotten us.[63]

The Princess's speechwriter's reference to the Crown, and to Britain as a mother country, in the setting of Ulster in a partitioned Ireland, typified the attitude of the English establishment towards the Irish aspiration for self-government. In discussing an earlier British attitude to Indian independence, Nicholas Mansergh makes a comparison with Irish self-government, which he believed 'was viewed with the same air of confident superiority, the same lack of instinctive sympathy for another and an older civilization. Even Liberals, in common with the vast majority of their fellow countrymen, did not comprehend the existence of an Irish mind and a distinctive Irish outlook.'[64] A year later, Ireland became a republic and 'was no longer, on any interpretation, part of His Majesty's dominions'.[65]

In contrast to the reporting of the royal visit, two short paragraphs in the *News-Letter* appeared to forecast the impending demise of the Empire. Both items were reports of statements by the leader of Australia's Liberal party, Sir Robert Menzies, a staunch imperialist. On Empire Day in 1948, he warned that 'the Empire will pass into history in 15 years unless the British people all over the world begin furiously to think of their relationship one with another'.[66] A year later, commenting on India's independence, Mr Menzies lamented that:

> the formula produced to keep India within the British Commonwealth has reduced the Crown from a pulsating reality to a heartless lawyer's document. There might not be an Empire Day next year. It might be called Commonwealth Day; it might even degenerate to something even less descriptive of the great human association under the Throne.[67]

In the event, Mr Menzies's anxious crystal ball gazing was perfectly accurate; it was announced in the British Parliament on 28 December 1958 that Empire Day was to change its name to Commonwealth Day, while the movement founded by the Earl of Meath in 1903 which had carried Empire Day's name through six decades finally ceased to exist on 1 March 1962. Exactly ten years to the day after Menzies's gloomy foreboding, the *News-Letter* reported a sermon by a prominent liberal Methodist, the Reverend Eric Gallagher, at a Commonwealth Day Service in the Grosvenor Hall, Belfast, which was headlined 'No Master Race in the Commonwealth'. Gallagher stated: 'Our concept of Commonwealth gives the lie to any claims to national or racial superiority. Today, we have a community of nations, and we have disowned any idea of an Empire ruled by a master race.'[68] Perhaps this was a fitting epitaph to the whole concept of empire.

R.T.C. LIBRARY LETTERKENNY

Before concluding, we ought to remind ourselves of the psychological, emotional and political importance that the English, and for that matter, the Scots too, have placed on keeping what can best be described as a foothold in Ireland; a feeling no doubt inherited from the history of the plantations, along with a sense of common destiny at times of war and other crises in the Empire. Writing in an unsigned article in the *Quarterly Review* of 1883, the third Marquis of Salisbury, later Conservative and Unionist Prime Minister, expressed the belief that:

> The highest interests of the Empire, as well as the most sacred obligations of honour, forbid us to solve this [Irish] question by conceding any species of independence to Ireland; or in other words, any licence to the majority in that country to govern the rest of Irishmen as they please. To the minority, to those who have trusted us ... it would be a sentence of exile or of ruin. All that is Protestant – nay, all that is loyal – all who have land or money to lose ... would be at ... the mercy of ... adventurers.[69]

Thirty-four years later, at the height of the First World War, Charles Frederick D'Arcy, Bishop of Down, emphasising his commitment to the Unionist philosophy at his Diocesan Synod in Belfast in 1917, said:

> We cannot realise the best thing in us as a people except through association with England. We are not a separate race from the English ... The British Empire is an Irish Empire as well as an English Empire. We share in all the wealth of that grand inheritance which they, with our help, have created.[70]

In expressing a similar conviction from a different perspective, Dr Henry Montgomery, the Moderator of the Presbyterian General Assembly in 1912, wrote: 'There are two nations in Ireland, differing in race, religion and in their sense of civic responsibilities; the fusion of the two is an absolute impossibility'.[71] On this the *Witness* commented: 'If Ireland should be separated from Britain, Ulster should be separated from Ireland'.[72] Perhaps the final word on this subject should go to Canon Dudley, preaching a year later in his parish church in Coleraine, County Londonderry: 'There is no better Englishman than an Irishman who is possessed of the true Imperial sentiment'.[73]

In contrast to the apparent certainty of such sentiments, it is possible that it is the absence of an empire concept as a stimulus and inspiration which has made many contemporary Ulster loyalists question their sense of identity and purpose in the life of the nation. Steve Bruce, in an analysis of the origins of Ian Paisley's Free Presbyterianism and the Democratic Unionist Party, argues that 'these Ulster Protestants seem closer to Victorian Britain than to their twentieth century descendants'. Bruce asserts that Ulster loyalists would still like to be part of a

British Empire whose world domination 'was displayed on school wall-maps with huge areas of red' and concludes that 'their zeal in claiming to be British is both a mark of the uncertainty they feel about their identity and a response to the obvious unwillingness of many British people to accord them that identity'.[74] Nicholas Mansergh seems to confirm part of this analysis, when writing of Ireland's attitude to the Commonwealth in 1949, which he felt had elicited very little appreciation from Whitehall and no enthusiasm whatsoever in Belfast, where 'the Unionist stance was, and remained, less Commonwealth than imperialist'.[75] Finlay Holmes may have put his finger on the reason for the apparent alienation between the people of Britain and Northern Ireland, when he wrote of the contemporary political scene in 1990:

> Presbyterian suspicion of Irish nationalism on political grounds, as a subversive force dedicated to the destruction of Northern Ireland ... and fear of Roman Catholicism on theological grounds ... united to promote *sectarian apartheid* in Northern Ireland ... Irish Presbyterians in general remain committed to the political status quo ... that is, the partition of Ireland and the Union of Northern Ireland with Britain.[76]

The debate about the relative merits of the Empire will no doubt continue. In 1903 the radical economic theorist J. A. Hobson argued that imperialism abroad not only drained off capital and stunted the growth of social welfare at home but was 'a huge business blunder'. On the moral argument he wrote: 'The acquiescence, even the active and enthusiastic support, of the body of a nation in the course of policy fatal to its own true interests is secured partly by appeals to the mission of civilization, but chiefly by playing upon the primitive instincts of the race'.[77] At the time Hobson wrote this, Lord Meath was just setting out to promote Empire Day in the schools of the United Kingdom and the dominions 'to elevate the British character, strengthen and consolidate the British race, and render the Empire safe from internal rebellion and external attack from the many barbarous and semi-barbarous countries surrounding it ... containing semi-civilized and savage races'.[78] Perhaps it is not too unkind to conclude that all that remains of the latter conviction is a window dedicated to the memory of the twelfth Earl of Meath in one of England's great shrines, St Paul's Cathedral. Clearly, empires have only an ephemeral ability to impart a sense of purpose into the life of nations, in contrast to the sense of identity and belonging provided by nationalism, which for good or ill, shows a remarkable degree of resilience.

Notes

1   *The Times*, 28 December 1896.
2   See Royal Commonwealth Society (RCS), *Library Notes*, New Series No. 259 (February 1984), for more details on the origins of Empire Day.
3   Meath, 'British youth and the Empire' in *King and Country*, London, December 1902, p. 23 (Meath archives).
4   Meath, *Memories of the Twentieth Century*, London, 1924, p. 144.
5   RCS *Library Notes*, New Series No. 259 (February 1984).
6   In 1550 Sir William Brabazon, from Leicester, England, was appointed by King Henry VIII to the commission which dissolved the monasteries in Ireland. He acquired the estate at Killruddery, County Wicklow, which had been monastery land since 1170. Sir William was three times Lord Justice of Ireland. His son Sir Edward Brabazon was made Baron Ardee in 1616, and Sir William's grandson became the first Earl of Meath in 1627 (*Burke's Peerage*, 1949).
7   Meath, *Memories of the Nineteenth Century*, London, 1923, p. 25.
8   Lady Mary Jane Maitland, the only surviving daughter of the eleventh Earl of Lauderdale, married Lord Meath in 1868. They had three sons and two daughters. Lady Meath died in 1918.
9   *Who's Who*, 1920.
10 Lord Meath kept meticulous, detailed records of all his public activities, in forty leather-bound volumes, presently in the archives at the Meath family home at Killruddery, Bray, County Meath.
11 Meath, *Memories of the Twentieth Century*, p. 77.
12 *The Sphere*, London, 29 May 1926 (RCS Library, Cambridge).
13 Meath, *Memories of the Twentieth Century*, p. 6.
14 First published with the title *Belfast News-Letter & General Advertiser* as a weekly on 1 September 1737, it claims to be the oldest surviving newspaper in the British Isles. It is strongly orientated towards the business community, while politically its principles were declared in 1851 to be: 'Loyalty to the Throne, devotion to the religion of the Bible and unswerving attachment to the Protestant Constitution of these lands'. In 1967 the owner Captain O. W. J. Henderson confirmed the *News Letter* (its present title) 'as a constant upholder of the Union of Great Britain and Northern Ireland … and most particularly the people's devotion to Queen and Country'. *News Letter*, 250th anniversary edition, 3 September 1987.
15 *Belfast News-Letter* (hereafter *BNL*), 25 May 1904.
16 Petrie, *The Victorians*, London, 1960, p. 109. Petrie was President of the Military History Society of Ireland.
17 *Northern Whig*, 25 May 1904.
18 *Irish Times*, 25 May 1904.
19 Meath, *Memories of the Twentieth Century*, p. 102.
20 In 1871, the Church of Ireland consisted of just over 12 per cent of the population, and this figure has remained more or less static. It was relatively strong in the business and professional worlds, and so had an urban bias, although the geographical distribution was unequal across the country. Over half the membership was in Ulster, and it was relatively strong in the more prosperous parts in and around Dublin and the central plain (R. B. McDowell, *The Church of Ireland 1869–1969*, London, 1975, pp. 2–3).
21 *Church of Ireland Gazette*, May 1904, p. 5.
22 *BNL*, 14 June 1904.
23 *Ibid.*, 25 May 1907.
24 The Church of Ireland clergy in the nineteenth century were drawn from establishment families, the aristocracy and the landed gentry. Over half of the incumbents were the sons of professional men, army and naval officers, lawyers, doctors, schoolmasters and clergymen, with only 11 per cent sons of businessmen and 4 per cent farmers' sons. Of the clergy who had attended a university, 90 per cent had been to

Trinity College, Dublin (McDowell, *The Church of Ireland*, pp. 13–14).

25 The *Witness* was first published in 1874 and ceased publication in 1941.

26 David Kennedy, 'Aspects of the northern situation' in Michael Hurley (ed.), *Irish Anglicanism 1869–1969*, Dublin, 1970, p. 164.

27 *Empire Day*, an Empire Day Movement pamphlet, 1912, (RCS Library, Cambridge).

28 *BNL*, 25 May 1907.

29 'How to Improve the Race' in *Prevention*, January/March 1913 (Meath archives).

30 Mark Bence-Jones, *Twilight of the Ascendancy*, London, 1987, p. 156.

31 *BNL*, 24 May 1912. The Bishop of Derry, Dr George Alexander Chadwick, was a graduate of Trinity College, Dublin.

32 *BNL*, 24 May 1912. The Bishop of Clogher, Maurice Day, came from a family of landowners in County Kerry. He was educated at Queen's College, Cork, and Trinity College, Dublin.

33 Bonar Law was the son of the Reverend James Law, a Presbyterian minister from Coleraine, County Londonderry, who had emigrated to Canada in 1845 and returned to Ulster in 1877. Bonar Law was born in New Brunswick, and later settled in Scotland, where he became an iron merchant in Glasgow (A. T. Q. Stewart, *The Ulster Crisis*, London, 1967, p. 38).

34 *BNL*, 10 April 1912. Lieutenant Colonel Robert Lundy was the military commander during the siege of Derry in 1689 who saw little hope in defending the city and wanted his officers to withdraw. He was overthrown by a citizens' revolt and has gone down in popular mythology as a traitor to King William of Orange's cause.

35 *BNL*, 25 May 1913. Sir Robert Kennedy had spent nearly forty years in the British Diplomatic Service, retiring in 1912 as Minister to Uruguay.

36 *BNL*, 25 May 1913. Reverend William S. Kerr, Rector of St Paul's, Belfast, was a graduate of Trinity College, Dublin. He served on the board of the government's Teacher Training College at Stranmillis, Belfast, and from 1946 to 1955 was Bishop of Down and Dromore.

37 *BNL*, 25 May 1914.

38 *Ibid.* Reverend C. T. P. Grierson B.D. was Chaplain to the Lord-Lieutenant of Ireland from 1896 to 1916, and Bishop of Down, Connor and Dromore, 1919 to 1934.

39 *Northern Whig*, 25 May 1914.

40 Hugh Shearman blames the heavy losses on the fact that 'no corresponding advance was made on either side of the Ulster Division, so they were left under heavy attack from three sides and had to retreat'. He adds: 'In Ulster there were those who saw the disaster, not as an exhibition of incompetence and lack of co-ordination among British generals, but as Liberal England's way of trying to solve the Ulster question. The event lingered on in popular memory.' (Shearman, 'Ulster at War', *News Letter*, 250th anniversary edition, 3 September 1987, p. 91).

41 Jonathan Bardon, *A History of Ulster*, Belfast, 1992, pp. 455–6. July 12 each year is celebrated by Protestants as the anniversary of the Battle of the Boyne in 1690, in which King William of Orange defeated King James II.

42 RCS, *Library Notes*, New Series No. 259 (February 1984).

43 *Irish Times*, 25 May 1916.

44 *BNL*, 25 May 1920.

45 *Ibid.*, 24 May 1921.

46 *Irish Times*, 25 May 1920.

47 *Ibid.*, 25 May 1924.

48 Bardon, *A History of Ulster*, p. 67.

49 *BNL*, 25 May 1922.

50 *Ibid.*, 25 May 1922.

51 *Ibid.*, 24 May 1923.

52 *Ibid.*, 25 May 1924.

53 *The Times*, 25 May 1924. Dr Randall T. Davidson was Archbishop of Canterbury from 1903 to 1928.

54 *Exeter Diocesan Magazine*, May 1924, p. 2.

55 *Irish News*, 26 May 1927.

56 *Irish Times*, 25 May 1935.
57 *BNL*, 25 May 1932. The 1931 Statute of Westminster saw the end of the long-cherished principle of British parliamentary supremacy in the dominions (Nicholas Mansergh, *The Commonwealth Experience*, II, London, 1982, pp. 31–5).
58 *BNL*, 25 May 1937.
59 *Irish News*, 24 May 1941.
60 Hugh Shearman notes: 'Memories of World War 1 had caused people to say that what Britain needed from Ulster was not so much infantry as generals ... such soldiers as [Field Marshals] Alanbrooke, Alexander, Templer and Montgomery came from Ulster families and made historic contributions to victory' (Shearman, 'Ulster at War').
61 *BNL*, 25 May 1948.
62 John Mackenzie, *Propaganda and Empire*, Manchester, p. 193.
63 *BNL*, 25 May 1949.
64 Nicholas Mansergh, *The Irish Question 1840–1921*, London, 1975, p. 72.
65 Mansergh, *Commonwealth Experience*, p. 143.
66 *BNL*, 25 May 1948. Sir Robert Menzies was Prime Minister of Australia 1939–41 and continuously from 1952 to 1966. 'He had a vision of Empire and Commonwealth which belonged to the days when it was British in name, in loyalties, largely in composition and in its united purposes' (Mansergh, *Commonwealth Experience*, II, p. 253).
67 *BNL*, 25 May 1949.
68 *Ibid.*, 25 May 1959.
69 Anon [Lord Salisbury], 'Disintegration', *Quarterly Review*, 312 (October 1883), p. 594. See also Mansergh, *The Irish Question*, p. 231. Lord Salisbury's authorship was later revealed without his permission, to his political embarrassment.
70 *Report of Diocesan Synod, 30 & 31 October, 1917*, p. 8 (Down and Dromore Diocesan Archives, Belfast). D'Arcy, then Bishop of Down, Connor and Dromore (1911–19), was Archbishop of Dublin (1919–20), and became Archbishop of Armagh and Primate of all Ireland from 1920 to 1938. He frequently spoke out in favour of the Union.
71 *Witness*, 12 May 1912.
72 *Ibid.*
73 *Coleraine Chronicle*, 31 May 1913.
74 Steve Bruce, *God Save Ulster*, Oxford, 1989, p. 252.
75 Nicholas Mansergh, *The Unresolved Question*, Yale, 1991, p. 337.
76 R. F. G. Holmes, 'The General Assembly and Politics', in R. F. G. Holmes and R. Buick Knox (eds), *The General Assembly of Presbyterian Church in Ireland 1840–1990*, Coleraine, 1990, pp. 178 and 182 (my italics in the text). Dr Holmes was Moderator of the General Assembly of the Presbyterian Church in 1990, its 150th anniversary, and was the Principal of Union Theological College, Belfast, from 1987 to 1992.
77 J. A. Hobson, *Imperialism – A Study*, London, 1968 edn, p. 212.
78 Lord Meath in *King & Country* (May 1902) p. 23 (Meath archives).

CHAPTER SEVEN

Businessmen in Northern Ireland and the imperial connection, 1886–1939

Philip Ollerenshaw

The role of the business community in modern Ireland has never been the focus of sustained research by historians. This essay concentrates upon one aspect of this role and one geographical region, the north-east. It examines the views of that region's businessmen on the British Empire, including their perception of Empire, the role of Empire as an economic unit, and looks at the status of Northern Ireland within the Empire itself. Our discussion concentrates on the half century after the introduction of the first Home Rule Bill in 1886.[1]

In strictly economic terms, businessmen were interested in the Empire as a source of raw materials and as a market for goods and services. During the second half of the nineteenth century competition within the international economy intensified and in the period from the 1870s to 1914 such competition was both cause and effect of the 'new imperialism'. The dominant position of the United Kingdom came under threat from a small number of other powers, especially the post bellum United States and a newly united Germany. Coupled with improvements in ocean and rail transport, the rising tide of protectionism in foreign markets, and more pronounced economic instability in the international economy, these developments tended to stimulate a reconsideration of the benefits to be derived from an imperial system of trade and finance.[2] Even within the Empire, some of the more independent countries such as Canada and Australia began to impose protective tariffs on UK as well as on foreign products.[3]

The impact of economic nationalism in imperial and foreign markets before 1914 was offset by the long-term growth of world trade, and even if the UK economy captured a gradually smaller proportion of that trade it could at least rely on its service sector to bring respectability to its balance of payments figures. As Table 1 shows, the Empire was of growing importance as a source of imports and as a destination for exports. Furthermore, in the longer term, UK–Empire trade grew at a

[169]

Table 1: Distribution of overseas trade of the United Kingdom, 1870 and 1914

| | 1870 | | 1914 | |
	£m	% share	£m	% share
Imports from:				
Foreign	238.4	78.6	508.8	73.0
Empire	64.4	21.4	187.8	27.0
Total	302.8	100.0	696.6	100.0
Exports to:				
Foreign	188.7	77.3	342.3[a]	65.1
Empire	55.4	22.7	183.9[a]	34.9
Total	244.1	100.0	526.2[a]	100.0

Note: [a] includes re-exports
Source: Forrest Capie, *Depression and Protectionism*, London, 1983, p. 13

far faster rate than UK–foreign trade, the annual average figures for period 1904–38 being 2.3 and 0.6 per cent respectively.

In 1870 the three principal sources of imports from the Empire to the UK were India, Australia and the North American colonies, and this remained the position in 1914, with southern Africa and New Zealand gaining ground in the intervening period. As far as exports from the UK to the Empire were concerned, the same areas tended to dominate between 1870 and 1914, and they also accounted for well over three-quarters of total Empire trade.[4]

The size of the Empire and the increasingly serious foreign challenge faced by UK exporters made it inevitable that more attention would be given to the question of how imperial self-sufficiency could be maximised. Various ideas were put forward, one of which was the creation of an imperial Zollverein, or customs union. However, given the fiscal autonomy enjoyed by important parts of the Empire, the prospects for the imposition by London of imperial free trade and/or protection against foreign imports were obviously poor, and indeed became progressively poorer. Speaking in 1887, Lord Salisbury believed a customs union was not impossible in principle, instancing that which had long existed between Great Britain and Ireland, but he thought it would require a fundamental shift in attitude and policy by constituent parts of the Empire to achieve it in practice.[5]

Discussions on how to protect and promote overseas trade were bound to be followed closely in the north-east of Ireland since the leading industries were export-oriented, and all the major products tended to be re-exported through British ports. Self-interest suggested that any ideas for the promotion of imperial trade would be given a positive reception in the north-east. An example of this was the publicity afforded to the United Empire Trade League, set up in the early 1890s to promote imperial self-sufficiency. The leading linen trade publication, the *Irish Textile Journal*, confirmed that in an increasingly protectionist and internationally competitive world it fully supported the League's determination to 'see the commerce and trade of the Old Country and the Colonies so arranged as to prove primarily beneficial to both mother and daughters'.[6] It was also probably impressed by the fact that the League's first published leaflet defined the 'mother country' as Great Britain and Ireland, and went on to declare that the Empire itself had mainly been acquired in the past 150 years 'either by adventurous settlement or conquest by the blood of England, Wales, Scotland, and Ireland spilt in foreign wars'.[7] By thus including Ireland as part of the mother country, the League was sure to strengthen its claim for attention in the north-east.

The industrial enclave around Belfast became more clearly delineated during the later nineteenth century as iron and steel shipbuilding, heavy engineering and others joined the more traditional export-based textile sector to underpin the prosperity of the regional economy. This region was also geographically coterminous with the heaviest concentration of the Protestant population, leading many to draw a strong positive correlation between prosperity and Protestantism. Indeed, in the light of British imperial expansion and massive post-Famine Catholic emigration, many evangelical Ulster Protestants went further and viewed the battle between their faith and Catholic superstition as an international one. Hempton and Hill have made the important point that this view enabled evangelicals to perceive of 'a clash of two world empires, one of commerce, Christianity and civilisation as exported by Great Britain and the other a sordid, embittered and disloyal Irish Catholic migration, particularly in the United States, where it created a culture in its own image'.[8]

A related, and reinforcing point was also increasingly made in the later nineteenth century: that the roots of industrial success could be traced back to the Act of Union and the benign legislation of the imperial Parliament. As the Belfast Chamber of Commerce put it in 1893: 'All our progress has been made under the Union. We were a small insignificant town at the end of the last century, deeply disaffected and hostile to the British Empire. Since the Union, and under equal laws, we have been welded to the Empire and our progress has been second to none.'[9] That progress, it was stressed, was all the more remarkable in the absence of locally available coal and iron. The common export orientation, geographical compactness and religious homogeneity combined to instil an assertiveness and unity of purpose amongst the businessmen in the Belfast region which developed into a formidable political force during the late nineteenth and early twentieth centuries.

Given that the Union made Ireland an integral member of the United Kingdom and that tangible benefits, including access to foreign and imperial markets, were held to have derived from the Union, the reaction of businessmen in the north-east to the prospect of Home Rule was predictable. As Alvin Jackson has recently argued, the debate on Home Rule always contained an imperial element. That element included those loyalists who spouted imperial rhetoric in order to appeal to English Conservatives, or who feared lest any Home Rule Act would 'downgrade their homeland to the status of a colony with themselves, one-time members of an imperial governing race, as mere colonials'.[10] It also included others with a broader commitment to the concept of empire, and who saw Home Rule as having a corrosive effect on imperial unity.

Within the business community of the north-east, attachment to the Westminster Parliament and to the Empire as a whole strengthened in the later nineteenth century not merely because of the need to maintain existing trade links, but also in order to protect itself from the unwelcome uncertainty that the Home Rule debate injected into business life. The widespread decline in Irish share values in both 1886 and 1893 offered a powerful argument against Home Rule, while the emergence of Sinn Fein with its ideas of state-aided reorganisation of industry behind a protective tariff wall was, to say the least, regarded with profound suspicion.[11] The prospect of an inward looking, Catholic-dominated, agriculture-oriented Dublin government was sufficient to galvanise business leaders in the north-east into wholehearted opposition. It is also worth noting that both the first and second Home Rule Bills were discussed against a background of acute trade depression which was international in scope.[12] The consequent unemployment and decline in profits may well have heightened the insecurity of an already unsettled Protestant business and working class. Although the passage of the Bills and the trade depressions of 1886 and 1893 were of course entirely unrelated, the coincidence of the two seemed to justify Presbyterian fears that Home Rule would indeed 'empty their mills, clear their rivers and shipyards, would stop their looms, would make the voice of their spindles silent and would cause a complete destruction of the industry that has made the province so prosperous'.[13]

Amongst the leaders of business opinion in the Belfast region was

Thomas Sinclair, before 1885 a stalwart of Gladstonian Liberalism but thereafter until his death in 1914 a leading figure in Liberal Unionism in Ulster. Sinclair was a provision manufacturer and merchant with business interests in Ireland, Britain, the United States and elsewhere and he was typical of many of his fellow businessmen in his loyalty to Ulster and his attachment to the United Kingdom and the Empire. Individuals such as Sinclair, and business organisations with which they worked closely (especially the Belfast Chamber of Commerce), played a major role in putting the case for the Union.[14] This role involved both public comment and more covert lobbying. An example of the former was Sinclair's response to the assertion of Chief Secretary Augustine Birrell in 1913 that on the Home Rule issue 'Britons did not even know the opinion of the business men of Ulster, all that they had heard represented the political spirit'. Sinclair, in a letter to *The Times*, spelled out in detail the different ways in which the business community had striven to oppose Home Rule and ridiculed Birrell's ignorance of all of these, which included a deputation to Asquith in 1912 described by the Prime Minister himself as 'one of the largest deputations from one of the greatest industrial communities in the United Kingdom'.[15]

In answer to another of Birrell's comments, that minorities (in this case Unionists in Ireland) must suffer because of their numerical inferiority, Sinclair wrote that:

> a minority in the United Kingdom is not to be measured by mere numbers; its place in the Constitution is to be estimated by its contribution to public well being, by its relation to the industries and occupations of its members, by its association with the upholding of national character, by its fidelity to law and order, and by its sympathy with the world mission of the British Empire in the interests of civil and religious freedom. Tried by all these tests, Ulster is entitled to retain her full share in every privilege of the whole realm.[16]

He rejected the very idea of a single Irish nation, believing that there were instead two nations 'utterly distinct' in racial characteristics, practical ideals, religious beliefs and 'sense of civic and national responsibility'. Peaceful coexistence between the two was impossible without an even-handed central authority in which both Irish 'nations' had full co-partnership.

Sinclair's definition of 'Ulster' was essentially sectarian: the six north eastern counties, together with the significant Unionist populations of counties Cavan, Donegal and Monaghan. In this area commerce and manufacturing was led by 'Unionist energy, enterprise and industry'.[17] An admiring obituary notice in the *Northern Whig* which, like Sinclair himself, had deserted the Liberal Party in 1885 and become consistently Unionist thereafter, pointed to his loyalism and support for Empire:

> Mr Sinclair was essentially an Ulsterman, and he was intensely proud of the fact. But though his work was done here it was in no sense provincial. Mr Sinclair was a strong imperialist and his love of imperial unity was one reason why he was such a strong opponent of the disintegrating effect of Home Rule.[18]

The First World War provided a politically opportune occasion for Ulster Unionists, and not least the businessmen among them, publicly to reaffirm their commitment both to the Union and the Empire. This was especially the case during the proceedings of the ill-fated Irish Convention in 1917 where the Unionist delegation included some prominent businessmen, including Hugh Pollock who represented the Belfast Chamber of Commerce and who later served as Minister of Finance in the government of Northern Ireland between 1921 and 1937. The delegation pointed to Ulster's whole-hearted provision of men and munitions during the conflict, and further declared its satisfaction with the Union as the form of government 'best suited to the needs of Ireland and best calculated to maintain the stability of the Empire'. Indeed, the Convention itself was seen as something of an unnecessary diversion from the 'vital national issues on which the very existence of the Empire depends'.[19]

If partition and the guaranteed Unionist majority in the new state of Northern Ireland allayed many of the fears of the business community, the pressing need to promote their interests in an increasingly unstable world economy remained. It was here that the Empire could serve an important role. One of the most visible and important ways that business interests could link with specifically 'imperial' events between the wars was through participation in British Empire exhibitions and imperial economic conferences. As we will see, involvement in both types of event revealed much about how northern businessmen perceived the Empire and used their own government, and especially the Ministry of Commerce, to extract maximum psychological and material benefit for the fledgling state of Northern Ireland.

Given the recent partition of Ireland, it is hardly surprising that uppermost in the minds of officials in the Ministry of Commerce was the need to be seen to participate in the British Empire Exhibition at Wembley in 1924. The Ministry established an advisory council, chaired by R. J. McKeown MP, one of the leading figures in the linen industry, to provide guidance to an executive committee whose specific brief was to determine precisely how the business interests of Northern Ireland would be represented at the event. The businessmen on the council included Lord Pirrie of Harland and Wolff shipbuilders, who judged it essential that Northern Ireland be 'well represented' at the Exhibition.[20] It was decided that the Ulster Pavilion should be housed in the United Kingdom Hall, with individual industrial exhibits in their appropriate UK industrial sections. Subject to a good level of support from northern manufacturers, the government of Northern Ireland agreed to finance the construction of the Ulster Pavilion. As Cecil Litchfield, Permanent Secretary at the Ministry of Commerce and Chairman of the Executive Committee, declared, 'the object of placing the Ulster Pavilion in the United Kingdom Hall was to ensure that Northern Ireland should still be regarded as part of the United Kingdom'.[21]

Apart from the opportunity to demonstrate the continued integration of Northern Ireland with the rest of the United Kingdom, Empire exhibitions also enabled Northern Ireland to emphasise the distinction between itself and the dominions. This may be illustrated by reference to the debate in the Northern Ireland Cabinet in February 1924 as to which flag should be displayed at the Ulster Pavilion at the British Empire Exhibition later that year. Edward Archdale, Minister of Agriculture and Commerce, judged that a distinctive flag 'should be displayed similar to Canada and the other overseas dominions'. This would be the Red Ensign with an inset containing the Red Hand of Ulster, and would thus be similar to the special flags used by Scotland and Wales at such exhibitions. In opposition to this idea, J. M. Andrews, Minister of Labour, thought it important to stress the distinction between Northern Ireland and the overseas dominions, and that 'we should therefore emphasise our union in the United Kingdom by flying the Union Jack without any special symbol'. The upshot was that *both* the Union Jack and the Red Ensign with the Red Hand symbol were displayed.[22]

The eventual choice of both flags illustrates that pre-partition strands of both loyalism and Unionism continued to survive among leading politicians within Ulster during the 1920s. At about the same time there was also an opportunity for Ulster Unionists to declare their support for 'imperial' organisations which aimed to strengthen imperial unity. One such body was the British Empire Union which had been established in 1915 'to make our people increasingly more Empire-minded' in a number of ways including the energetic promotion of imperial history in schools and of the idea of Empire Day within the population as a whole.[23] In 1923 the Union wrote to J. M. Andrews asking him to send a message for publication, expressing his official approval of its views. At the Cabinet discussion of this matter it transpired that although another minister had already given such a message, 'it would be better for ministers to exercise considerable caution in regard to these semi-political organisations'.[24]

In terms of a forum to publicise Northern Ireland itself and its products, the greatest stage in the 1920s was undoubtedly the Imperial Economic Conference of October–November 1923. Held in London against a background of profound industrial and monetary dislocation in Europe, the conference held no fewer than twenty-three plenary sessions, and optimists hoped that a more unified and coherent Empire would emerge to form a powerful contrast with the bitterness and economic disruption in Europe.[25] For Northern Ireland business interests, through the Ministry of Commerce, the principal aim was representation to ensure preservation and extension of their industry and trade. The Belfast government thought it crucial for Northern Ireland to be distinct from the other dominions and thus did not seek voting powers. In any case, giving Northern Ireland the same status as a dominion

> would be entirely contrary to the best interests of Ulster and would create dismay in the minds not only of the business community which finds its surest foundation in being an integral part of the United Kingdom, but also in the minds of those loyal Ulster people whose patriotic allegiance to British customs would make such a policy impossible of fulfilment.[26]

There was, however, a real fear that lack of representation would lead to the interests of Northern Ireland simply being subsumed under the very wide remit of the Board of Trade. Therefore there was 'no element of more importance at the Conference than the element of personal touch'.[27] After James Craig, Prime Minister of Northern Ireland, had raised the matter with an ever-supportive Bonar Law, Edward Archdale and Cecil Litchfield were named as 'Advisers for Ulster' to Sir Philip Lloyd-Greame, President of the Board of Trade. This arrangement enabled Northern Ireland's commercial representatives to enjoy all the advantages of the British government and the dominions: membership of several key committees, receipt of all conference papers and an invaluable base in the offices of the Board of Trade.

The Northern Ireland representatives worked in great secrecy at the conference, and their role was known neither to the Commons nor to the Senate of the Parliament in Belfast. Careful observation and energetic lobbying before and after the meetings enabled Archdale and Litchfield to establish sufficiently close relations with different delegations to enable 'an exchange of views and difficulties'. Moreover they sought 'a possible quid pro quo that would arouse material interest in the Delegations for self-benefit' and this was found in the proposed commercial development of pedigree flax seed within the Empire.[28]

Table 2: Sub-committee of the Ministry of Commerce Advisory Council for the Imperial Economic Conference, 1923

F. Anderson	Linen
D. Cheyne	Retail trade
W. F. Clokey	President, Wholesale Merchants' and Manufacturers' Association
Sir W. F. Coates	President, Belfast Chamber of Commerce
S. Ferguson	Banking
G. H. Fulton	President, Ulster Trades' Defence Assn.
W. Grant MP	Labour
J. Grey	Linen
J. Johnston	Linen
J. Mackie	Engineering
Prof. H. O. Meredith	Queen's University, Belfast
A. Scott	Linen
W. H. Webb	President, Association of Chambers of Commerce
W. E. Williames	Chairman, Belfast Harbour Commissioners
H. Wilson	Rope
W. J. P. Wilson	Secretary, Belfast Chamber of Commerce

Source: Confidential Report by the Minister of Commerce on the Imperial Economic Conference, 1923, and in particular in its relation to Ulster, pp. 8–9, PRONI CAB 8F/11/1

A sixteen man sub-committee of the Ministry of Commerce Advisory Council prepared Ulster's case and it contained a cross section of influential business opinion (see Table 2). One of their major tasks was to ascertain the relative significance of Empire markets for products manufactured in Northern Ireland in the early 1920s. These data, set out in Table 3, afford a rare glimpse of the approximate quantitative importance of imperial trade to the province and were used as a basis for discussion with dominion and colonial delegations with a view to identifying where 'foreign' competition in any particular market was greatest and which therefore required some protection in the form of increased preferences. Clearly in this respect the Ulster representatives placed much hope in personal economic diplomacy and Archdale specifically instanced several cases where he expected to reap dividends from this diplomacy.

Of all the delegations, only that of South Africa, led by Smuts, officially invited the British government to suggest how trade with the United Kingdom might be promoted.[29] As far as Northern Ireland was concerned, Archdale was confident that South Africa would increase

Table 3: Industries of Northern Ireland

Industry	Principal markets	Percentage of exports sent to Empire	Principal countries other than UK from which supplies of raw material are drawn
Linen goods of all classes	British Empire, USA, S. America, Europe and United Kingdom	22	Russia, Baltic States, Belgium, Holland, Canada, France, Kenya
Handkerchiefs	British Empire, N. America, S. America, Malay Straits, China	55	
Rope	British Empire, Scandinavia, S. America and United Kingdom	17–20	Philippines, Russia, Italy, East Africa, India, New Zealand, Mexico, Java
Mineral waters	USA, S. America, British Empire and United Kingdom	–	Cuba, Mauritius, and Dependencies, West Indies, Italy
Whisky and stout	British Empire, United Kingdom and USA	80	Canada, USA, South Africa, South Russia, Roumania
Soap and candles	South Africa and United Kingdom		W. Africa, Argentine, New Zealand, Australia, USA, Egypt, India, France
Tobacco, etc.	USA, British Empire, Scandinavia and United Kingdom	75–80	USA, Egypt, Turkey, Australia, India Rhodesia
Shirts and collars	British Empire, Scandinavia, South and Central America, China and United Kingdom	20	
Ready-made clothing	S. Africa, New Zealand, Canada, Australia, United Kingdom & Free State	15–20	
Hosiery and underwear	United Kingdom and British Empire	$4^{1}/_{2}$ (of total sales)	France and Belgium
Woollen piece goods	British Empire, North and South America, China, Japan, United Kingdom	20	Australia
Agricultural produce and provisions	United Kingdom and Free State		

Industry	Principal markets	Percentage of exports sent to Empire	Principal countries other than UK from which supplies of raw material are drawn
Machinery:			
Textile	United Kingdom, France, Belgium, Germany, USA, Japan	3	Canada
Electrical	United Kingdom	$7^1/_2$	Belgium, Italy, Canada, Germany
Heating, ventilation and tea drying	United Kingdom, British Empire and China	12	
Roofing material, felt, etc.	United Kingdom, British Empire and Continent of Europe		USA, India, Canada, Belgium and Russia
Chemicals	United Kingdom		Germany
Chemical manures	United Kingdom	nil	North America, Africa, Germany, France, Belgium
Biscuits	West Africa, United Kingdom, Free State		USA, Australia, Canada, Cuba, Mauritius
Jams	United Kingdom, Free State		Canada, USA, Spain, Cuba, Mauritius
Paper making	United Kingdom, France, Belgium, British Empire		Sweden, Norway and Germany
Cement	United Kingdom		
Match Manufacturing (new industry)	United Kingdom		
Fancy box making, Gelatine signs	United Kingdom		Sweden, Norway and Canada
Making-up trade (textile)	British Empire, S. America, Denmark, Holland, Italy, Scandinavia		

Source: Confidential Report by the Minister of Commerce, on the Imperial Economic Conference, 1923, Appendix 1, PRONI CAB 8F/11/1

its preferences for rope products and soap. Similarly, it was hoped to secure a very substantial reduction in the tariffs on linen entering the Australian market. In addition to the hope that the important Canadian market for binder twine from Northern Ireland would in future become open, there was also the expectation that trade in a whole range of articles between New Zealand and Northern Ireland would benefit because of the personal interest shown by W. F. Massey, the New Zealand Prime Minister.[30] Massey was an Ulsterman, the son of a Presbyterian farmer from Limavady, County Londonderry. Having emigrated to New Zealand in 1870 at the age of fourteen, Massey had become Prime Minister in 1912 and was a staunch supporter of the United Kingdom during the First World War, becoming a member of the Imperial War Cabinet. At the conference, Massey was 'very vocal and in all Empire matters more loyal than the King'[31] and he could be relied upon to support Northern Ireland's position within the Empire in general, and the promotion of its trading links with New Zealand in particular. Indeed, during the conference Litchfield and the New Zealand High Commissioner, Sir James Allen, confidentially exchanged information on trade between Northern Ireland and New Zealand with the aim of increasing the volume of trade and improving commercial facilities.[32]

Apart from specific examples of bilateral trade improvements, there were a number of other more general ways in which business interests in Northern Ireland might benefit from the Economic Conference. These included the planned formation of the Imperial Economic Committee to which the Minister of Commerce secured an invitation, the improvement of commercial intelligence within the Empire and the compilation of detailed imperial statistics under the auspices of the Board of Trade.[33] The most important export industry in Northern Ireland, linen, was expected to benefit substantially through the planned Empire Flax Scheme (discussed below) and also from its inclusion on the list of industries singled out for protection following Baldwin's declaration that certain industries in the United Kingdom would receive special treatment in this respect.

The work of the sub-committee noted earlier was facilitated during the conference by ad hoc advice from other business representatives from Northern Ireland, and this was seen as a 'strictly practical illustration of the co-operation that exists between the Ministry [of Commerce] and the business community'. In Archdale's view, Northern Ireland had reaped enormous benefit through participation at the conference, and he judged that the province would have 'suffered greatly within the Empire' had it not been so represented. As he himself put it,

We were part of a great Empire gathering and we felt we were. Running through the cordiality was a consciousness that we represented a part of the Empire that had stood unflinchingly for those ideals which were the very basis of our gathering. Ulster has, I believe, further consolidated her position in the Empire; she has assured herself of participation hereafter in the Councils of Empire, and she has done so without departing, in one jot, from her great traditions.[34]

Such a comment underlines the fact that, in the eyes of the Ministry of Commerce and the businessmen with whom it worked closely, the purpose of the Imperial Economic Conference was not merely to max-imise material advantage but to raise the profile of Northern Ireland on an international stage. David Harkness has written that the Economic Conference was unsuccessful, and that most of the questions discussed by delegates were either too large or too small for satisfactory treat-ment. The format of the conference would not be repeated.[35] While this may generally be the case, Harkness's view does tend to ignore the real, if unquantifiable, psychological boost that participation gave to both businessmen and government officials from a province whose identity and security were still in doubt.

All the evidence points to unalloyed enthusiasm for the conference by Ulster's representatives and great satisfaction at the positive recep-tion they received. For example, at a dinner for over a thousand people representing chambers of commerce throughout the UK, as well as leading conference delegates, Archdale was introduced as Minister of Commerce and Agriculture for Northern Ireland. 'The whole room cheered ... for about five minutes.' Afterwards Mackenzie King, Prime Minister of Canada, the Maharajah of Awar and several others told Archdale 'how glad they were to meet a representative of loyal Ulster'. Massey, too, was clearly pleased at the reception. Archdale himself noted in an effusive letter to Craig that since the Duke of Devonshire (Colonial Secretary) and Lord Peel (Secretary for India) and many more influential figures were there, 'it will do us a lot of good'.[36]

The search by businessmen and officials from Northern Ireland for improved trade links during the 1920s cannot be divorced from the severe economic downturn which affected the industrial north-east from the spring of 1920. If the years before partition had generally been prosperous, the reverse was true for two decades thereafter.[37] As men-tioned earlier, the principal manufacturing industry in Northern Ireland, linen, was strongly represented on the Ministry of Commerce sub-committee advising on the Economic Conference of 1923. One promising result of that conference was the stimulus it gave to the development of an Empire Flax Growing Scheme. This scheme may be regarded as part of a more general recognition, generated by the war, that the United Kingdom should harness more effectively the potential of the Empire in order to try to wean itself from unreliable 'foreign' sources of both demand and supply.[38]

In the vitally important UK textile sector, the woollen and jute industries drew very largely upon colonial and dominion sources, while cotton and linen relied heavily on foreign supplies. In 1916 a government-appointed committee began to consider the potential for the promotion of all textile industries within the Empire, and its report was published the following year. Promotion of imperial textile production had three main goals. Firstly, to safeguard the future needs of the Empire and secondly to enable fulfilment of promises made during the Allies' wartime economic conference in Paris that they would have 'a prior claim to the supply of raw materials' during the immediate post-war reconstruction period. A third aim was more closely related to the acknowledged power of the Empire in world production of textile raw materials. Once the needs of the Empire had been met and pledges to Allies honoured, imperial resources would still be large enough to constitute a powerful bargaining counter with foreign powers (and not least with Germany) in the negotiation of post-war tariff barriers. In short, this strategy, which was based upon close co-operation between London and other parts of the Empire, envisaged the explicit use of imperial textile resources as a useful weapon in the economic diplomacy of the post-war world.[39]

One of the first results of this was the formation under Royal Charter of the Empire Cotton Growing Corporation in 1921. Financed by a British government grant of £1 million, and empowered to levy 6d per bale on cotton spinners, the aims of the scheme were to strengthen the agricultural departments in the dominions and colonies, to disseminate information and to assist in marketing the crop.[40] For the linen industry the report recommended research into flax cultivation and preparation, the encouragement of flax production in Canada, India and anywhere else in the Empire where conditions seemed promising, and the conservation of flax by the Allies for their own use in preference to non-Allied trade. Of all the textile industries, linen faced the most difficult raw material supply problems during and after the First World War.

Cheap flax from Russia, and better quality fibre from Belgium and Holland had enabled the Ulster linen industry to function effectively before 1914. Although there were some who argued that the high degree of dependence on foreign supplies was too great, and that greater efforts should be made to stimulate Empire supplies and markets, these were in a definite minority until the First World War and Russian Revolution.[41] Before the 1920s, some very limited effort had been made to develop flax growing in the Empire, especially in Canada, India, Kenya and Tanganyika, but in terms both of quality and quantity the results had been disappointing.[42] The revival of interest in the Empire by Ulster linen manufacturers in the 1920s had little to do with enthusiasm for the Empire *per se*; rather it stemmed from the gradual realisation that only the Empire seemed capable of providing a cheap and reliable source of raw material in the future. Optimists hoped that in terms of flax supplies the post-war British Empire would be able to play the role of the pre-war Russian Empire.

The aim was to base expanded imperial flax production upon the new pedigree seed produced in the United Kingdom by the Linen Industry Research Association so that yields would improve and costs decline. The scheme envisaged that the areas within the Empire would eventually produce their own seed and thus be a further guarantee of future flax supplies. This, however, was a long term aim. In the short term, Cecil Litchfield confided that he hoped to use the scheme as leverage for granting of increased preference to the linen trade in different parts of the Empire.[43] Although some progress was indeed made in opening imperial markets, the Empire never produced anywhere near the expected amount of flax. For some critics the main problem was one of lack of commitment. As one of them put it in 1924, 'we still proceed in our old fatuous policy of neglecting our own kith and kin and pampering the unreliable foreigner for linen's raw material'.[44]

For Northern Ireland, the decade after partition was one of generally high unemployment in its staple industries and this problem became much worse in the slump of 1929–32. The devaluation of sterling following departure from the gold standard in September 1931 was expected to improve the competitiveness of UK products in international markets, but those markets were themselves contracting and subject to ever-higher tariff barriers. In these circumstances the opportunity to improve Empire trade offered by the Ottawa conference in 1932 was particularly welcome.

Ottawa represented imperial economic affairs on the grand scale, and the interests of Northern Ireland were overseen by a delegation headed by Hugh Pollock as Minister of Finance. Pollock had been active in the anti-Home Rule campaign before the war, at which time his business interests included linen and rope manufacture, flour and grain merchanting, shipping and insurance. He had also been a Harbour Commissioner and President of Belfast Chamber of Commerce. The range and type of Pollock's business experience made him an ideal choice to represent the international economic interests of Northern Ireland. Amongst others the group included Sir Basil Brooke (the future Prime Minister) to advise on agriculture, three civil servants and two special advisers on tariffs and linen respectively.[45] Having recovered from the initial shock of being booked on the same ship as the delegation from the Irish Free State, the party from Northern Ireland set about its task under the distinct impression that the British representatives were aloof and the Canadians particularly well disposed to delegates from the Free State. Although the delegation was far more 'official' than had been the case in 1923, it still found its position, which was neither independent nor fully integrated into that of Britain, somewhat problematic. As in 1923, however, the Northern Ireland delegation attempted to overcome this difficulty by informal personal contact with dominion representatives, this time by setting up a private bar in one of the hotel bedrooms. This strategy was judged to have been 'of exceptional value'.

As in 1923, the delegation from Northern Ireland prepared its case carefully. A detailed memorandum was written and circulated for the information of delegates representing the United Kingdom, reminding them that the government of Northern Ireland had no power to legislate on tariffs or any aspect of external trade relations. In addition to providing details on trade between Northern Ireland and the overseas dominions, a feature of the memorandum was the space devoted to the protectionist stance of the Irish Free State, and in particular the Customs Entry Duty imposed under the Finance Act of 1924. Free State duties had caused extensive damage to manufacturers and traders in Northern Ireland, especially in border areas such as Derry and Strabane, and this situation was not only detrimental but also grossly unfair given the unrestricted entry of Free State products into the North. The memorandum was under no illusion as to the rationale for the duties, quoting a report of remarks by de Valera that 'in our scheme of industrial development a rigorous Customs Barrier becomes necessary. The people in the North may eventually see an economic advantage in union with the South.'[46] Thus the representatives from Northern Ireland ensured that the UK delegation understood their hostility to Free State tariff policy, though this was in fact merely one aspect of a more deep-seated hostility towards the Free State in general which surfaced on many occasions at Ottawa.[47]

The adviser on linen was Lewis Gray, a director of William Ewart and Sons Ltd., one of the leading firms in the industry. Already under severe pressure in the all-important US market, and increasingly excluded by competitive linen industries in Europe, linen manufacturers hoped for respite from the dominions where the UK normally captured over 90 per cent of the market. In fact linen was subject to a whole range of duties in different dominions and, for Northern Ireland, the outcome of the Ottawa conference provided only limited grounds for satisfaction. South Africa proved unwilling to extend even a modest preference of 10 per cent to a whole range of goods, including linen.[48] A token reduction of already-low duties was made by New Zealand, more substantial concessions were made by Australia, and most of all by Canada.[49]

Manufacturers and government officials in Northern Ireland welcomed all concessions and those made by Canada were valued highly, and this in turn made them particularly well disposed to economic co-operation with Canada. On a modest, but symbolically important, level we can illustrate this mood of reciprocity with reference to the opening in Belfast in 1934 of a shop to sell Canadian produce. The public discussion preceding the actual opening of the shop demonstrates the significance not only of the principle of complementarity of production that lay at the heart of imperial economics, but also reciprocal trade arrangements and ancestral links between different parts of the Empire.

Speaking in Belfast of the desirability of promoting trade between Northern Ireland and Canada, James Craig was careful to point out that this did not represent a threat to employment in the province. He reminded his audience of the recommendation of the Ulster Industrial Development Association: that purchasers prioritise their spending by buying Ulster goods first, then British and then Empire products. However, he saw considerable scope for trade in goods that neither Northern Ireland nor Canada could produce independently. This was the 'soundest foundation on which to base business between friends'. He paid explicit tribute to the favourable treatment received by the Ulster delegation at Ottawa from the Canadian Prime Minister, R. B. Bennett, and to the way in which the Canadians had tried 'in every possible way' to encourage the free import of linen. In return, people in Northern Ireland 'could purchase Canadian products which did not clash with their own locally produced goods, and the people of Canada were not asking any more'.[50]

Mutual gains from trade were a key theme in the public statements of the Director of Canadian Trade Publicity, D. G. Geraghty whose family came from County Down. The year after import restrictions on linen goods into Canada had been eased, there had been a £50,000 increase in the value of linen exports from Ulster. Strengthening the claim for better trade, Geraghty stressed that 'we do not at any point conflict with Ulster industries ... We sympathise with your "Buy Ulster goods" movement and we do not want to be regarded as competitors'. At the official opening of the shop in April 1934, Ulster-Canadian diplomatic, business and family links were re-emphasised by Craig.[51] Ulster had provided one Governor-General to Canada, the Marquis of Dufferin and Ava. Moreover, Timothy Eaton, founder of a major company in the Canadian retail sector, had been born near Ballymena, County Antrim.[52]

Although the shop remained open only a short time, some sixty thousand people from Ulster visited it and the following year a decision was taken to repeat the success. In order to demonstrate the importance of the occasion, Craig was joined at the second ceremony by several Cabinet colleagues including Hugh Pollock, Minister of Finance, J. M. Andrews (Labour), Sir Basil Brooke (Agriculture), as well as Sir Frederick Cleaver of the Ulster branch of the Overseas League. Frederick Rudd, the Chief Trade Commissioner of the Canadian Government, said that in 'coming to Belfast, they took still another step forward on the highway of imperial cooperation'. In response, Craig observed that Canada 'was really half Ulster to begin with and in one of the provinces of the Dominion he would not know whether he was in their town or his town'. Regretting the unavoidable absence of Godfrey Ferguson, the Canadian High Commissioner, Craig concluded that Ferguson was not only a great personal friend and 'a great Orangeman, but ... also a tremendous believer in Ulster's stand and fight to remain in the Empire. He hoped they would yet have the privilege of welcoming one of the great men of Canada and the Empire and that his visit was only postponed.'[53]

In assessing whether participation in any particular imperial event was worthwhile, Northern Ireland businessmen and the Ministry of Commerce had to try to evaluate costs and possible benefits, and it is clear that sometimes the cost was considered too high to justify a presence. This was the case in the British Empire Exhibition held at Johannesburg in 1936 to celebrate the jubilee of that city and to demonstrate the unity of Empire. South Africa had taken a leading position as a destination for UK exports, having moved ahead even of India in the first quarter of 1936. As the *Northern Whig* noted, it would be unfortunate if Northern Ireland 'was not represented at such an important event in a part of the Empire with which the Mother Country is linked by fine liners built on the Lagan'.[54] Pressure for involvement also came from the Ulster branch of the Overseas League which offered to help bring Ulster 'to the forefront in this exhibition'.[55]

Official representation at Johannesburg was, however, rejected on financial grounds, although the Ministry of Commerce did respond positively to a request for a message of support.[56] Even if South Africa had conceded very little at Ottawa, Craig was advised that the two staple industries of Northern Ireland had benefited directly from the growth in UK–South African trade. By 1936 South Africa ranked third as a market for linen within the Empire and sixth in importance as an export market.[57] Moreover, but for rising prosperity in South Africa,

[186]

Northern Ireland would have lost the 'vast amount of employment' provided by the construction of a substantial number of Union-Castle liners turned out from Belfast shipyards.[58]

The link between shipbuilding in Belfast and the growth of South African trade stretched back well before the First World War. Harland and Wolff had designed some particularly successful vessels for the Union Line in the 1890s, a fact which helped to increase the competitiveness of the latter in its rivalry with Castle Line on the South Africa run. The connection was strengthened by the appointment of Gustav Wolff as a director, after which all new ships were ordered from the Belfast yard. Another key figure in developing this aspect of Ulster's 'imperial' business was Donald Currie, born into a Presbyterian family in Greenock and brought up in Belfast. Founder of the Castle Line in the 1860s, and knighted in 1881, Currie went on to build a business empire which included the formation of Union-Castle in 1900, the dominant force in South African shipping by the turn of the century. Though undoubtedly of less significance than it had been, Wolff's influence survived in Union-Castle, and the shipyard continued to be one of a number of UK firms catering for this major shipping line both before and after the First World War.[59] This was an important reason why Craig acknowledged in 1936 that Northern Ireland had 'every reason gratefully to wish South Africa continued prosperity'.[60]

By the end of the 1930s, links between industry and trade in Northern Ireland and the Empire retained their psychological and material importance. Businessmen, through the Ministry of Commerce, played an active role in sustaining those links. In the period before partition and the onset of severe economic dislocation, attachment to the Empire had been very much part of the anti-Home Rule campaign. Explicit cultivation of Empire resources and markets was far less in evidence than during the years following. Not only did the political insecurity of Northern Ireland require a more overtly pro-British and pro-imperial stance on the part of business leaders and politicians, economic circumstances, especially rising unemployment and closing foreign markets, worked in the same direction. In contrast to Britain, within Northern Ireland the seat of government, Belfast, was also the centre of manufacturing. This, together with the fact that Unionist politicians with business backgrounds were much in evidence at every level of government, meant that industry–government connections remained strong and enduring.[61]

During the period from 1885 to 1920 the business community played a central role in organising and financing the opposition to Home Rule. Lobbying and organisational skills developed then were put to good use after partition in order to raise the political and economic profile of Northern Ireland on the imperial stage. Without those efforts, the sense of insecurity and isolation in the early years of the new state would doubtless have been much more acute, and economic difficulties even more pronounced, than they actually were.

Notes

1 The helpful comments of Kent Fedorowich on an earlier draft of this chapter are gratefully acknowledged. Thanks are also due to the staff of the Public Record Office of Northern Ireland (PRONI) for their assistance, and to the Twenty Seven Foundation of the Institute of Historical Research for a grant in aid of research.

2 The best survey of an extensive literature is P. J. Cain & A. G. Hopkins, *British Imperialism: Innovation and Expansion 1688–1914*, London, 1993, Ch. 7. See also James Sturgis, 'Britain and the new imperialism', in C. C. Eldridge (ed.), *British Imperialism in the Nineteenth Century*, London, 1984, pp. 85–105.

3 Roger Weiss, 'Economic nationalism in Britain in the nineteenth century', in Harry G. Johnson (ed.), *Economic Nationalism in Old and New States*, London, 1967, p. 43.

4 Forrest Capie, *Depression and Protectionism*, London, 1983, pp. 14–15.

5 E. A. Benians, 'Finance, trade and communications 1870–1895', in the *Cambridge History of the British Empire, III, The Empire-Commonwealth*, Cambridge, 1959, p. 220.

6 *Irish Textile Journal*, 15 June 1894, p. 63.

7 *Ibid.*, 15 July 1894, p. 81.

8 David Hempton & Myrtle Hill, *Evangelical Protestantism in Ulster Society 1740–1890*, London, 1992, p. 182. For a hard-hitting rejection of the alleged link between Protestantism and the prosperity of Ulster, which stressed instead favouritism and good fortune see T. M. Kettle, 'The business genius of Ulster?', *English Review*, XVII (1914), pp. 540–51.

9 Government of Ireland Bill: Report of the Council presented to and adopted by an Extraordinary General Meeting of the Belfast Chamber of Commerce, 17 March 1893, in *Irish Textile Journal*, 15 April 1893, pp. 43–4. See also *Mr Gladstone and the Belfast Chamber of Commerce*, Belfast, 1893, pp. 5, 32. The reference to disaffection in the late eighteenth century recalled the involvement of Presbyterian manufacturers and merchants with the United Irishmen. For illuminating comments on this see Nancy J. Curtin, 'The transformation of the United Irishmen into a mass-based revolutionary organisation, 1794–6', *Irish Historical Studies*, xxiv, no. 96 (1985), pp. 463–92.

10 Alvin Jackson, *The Ulster Party: Irish Unionists in the House of Commons 1884–1911*, Oxford, 1989, p. 120.

11 For a useful brief summary of Sinn Fein's ideas on protectionism and state-aided industrial development see Richard Davis, *Arthur Griffith*, Dundalk, 1976, pp. 13–14.

12 Angus Maddison, *Phases of Capitalist Development*, Oxford, 1982, pp. 74–5.

13 Quoted in Hempton and Hill, *Evangelical Protestantism*, p. 173.

14 D. C. Savage, 'The origins of the Ulster Unionist party 1885–6', *Irish Historical Studies*, XII, no. 47 (1961), pp. 198–9, 208.

15 The text of the letter is in Belfast Chamber of Commerce Letter Book, 30 June 1913, PRONI D 1857/1/BA/8. There is a summary of, and critical reaction to, Birrell's speech in the *Textile Mercury*, 5 July 1913, pp. 5–6.

16 Thomas Sinclair, 'The position of Ulster', in S. Rosenbaum (ed.), *Against Home Rule: the Case for the Union*, London, 1912, p. 173.

17 *Ibid.*, p. 170.

18 *Northern Whig*, 16 February 1914. On the politics of this, and some other northern newspapers see Dennis Kennedy, *The Widening Gulf: Northern Attitudes to the Independent Irish State 1919–49*, Belfast, 1988, Ch. 1, esp. p. 13.

19 'Report of the Ulster Unionist delegates to the Irish Convention', in *Report of the Proceedings of the Irish Convention*, p. 31 [Cd. 9019] H.C. 1918, x, 727.
20 Minutes of a meeting of the Ministry of Commerce Advisory Council, 6 March 1922, PRONI CAB 9F/4/1.
21 *Ibid.*, 29 June 1923.
22 Cabinet conclusions, 15 February 1924, PRONI CAB 4/100.
23 John M. Mackenzie, *Propaganda and Empire: The Manipulation of British Public Opinion 1880–1960*, Manchester, 1985, pp. 156–7.
24 Cabinet conclusions, 29 October 1923, PRONI CAB 4/91.
25 David Harkness, *The Restless Dominion: the Irish Free State and the British Commonwealth of Nations 1921–31*, London, 1969, pp. 46–7.
26 Confidential Report by the Ministry of Commerce on the Imperial Economic Conference, and in particular in its relation to Ulster (November 1923), PRONI CAB 8F/1/1 (hereafter, Confidential Report), pp. 1–3.
27 *Ibid.*, p. 2.
28 *Ibid.*, Eighth Report pp. ii–iii, and Appendix XVIII.
29 Confidential Report, p. 10.
30 *Ibid.*, p. 12.
31 R. MacGregor Dawson, *William Lyon Mackenzie King 1874–1923*, London, 1958, p. 461. There are further details on Massey in the *Dictionary of National Biography 1922–30*, London, 1937, pp. 565–6 and in the *Oxford New Zealand Encyclopedia*, Oxford, 1965, p. 242. Massey received an honorary degree from Queen's University, Belfast and the freedom of the city of Londonderry.
32 Confidential Report, p. 12.
33 *Ibid.*, pp. 14–15.
34 *Ibid.*, p. 17.
35 Harkness, *Restless Dominion*, p. 49.
36 Archdale to Craig, 25 October 1923, PRONI CAB 8F/11/1.
37 For a good survey of these problems see D. S. Johnson, 'The Northern Ireland economy 1914–39', in Liam Kennedy & Philip Ollerenshaw (eds), *An Economic History of Ulster 1820–1939*, Manchester, 1985, pp. 184–223.
38 *Report of the Departmental Committee Appointed to Consider the Position of the Textile Trades After the War*, pp. 30–3 [Cd. 9070] H.C. 1918, xiii, 672–5.
39 *Ibid.*, pp. 121, 125.
40 Memorandum on the Empire Cotton Growing Corporation, 1924, PRONI COM 62/1/325/2.
41 *Report of the Tariff Commission, II: The Textile Trades part 7: Evidence on the Flax, Hemp and Jute Industries*, London, 1905, para. 3615.
42 Flax Growing within the Empire: Memorandum by Ministry of Commerce Explanatory of the Draft Scheme, 21 January 1924, p. 3, PRONI CAB 4/97.
43 See note 28.
44 *Textile Recorder*, 15 February 1924, p. 65.
45 This account relies on Brian Barton, *Brookeborough: the Making of a Prime Minister*, Belfast, 1988, pp. 75–6. Information on Pollock's business interests is in *Textile Mercury*, 5 July 1913, p. 6; and John F. Harbinson, *The Ulster Unionist Party 1882–1973*, Belfast, 1973. At the time of the Ottawa conference Pollock was eighty years old.
46 Imperial Economic Conference, Ottawa, 1932: Notes on matters specifically affecting Northern Ireland, PRONI CAB 4/302/1.
47 Deirdre McMahon, *Republicans and Imperialists: Anglo-Irish Relations in the 1930s*, New Haven & London, 1984, pp. 74–5.
48 Ian M. Drummond, *Imperial Economic Policy 1917–39: Studies in Expansion and Protection*, London, 1974, pp. 245–6. Drummond notes that South Africa was 'not very interested' in the Ottawa conference and that her concessions were 'worth almost nothing'.
49 Details on the linen industry are taken from *Textile Recorder*, 15 November 1932, p. 21; 15 January 1933, p. 27.
50 *Belfast News-Letter*, 20 January 1934.

51 *Belfast Telegraph*, 16 January 1934, *Northern Whig*, 17 January 1934.
52 *Belfast News-Letter*, 20 January 1934.
53 *Ibid.*, 6 April 1935, *Northern Whig*, 6 April 1935.
54 *Northern Whig*, 16 July 1935.
55 Phyllis Cowan (Secretary of the Ulster branch of the Overseas League) to W. D. Scott (Secretary of the Ministry of Commerce), no date but *c.* 17 July 1936, PRONI COM 62/1/548/1.
56 *Ibid.*, Scott to Cowan, 21 July 1936.
57 *Northern Whig*, 16 July 1936.
58 J. Milne Barbour, 'Northern Ireland shares in trade recovery', *The Imperial Review and Empire Mail*, May–June 1937, p. 198.
59 Andrew Porter, *Victorian Shipping, Business and Imperial Policy: Donald Currie, the Castle Line and Southern Africa*, Woodbridge, 1986, pp. 1, 13–18, 239.
60 Barbour, 'Northern Ireland'.
61 For an illustration see Philip Ollerenshaw, 'Textiles and regional economic decline: Northern Ireland, 1914–70' in Colin Holmes & Alan Booth (eds), *Economy and Society: European Industrialisation and its Social Consequences, Essays Presented to Sidney Pollard*, Leicester, 1991, esp. pp. 72–9.

CHAPTER EIGHT

Ulster resistance and loyalist rebellion in the Empire

Donal Lowry

R.T.C. LIBRARY, LETTERKENNY

In 1886, Thomas McKnight, editor of the *Northern Whig*, described the position of Ulster loyalists in a classic statement of conditional allegiance that would find later echoes among the British of Rhodesia, Kenya and Natal:

> When the Ulster settlements were made, there was an implied compact that they who crossed the Irish Sea on what was believed to be a great colonising and civilising mission should not in themselves, nor in their descendants, be abandoned to those who regarded them as intruders and as enemies.[1]

We are not concerned here with the details of the Ulster resistance to Home Rule between 1886 and 1914, but with the sentiment of conditional loyalty, the claims to uphold the true interests of the Empire in the face of apparent metropolitan abdication, the obligations of the imperial government to uphold the interests of its kith and kin over those of non-British peoples, whether in Ireland or in the colonial Empire, and the precedent which the Ulster resistance to Home Rule set for British communities elsewhere which felt threatened by indigenous peoples. We are not concerned, then, with whether these imperial crises are objectively similar – indeed, there were differences between each of these territories – but with the significance of their identification with each other on the grounds of a common ethnic and political sentiment.

For centuries before 1886, in Ireland, North America, the Caribbean and India, imperial authorities in England had confronted determined opposition from settlers who claimed to be acting out of loyalty, Ulster emigrants not least among them. Analogies between Ulster loyalists and zealous British settlers were frequently drawn.[2] In 1901, for example, Sir William Harcourt in a letter to the Liberal leader, Sir Henry Campbell-Bannerman, feared that Lord Milner, British High

Commissioner at the Cape, was placing himself at the head of a pro-
British party – what Harcourt called 'the new Orangemen of a Greater
Ireland'.[3] What made the revolt of the Ulster loyalists unique was the
complicity of the Conservative Party in Britain in Ulster intrigues and
the Unionist movement's harnessing of the self-consciously modern
tactic of 'direct action'.[4] The telegraph also brought the crises of 1886,
1893 and particularly 1912–14 to within a day's newspaper reach of the
remotest of white colonies. In 1912–14, not only Ulstermen but Empire
loyalists generally witnessed what they regarded as the unfolding of an
emergency of supreme importance to the survival of their Empire. The
imperialist derring-do and efficiency of Ulster loyalists gripped the
patriotic imagination with accounts of their volunteer force staffed by
gallant former Indian army officers, and shielded the illustrious imperial names, Roberts of Kandahar, Milner of Cape Town, Jameson of the
Raid, and Rudyard Kipling, who joined the loyalists' campaign to defeat
the Liberal government's third Home Rule Bill.[5] 'If we die we die',
Kipling reflected, 'but at least we can die decently ... We make a great
mistake if we think we can hold the Dominions to us by a policy of
compromise which they call funk'.[6]

Mass anti-Home Rule meetings were held across Canada, Australia
and New Zealand, with heavily subscribed petitions and pledges of volunteers from prairie, veldt and outback in the event of hostilities breaking out between the Ulster loyalists and the British army.[7] A meeting of
the Melbourne Orange Lodge was told that this 'was an imperial
struggle, and every man in Australia was as concerned as much as the
man in Ireland. It all seemed to indicate the disastrous possibility that
the virility of the British race was departing. The British lion seemed to
have gone to sleep'.[8] '[W]e are on the edge of [the Glorious Revolution
of] 1688', Kipling warned.[9] 'You aren't watching a skirmish of politicians ... [Y]ou are watching the revolt of the English ... This Ulster
business is the beginning of the counter-revolution ... Our game is
organised resistance *to the end*'.[10]

An Ulster committee was formed in Johannesburg to raise volunteers, where a future Prime Minister of Northern Ireland, Captain Sir
Basil Brooke, was preparing to desert his British army regiment so that
he could lead the Ulster Volunteer Force in his native Fermanagh. He
had lately been busy helping to crush a serious white miners' strike on
the Rand. Now he was contemplating a 'country house' form of syndicalism, one which was led by imperial-minded gentlemen with powerful connections in the metropolitan establishment.[11] 'Desertion is not a
course a professional soldier contemplates easily', Brooke later recalled,
'but my loyalties were to my home and my people'.[12] By the summer of
1914, Britain and Ireland teetered on the brink of constitutional

collapse. 'Civil war ... is certain', concluded the imperial-minded South African *Journal*.[13] Its South African-born London correspondent noted: 'Civil war is a terrible thing certainly, but it is preferable anyway to giving a Cabinet, such as we have, unlimited power over the lives and liberty of the subject ... We are no longer under constitutional government at all, but under a tyranny'.[14] For those loyalists for whom the imperial government's Home Rule plans marked Greater Britain's death-knell, this was at once their Empire's most perilous and finest hour. The *Natal Witness* warned at the height of the crisis: 'If it is true and right to say that "Ulster will fight and Ulster will be right", will this be lost upon other discontented elements of society, not only in the United Kingdom but in the British dominions overseas?'.[15] The white settlers of Rhodesia, Kenya and Natal were profoundly influenced by Ulster's action. Like Ulster, these communities' local origins and identities were closely bound up with Britain's imperial expansion. They came to feel acutely alienated from the British metropolis when the relative decline of Empire became apparent in the closing years of the nineteenth century, and, although they had normally worshipped established authority, they ultimately justified illegality in a patriotic cause. They each claimed allegiance to what they regarded as the higher principles of racial solidarity and the values of traditional imperialism. They felt a sense of pan-Britannic unity at times of crisis and they borrowed ideas from each other, reminding us that the 'national' identities of the settler colonies can be most profitably analysed in their imperial context.[16]

The first ideological tremor from the Ulster revolt had already occurred in Southern Rhodesia in 1911, where the Colonial Office feared an Ulster-style uprising by white farmers against the ruling British South Africa Company's monopoly control of African labour.[17] In 1914, these ultra-loyalist white settlers were opposed to imperial government plans to integrate the territory into the Union of South Africa. Fearing domination by anti-imperialist Afrikaner nationalists and a major influx of poor whites, a prominent solicitor warned the settlers that they might have to arm themselves and say 'Rhodesia will fight and Rhodesia will be right'. At the height of the Ulster crisis, Henry Cullen Gouldsbury, one of Rhodesia's leading balladeers (incidentally an English Catholic) titled a poem 'To England from the Outposts':

> Cast out the smoothed-mouthed traitor,
> Cast out the prating fool,
> Cast out the speculator
> Who plots against your rule –
> Trust to the simpler school

Of the men who love your name,
And if you prize us, Mother, spare
us eternal shame ...

Think of the lonely stations
That hem your borders round!
In the history of the nations
Each spot is holy ground!
Would you have your Wardens bound
By coward traitor-hands?
Shame upon 'Little England' while
Greater England stands!

Shall they grind us down with the harrow,
Digging us into the dust,
While British bones and marrow
Are faithful to their trust?
We will perish if we must,
But rather in sheets of flame
Than yielding to Those Others the
glory of our name.[18]

Gouldsbury's sentiments bore a remarkable resemblance to those expressed by Rudyard Kipling in his poem 'Ulster 1912', as the following stanzas demonstrate:

The dark eleventh hour
Draws near and sees us sold
To every evil power
We fought against of old.
Rebellion, rapine, hate,
Oppression, wrong and greed,
Are loosed to guide our fate
By England's act and deed.

The faith in which we stand,
The Laws we made and guard,
Our honour, lives and land,
Are given for reward,
To Murder done by night,
To Treason taught by day,
To folly sloth and spite,
And we are thrust away ...

The blood our father spilt,
Our love, our toil, our gains,
Are counted as for guilt
And only bind our chains.
Before an Empire's eyes

> The traitor claims his price.
> What need of further lies?
> We are the sacrifice.
>
> We asked no more than leave
> To reap where we had sown;
> Through good and ill to cleave
> To our own Flag and Throne ...
>
> The terror, threats and dread
> In market, hearth and field –
> We know, when all is said,
> We perish if we yield ...
>
> What answer from the North?
> One Law, One Land, One Throne.
> If England drives us forth,
> We shall not fall alone.[19]

Both balladeers shared that sense of history which was crucial to settler perspectives in this period. Like their Ulster exemplars, the Rhodesians believed that they had the right to disobey the decisions of British governments if they believed it was in the true interests of the British Empire.

After the Great War, events in Ulster continued to fuel feelings of 'direct action' by loyalists engaged in their own struggles in the British settler colonies. Even after the establishment of Northern Ireland in 1921, Ulster Unionists feared being abandoned and betrayed. It was rumoured that the Boundary Commission established to draw a border would transfer numbers of loyalists to southern jurisdiction. Sir James Craig, Prime Minister of Northern Ireland, immediately warned of what would have been in effect a loyalist 'unilateral declaration of independence'. Unionists may be obliged to summon 'their friends and supporters – more especially the members of the loyal Orange Institution – to come to their assistance by means of arms, ammunition and money from Great Britain, the Dominions and other parts of the world where people of Ulster descent are in strength and desirous of helping'.[20] To some English Tories Ulster's continued opposition to the Irish majority was righteous rebellion, 'for it was England placed in Ulster this little garrison of her own sons to uphold her throne and maintain her flag'.[21] This justification for illegal actions only served to encourage the gambling mentality among settlers in Africa in their own struggles with Whitehall.

During this period, meanwhile, the Southern Rhodesian settlers were resisting the plans of the imperial government, the South African government and the ruling British South Africa Company to incorporate their territory as a fifth province of the Union of South Africa. In 1919, at a time when the imperial government was supporting such a scheme, the *Gwelo Times* argued that King George was 'far too enlightened to wish to coerce any part of the British Empire into a course repugnant to them, and [they would not] be treated as pawns in a game of which [they knew] nothing'.[22] Leopold Moore, editor of the *Livingstone Mail*, accused the imperial government of putting aside the interests of British settlers. There was, he wrote, little use in 'whining about the treatment meted out to a loyal population who have done their utmost, at a critical time, to support the Empire that now casts them off'. They could rely on no one at the head of the Empire who 'had the courage and determination ... to strive with all their might to maintain the mightiest heritage ever held by a nation', and he warned, in a broadside worthy of Sir Edward Carson and the Ulster Volunteer Force: 'Rhodesians are politely told that their desire to remain within the Empire cannot be gratified ... Rhodesians now know quite well that ... they are prepared, with arms in their hands, to proclaim a Republic'.[23] The Sons of England Patriotic and Benevolent Society based in Rhodesia lamented that: 'The Imperial Government, as indicated in the case of Ulster, seems rather to enjoy putting pressure on a small loyal English community to surrender its inheritance and its liberties to the majority disposal of a much bigger [community] that is – well – not so English and not so loyal'.[24] Another correspondent echoed contemporary Ulster loyalist sentiment: 'Rhodesians snatched this country from the wilderness ... and what they have they'll hold, true to their traditions of fearlessness ... [They will not] hand over their heritage for a mess of pottage to the enemy at their gate'.[25]

In Britain, similar connections were made. When King George met the Rhodesian self-government delegates in London in 1921, he remarked to Sir Charles Coghlan, the settler leader, that Rhodesia, in objecting to Union, appeared to be 'the Ulster of South Africa'. Coghlan, ironically a Cape colonial of Irish Catholic descent, replied – ominously, in the light of events half a century later – that Rhodesia would prove just as loyal as Ulster. 'We will not part from the British flag without fighting', he declared.[26] 'If 10,000 [Kenyan settlers] can give all that trouble [to the imperial government], what can we with 35,000 do if need be?', he wrote privately to a colleague.[27] In the treaty negotiations of 1921, Winston Churchill, Colonial Secretary then responsible for managing both Irish and Rhodesian policy, suggested to Michael Collins and Arthur Griffith that they emulate the South Africans' conciliatory approach to Rhodesia in their own attempts to woo Ulster.[28] Sir James Craig returned to the Rhodesian analogy later that year in a speech to the Northern Ireland House of Commons:

[I]t may be that a time will come when some Irishmen on Irish soil will be able to repeat the speech – made by General Smuts in Cape Town a few days ago, in which he said, 'The Union Government would welcome the early admission of Rhodesia into the Union. At the same time, they realise that in a matter of that kind, the initiative necessarily lies with the people of Rhodesia. It was for them to say whether and when they are prepared to become a part of that larger South Africa which is their destiny'.[29]

King George V had ample reason, then, to remind Ulster MPs at the first opening of the Northern Ireland Parliament in June 1921 that 'everything that touches Ireland finds an echo in the remotest part of the Empire'.[30]

One of the earliest to recognise the Ulster parallel for the refusal of this ultra-British community to join its southern neighbour was Ethel Colquhoun, the leading intellectual of early Rhodesia and first woman parliamentarian in the British Empire.[31] She founded the Responsible Government Association in the territory in 1917. As a prominent woman Unionist in pre-war England, she had supported the actions of the Ulster Volunteer Force.[32] Her propaganda thrived in such an atmosphere. She used the Irish settlement to embarrass Smuts, who had played a key role in bringing about the Irish Truce in 1921. Smuts was now at the height of his power, a Boer poacher turned Commonwealth gamekeeper who was revered by the British as a philosopher-king. Colquhoun, however, being a keen student of imperial affairs, had been following Smuts's definitions of dominion status and particularly his correspondence with Eamon de Valera on the subject. It was a case of guilt by association. Dominion status as set out in the Irish Free State constitution was, for her, as for many old school imperialists, the thin end of a wedge, which would lead to a sham Empire. She took Smuts to task for his approval of it and she received great applause at a public meeting in Salisbury where she repeated that 'far as loyalty to the throne is concerned we are in no way different to Ulster'.[33] Like Ulster Unionists, like the loyalists of Ontario, she saw her territory as a loyal imperial bridgehead which could intervene to contain sedition on its southern flank.[34] The country was to be a stronghold beyond the Limpopo: 'The average British-born Rhodesian feels that this is essentially a British country, pioneered, bought and developed by British people, and he wants to keep it so ... Rhodesians, as a rule, are intensely imperialistic'.[35]

Like the Ulster loyalists before the Great War, the Rhodesian settlers after it successfully resisted external pressure to be subsumed within a neighbouring polity.[36] Thus, in the early 1920s two largely self-governing entities of Northern Ireland and Southern Rhodesia came into existence with the reluctant consent of the imperial government, the former a self-governing part of the United Kingdom, while the latter was a self-governing colony. In both cases, however, the imperial government always retained the final constitutional authority, even if it rarely exercised its rights. These two states were characterised by a xenophobic attitude to their southern neighbours and a profound attachment to the monarchy, balanced by an often equivocal, suspicious and Whig-like attitude to Whitehall. An extreme example of this outlook was the case of Henry Hamilton Beamish, an Anglo-Irish neo-fascist and anti-semite with an international reputation, who sat in the Rhodesian legislature in the 1930s. During these years he issued warnings to Ulster and Rhodesia, the two loyal remnants of Britishness, not to obey the 'be-Jewed' House of Commons in London, whence the international 'Kosher War' was being directed.[37]

After the First World War, the British faced another threat of loyalist rebellion in Kenya.[38] There, the imperial government's plans to treat sympathetically the demands of Indians for equal rights with Europeans brought it into conflict with the white settlers, some of whose leaders had retired to Kenya after distinguished careers in the Indian Army. 'It was to be an original kind of rebellion', wrote Elspeth Huxley, 'a rebellion paralleled only by the situation in Ulster in 1914 – a rebellion which aimed not at breaking away from the Empire, but at remaining in it'.[39] The settlers formed themselves into a Vigilance Committee and organised a rebel force of ex-officers under the direction of Brigadier-General Philip Wheatley.[40] It was modelled on the Ulster Volunteer Force and echoed a similarly ambiguous loyalist sentiment under the motto of 'For King and Kenya'. Plans were made to kidnap the Governor and create a provisional government based on Carson's pre-war scheme to take control of Ulster. Declarations were issued, consciously modelled on the Ulster Covenant of 1912:

> That in the event of the Government of this Colony acceding to the political claims made by the Indian community, the white community will take such action as they may consider proper and necessary to prevent any legislation with that object from taking practical effect ...
>
> That the white community of this district bind themselves to support the Central Committee in any steps that they may consider necessary, and to carry out, or assist in carrying out, any instruction issued by them with the object of effectively accomplishing any programme they may adopt.[41]

This was the kind of threat of aristocratic direct action to which Britain had grown accustomed during the Home Rule crisis. Wheatley and his followers were in earnest. 'If ordered would British troops come, or should we have a second Curragh incident?', he asked:

It is a sad reflection on English political life but it is unfortunately a true one that for many years past any English government has yielded to force ... The problem before us in many aspects resembles that of the Ulster people ... Both communities are fighting to remain in the British Empire and to maintain its integrity.[42]

Lord Delamere, the settlers' leader in the Kenyan Legislative Council, also echoed the Ulster loyalists' definition of loyalty. He agreed that the advisers to the Crown had authority under the written law of a colony to impose immigration regulations without regard to the wishes of its inhabitants, but he submitted that there was something deeper than that which governed the British Empire:

Although the British people wherever they had been in the Colonies, had always been the most loyal and law abiding people, they had always re-served for themselves the sacred right of resistance if their rights were overridden by arbitrary acts which went over the constitution ... [The imperial government's authoritarianism in forcing through the immigra-tion measure] gave the people of this country an example in direct action which they might follow.[43]

On this occasion, it seems likely that the imperial government could have relied on the loyalty of its armed forces to crush any outbreak of rebellion, but the Colonial Office believed that any use of African soldiers would be 'unthinkable; [and] fatal to British prestige through-out Africa', while the employment of European troops would prove to be a be 'a costly enterprise, particularly unedifying to the public in this country and the Dominions'.[44] Rather than put these theories to the test, the imperial government compromised on the principle of Indian-European equality and full-scale revolt was thus avoided.

The South African province of Natal is our third example of a region on the imperial periphery where the effects of the Ulster campaign against Home Rule were felt. It provides us with the most explicit illus-tration of the Ulster influence. The white Natalians' imperial patriot-ism was epitomised by such organisations as the semi-secretive Sons of England Patriotic and Benevolent Society, dedicated to the mainte-nance of the British link and the Protestant succession to the throne, the British Patriotic Union, the Daughters of Empire, the Empire Group, the Flag (Vigilance) Committee and the New Guard. There was also the Union Jack Legion, and the eminently respectable, if eccentric, British Israelite cult, to which Jews and Catholics tended to be anath-ema, which argued that the British peoples were blood descendants of the Lost Tribe of Israel.[45]

Natal had joined the Union as one of the four provinces of the new Union of South Africa established by the British in 1910, but it proved to be an awkward member. This was especially the case when the Afrikaners, who had lost the Boer War, began to win the peace and gain effective power. In the 1920s the first major dissension occurred over the Union government's plans to introduce a new South African national flag. Natal would have nothing but the British flag and the controversy became so bitter that civil war, Ulster-style, was freely spoken about.[46] In August 1927, two of Natal's leaders, George Heaton Nicholls and William O'Brien, an Irish-born Protestant, travelled nearly two thousand miles to Livingstone, Northern Rhodesia, to ask the advice of Leo Amery, the colonial secretary, who was then on an Empire tour. Amery was a staunch imperialist and an admirer of the simple patriotism he had encountered in the pre-war Ulster resistance, which he had fully supported. But he had grown cautious. He urged the Natal delegation 'very earnestly to give no countenance to any talk of secession or any illegal action, reminding them of the unfortunate consequences in our own experience of our attitude with regard to Ulster'.[47] He advised them to keep their opposition within the bounds of the law. Secessionist sentiment, however, continued throughout the 1930s. In 1948, the Nationalist Party came to power in South Africa and proceeded to tamper with major sections of the constitution. Natal remained in the forefront of the campaign against the removal of 'coloureds' from the electoral roll, largely out of anti-Afrikaner rather than pro-coloured sentiment, especially as the Nationalist government made it clear that it intended to declare a republic eventually, following a referendum of the white electorate, and the precedent of Eire's exit from the Commonwealth in 1949 was frequently cited. This republican course, many British Natalians argued, would breach the social contract negotiated in the Act of Union in 1910, and would thereby dissolve their obligation to obey the government.[48] Typical of the Natal loyalist leadership at this time was Major-General Arthur Selby, CB, CBE, Chairman of the Federal Party, an Australian-born soldier who had served in the Royal Ulster Rifles.[49] In 1955, he, together with other Natal party leaders, launched an Anti-Republican League and called on all voters to sign a Natal Covenant. This document manifested the Natalians' keen sense of imperial history, since it was an abridged version of its Ulster predecessor:

> Being convinced in our consciences that a republic would be disastrous to the spiritual and material welfare of Natal as well as the whole of South Africa, subversive of our freedom, and destructive of our citizenship, we, whose names are underwritten, men and women of Natal, loyal subjects of Her Gracious Majesty Queen Elizabeth the Second, do hereby pledge ourselves in solemn covenant throughout this our time of threatened calamity to stand by one another in defending the Crown and in using all

means that may be found possible and necessary to defeat the present intention to set up a republic in South Africa.

And in the event of a republic being forced upon us, save with the free will and consent of the people of Natal, expressed by means of a separate referendum, we further solemnly and mutually pledge ourselves to refuse to recognise its authority. In sure confidence that God will defend the right we hereto subscribe our names. GOD SAVE THE QUEEN.[50]

Very appropriately the covenant was launched in Durban City Hall, strikingly similar in design to Belfast City Hall, so that the Ulster scene of 1912 was almost exactly reproduced. 'Few would maintain that the people of Northern Ireland had not right on their side in their determination to maintain their allegiance even at the cost of the division of Ireland', the Natalian Defenders of the Constitution argued, and Natal's moral right to exist in allegiance to the Crown was no less keenly felt.[51] Some 33,000 Natalians signed the covenant and petitions were sent to the Queen and the governments of the dominions.[52] For a time the Natalians seemed to be in deadly earnest, but they had not the Ulster stomach for battle, nor Ulster's allies in the metropolitan country. The British government declined to intervene on their behalf and their leadership refused to lead them into illegal action that could end in civil war against both the Afrikaner nationalists and very possibly the black majority. They were never granted a separate referendum and, having voted overwhelmingly against the republic in 1960 (the only province to do so), they conformed when it was declared in the following year. The Pietermaritzburg Club adopted the British flag as its emblem and Queen Victoria's statue still surveyed the city, but thereafter the Natalians confined their protest to half-humorous car stickers incorporating the Union Jack and the defiant boast, 'Last Outpost'.

By the mid-1960s there were few such loyalist outposts left. New Zealand, which once reminded Kevin O'Higgins, the Irish Free State cabinet minister, of Northern Ireland, 'for it produces the same type of jingo reactionary',[53] was now being quietly abandoned by a Britain seeking entry into the European Common Market. English Canada, once the heartland of pan-Britannic patriotism, scarcely counted any more, and though Ontario was still 'The Loyal Province', membership of the Orange Order was no longer a necessary passport to advancement in Toronto.[54] Now Rhodesia and Northern Ireland were the most prominent remnants, each with a recognisably dated variation of British imperial identity.

Despite the remarkable similarities, there had been little real direct contact between the two territories. Sir Robert McIlwaine, the father of the Rhodesian civil service, hailed from Larne. The third Duke of

Abercorn (1869–1953), Governor of Northern Ireland from 1921 to 1945, took an active part in the administration of Rhodesia, following in the footsteps of his father who had been a founder of the British South Africa Company. So attached did he feel to the country that he named his eldest daughter Mary Cecilia Rhodesia.[55] Charles Olley, big game hunter, sometime Mayor of Salisbury and member of the Legislative Assembly, editor of the opinion-forming *New Rhodesia*, an influential trade unionist and founder of the White Rhodesia Council, was a Belfast-born member of the Orange Order. He was one of the foremost right-wing thinkers in Rhodesia from the 1920s to the 1950s and a progenitor of the Dominion Party and the Rhodesian Front.[56] A number of MPs of Ulster origin sat in the Rhodesian House of Assembly in the 1960s and 1970s, including Paddy Shields (1974–85) from Larne, Jack Carey (1964–75), also from County Antrim, and Arthur McCater (1974–76), a former assistant editor of the *Belfast Telegraph*.[57]

Almost alone among former colonists the Rhodesians still used the fading vocabulary of Empire,[58] and the Belfast Protestant working class, in the decades following the Second World War, still referred to the Sandy Row district of their city as the 'heart of the Empire'.[59] These communities were characterised by an exceptional sense of pride in the British Empire and its 'civilising mission'. Both the Rhodesians and the Ulster Unionists reaffirmed their continued loyalty to the person of the monarch, whom they sharply distinguished from the British government of the day, especially one led by Harold Wilson. Neither group confused that loyalty with unconditional obedience to British governments, nor did they exclude the possibility of illegal action when they thought such action justifiable, for instance when the British government was perceived to be taking the part of subject peoples against its own 'kith and kin'.[60] The xenophobia of both these imperial peripheries posed problems for the British government, which had wider interests and priorities than the immediate concerns of its erstwhile 'Wards of the Outer Marches'. Both political entities had been created in the 1920s, when the imperial government was anxious to delegate authority and lighten the burden of Empire. By the 1960s, however, both territories had become for many British people embarrassing and anachronistic flotsam in an unfamiliar, post-colonial world, as the Ulster poet John Hewitt put it with his characteristic sense of history:

> ... now the empire-Commonwealth runs down;
> new flags, new faces fill the halls of state
> and in embattled company alone
> we misbelieve the vagaries of fate ...
> Some would pray our shrunken empire hold
> us closer to her flank beside the throne

and others, rasher, summon us to fold
our thin cloak round us close and stand alone ...[61]

An Ulster link with Rhodesia continued throughout the post-war period. The constitutional relationship of Northern Ireland to the rest of the United Kingdom was frequently used as a possible model for the relationship of Northern Rhodesia to its more powerful southern namesake. In the early 1960s, Sir Edgar Whitehead, Southern Rhodesian Prime Minister, advocated a subordinate relationship of Northern to Southern Rhodesia, which he called his 'Northern Ireland solution'.[62] In 1963, following his retirement, he advocated Rhodesia's entry into the United Kingdom on the same terms as Northern Ireland, retaining a government in Salisbury, but with representation at Westminster.[63] In this way, Whitehead hoped, black Rhodesians would become a minority within a predominantly white United Kingdom. White Rhodesia, thus, could then feel secure enough to make concessions to the blacks. This was reminiscent of Pitt's scheme for Catholic emancipation at the time of the Irish Act of Union in 1800–1. In 1968 Harold Wilson proposed just such a solution in the form of an Anglo-Rhodesian Union.[64] This was a final echo of the 'imperial federation' idea which dated back to the 1870s.[65] Perhaps Wilson thought such a dramatic solution would break the diplomatic logjam. A Northern Ireland constitutional connection was personified in Sam Whaley, a leading Salisbury lawyer from the 1960s to the 1980s, who was staunchly proud of his Enniskillen parentage. He was Chairman of the Rhodesian Senate Legal Committee and was largely responsible for the drafting of Rhodesia's 1965, 1969 and 1979 constitutions.[66]

By the 1960s the ideological trends in the Ulster-Rhodesian relationship went into reverse as Rhodesian political events and ideas found influence and echoes in Northern Ireland. The Rhodesian Unilateral Declaration of Independence (UDI) was the kind of direct action, country ranch syndicalism in the mould of its pre-1914 prototype, which Ulster Unionists could admire. Some Conservatives regarded Rhodesia as a kind of Second Troy where an ideal of Britishness survived with undiminished vigour. As one Tory MP put it, in language that echoed Lord Randolph Churchill's description of the Anglo-Irish and Scots-Irish populations as being 'essentially like ourselves, a dominant, imperial caste', Rhodesia had become the equivalent of Ulster in 1911–14, a place where the British soul could be redeemed: 'Rhodesia represents Britain in its halcyon days: patriotic, self-reliant, self-supporting, with law and order and a healthy society'.[67]

The question of whether British army officers would be willing to crush Rhodesia's UDI in 1965 also brought Ireland and Ulster to mind.

Robert Good, the American ambassador to Zambia during this period, recalls that on everyone's lips was the precedent of the Curragh 'mutiny' of 1914, when certain elements of Britain's regular army had refused to coerce the citizens of Ulster. It was said that discreet samplings had been taken of opinion among British units as to whether they would be willing to go to Rhodesia to fight. The results purportedly were largely negative. Rumours circulated concerning resignation at high levels in the armed forces if the decision were made to invade Rhodesia.[68] Denis Healey, the Defence Secretary at that time, gave the army chief of staff a severe warning about 'mutinous mutterings' among senior officers.[69] Even Lord Mountbatten, Chairman of the Chiefs of Staff Committee, did not escape speculation. Field Marshal Sir Henry Wilson would have felt at home among such patriotic intrigues. It was unthinkable to ask United Kingdom soldiers to go to Rhodesia and shoot Britishers. 'We were in fact', said a leading civil servant, 'kithier and kinnier than anyone realised'.[70] No doubt with the Curragh incident in mind, Douglas Hurd, later to become British Foreign Secretary, used this Rhodesian scenario as a backdrop to his fictionalised account of a British army coup, *Send Him Victorious* (1968), in which a 'Hands Off Rhodesia Movement', in the tradition of *Algérie Française*, attempts to persuade the British government not to invade Rhodesia. One member of the pro-Rhodesia lobby schemes to get the 'King' to dismiss his Prime Minister, a tactic Bonar Law had attempted with George V over Ulster in 1914. To complete the analogy of 1914 there is disaffection in the army, but the United Nations, international communism and black nationalism replace the Catholic Church and the Irish nationalists as the mortal threats to the British imperial soul. A pamphlet issued by these fictional mutineers was worthy of their Curragh counterparts.[71] According to Garret FitzGerald, sometime Irish Prime Minister, memories of the 'kith and kin' strains imposed on British army allegiances by the Rhodesian crisis played a role in the British Cabinet's decision to limit the security forces' role in maintaining order in the Ulster loyalist workers' strike of 1974.[72]

When Rhodesia declared UDI in November 1965, the parallel between the two communities was underlined with historical resonance in the House of Lords, where Lord Coleraine, son of Bonar Law, attacked Harold Wilson for his allegedly vengeful attack on Smith and Rhodesia: 'It is often said that rebellion is an ugly word and an ugly thing. I know of only one thing uglier, and that was when a people surrendered under threat of force its conviction, its tradition and its heritage'.[73]

The *Irish Times* also drew this connection:

[The Rhodesian] claim of unswerving allegiance to the British Crown, genuine or not, cannot in context be considered as other than an attempt to salvage sympathy in Britain. Bonar Law and his friends presented the Ulster crisis to their Unionist followers in the same light that Mr Smith sees the prospect of Rhodesia with a negro majority.[74]

There was also, however, an ominous aspect to these affinities. In August 1966, Captain Terence O'Neill, the Northern Ireland premier, lunched with Harold Wilson in Downing Street. 'I suppose', said Wilson, 'Northern Ireland is rather like Rhodesia'. 'Maybe it is', replied O'Neill, adding, in a reference to a deposed Rhodesian premier who had reformist tendencies, 'but I do not intend to be the Garfield Todd of Northern Ireland'.[75] O'Neill felt compelled to warn Unionists, including members of his own Cabinet, against a Rhodesian-style UDI to forestall metropolitan or United Nations intervention.[76] By December 1968, however, his reforms went too far for his party colleagues, some of whom were talking of a UDI to prevent interference from Westminster and thus preserve their Britishness. O'Neill, like Garfield Todd, was ousted. In a BBC television broadcast, 'Ulster stands at the crossroads', he warned against a UDI:

> There are, I know, today some so-called loyalists who talk of independence from Britain ... Rhodesia, in defying Britain from thousands of miles away, at least has an air force and an army of her own. Where are the Ulster armoured divisions and the Ulster jet planes? ... These people ... are not loyalists but disloyalists: disloyal to Britain, disloyal to the Constitution, disloyal to the Crown, disloyal – if they are in public life – to the solemn oath they have sworn to Her Majesty the Queen.[77]

Now, unlike the Ulstermen of 1912–14, neither Unionists nor white Rhodesians could rely on the whole-hearted support of politicians at Westminster, and this heightened their common sense of betrayal.[78] These frontiersmen would have given the same answer to the question posed by a Belfast Methodist minister in 1886, 'Shall the loyal be deserted and the disloyal set over them?'[79] and an identical reply to the admonition draped over the balcony at the Ulster Unionist Convention in Belfast in 1892: 'What England was, shall her true sons forget?'.[80]

This beleaguered outlook found concrete expression in the Vanguard Movement, founded in 1972 by William Craig, a former Northern Ireland cabinet minister, following the suspension of the Belfast Parliament by the British. Along with other loyalist groups, Vanguard forged links with the National Front and other far-right organisations in Britain and advocated a UDI to preserve 'British Ulster'.[81] Craig was openly sympathetic to Smith's Rhodesia. Typical of the mood of loyalists during this period was Reverend Robert Bradford MP's statement that 'The time may come when we may have to become Queen's rebels in order to remain citizens of any kind'.[82] To him and his supporters, Britain had changed irrevocably; still Ulster, like Rhodesia, had remained steadfast to the time honoured virtues of 'true' Britishness.

Although opposed to an Ulster UDI, Dr Ian Paisley's *Protestant Telegraph* also provided consistent support for white Rhodesia, which it regarded as a fellow victim of 'papist', ecumenical and 'leftist Labour government' conspiracies. The paper held Harold Wilson personally responsible for the decline of Empire, while the 'towers of Babel' of the Common Market and the World Council of Churches were seen as the most cunning of papal plots, held by many of Dr Paisley's followers to be clearly manifest in the Treaty of *Rome* of 1957.[83] Ian Smith was depicted as a loyal ally in the struggle against the Romanists, who were taking advantage of the 'cunning black revolution to liquidate God-fearing evangelicals'.[84] For Paisley's section of Unionist opinion, Rhodesia had become the symbol, the flagship of the Empire's recovery. The Labour government had, they argued, put Britishness into temporary abeyance, so that it had become incumbent upon the two loyalist communities to uphold the imperial cause. The language of the paper was characteristically intemperate. According to the *Protestant Telegraph*, both the Rhodesians and Ulstermen had 'primitive natives' to deal with; in Rhodesia cannibals believed in the throwing of bones, while in Ulster 'the Irish scum' believed in the throwing of holy water. Irish Catholics and black Rhodesians were frequently depicted as living in similar states of fecklessness, immorality and filth.[85] One Rhodesian reader of the paper wrote in to assure the Ulstermen that his country was very Protestant, 'forming a bastion in the African continent against communism ... the latest mask of the Jesuits'. The IRA was regarded as the inspiration behind African terrorism and the paper argued that where the 'native Irish papist' led, the blacks would soon follow. Irish missionary priests were depicted as subversive of 'Protestant Rhodesia' through their influence over blacks 'whose superstitious natures can more easily assimilate the errors and idolatry of Romanism'. There was enough evidence of Irish missionary support for the guerrillas to give credence to such arguments.[86] The paper sent its congratulations to the Rhodesian government on those occasions when Catholic missionaries were prosecuted for aiding the guerrillas, such as the case of Ballycastle-born Bishop Donal Lamont of Umtali who was deported in 1978 for failing to report the presence of guerrillas at one of the missions under his jurisdiction. Lamont was fond of likening Rhodesian white supremacism to Orange triumphalism and, not surprisingly, therefore, he was described by the *Protestant Telegraph* as an IRA man in disguise.[87] The paper ignored prominent Catholics who held office in Smith's Cabinet, as well as the traditional imperial allegiances of many white Rhodesian Catholics, both clerical and lay.[88] Instead, it noted that Desmond Lardner-Burke, the Rhodesian Justice Minister, was a known opponent of ecumenism.[89]

Britain's treatment of Rhodesia was presented as a precedent for a final 'sell-out' to the United Nations and ultimately the Irish Republic. Was it the 'end of the road for Ulster?', the *Protestant Telegraph* asked: 'Remember that Britain's ambassadors have gone on record as saying that Britain would accept UN decisions regarding Rhodesia and Gibraltar, and why not Ulster?'.[90] One of its Scottish correspondents discerned in Ulster 'the old familiar pre-independence pull-out tactics seen so often in Africa, Cyprus and Aden' and this became a common theme in its columns.[91] Ulster would be 'left to the mercy of the murdering Irish, with perhaps the UN as spectators'.[92] According to another correspondent, 'Rhodesia, like Ulster in 1912, took the necessary step of standing against tyranny and oppression'.[93] Foremost among the apologists for Smith's Rhodesia was Clifford Smyth, secretary of the Young Unionists and sometime Democratic Unionist MP. He contributed to the the *Covenant Message*, journal of the South African British Israelites, articles on alleged Vatican–Kremlin conspiracies. For him, Rhodesian and Irish issues were inseparable: 'Fundamental to any understanding of the Irish Question is our appreciation of the fact that the government of Northern Ireland, together with Rhodesia and South Africa, is based on the Protestant Ascendancy, and the last in the world to be so based'.[94] This alliance of sentiment, ideology and kin was not, however, always so reassuring. 'Prophesised' recoveries of the cause of white Rhodesia failed to materialise and these steadily gave way to ever gloomier predictions. Rhodesia's woes seemed to forebode a similar fate for Ulster, and the *Protestant Telegraph* seemed to offer little immediate comfort to those who worried about the future of both territories.

Support for Rhodesia was more widely spread than Craig and Paisley's followers and covered both the Ulster Loyalist and Ulster British strands of Unionism (as identified by Jennifer Todd). The Reverend Martin Smyth, MP, Grand Master of the Orange Order and member of the Ulster Unionist Council, could certainly see common features, and recalls many Unionists throughout Ulster feeling a strong sense of sympathy for the white Rhodesians, particularly because of their 'betrayal' by the Foreign Office, which they equated with the Anglo-Irish Agreement of the 1985.[95] Roy Bradford, a senior Unionist politician, was also in no doubt about a sellout:

I was [in Rhodesia] for some months in 1976 and certainly the parallels with Ulster are obvious. Their dilemma was the same as ours: to oppose the Crown is in fact to deny one's raison d'être, identity with Britain. The frustration was the same, as was the reluctance to adhere to a one-sided political contract, the feeling of lost self respect.[96]

This parallel can still arouse strong feeling in Ulster because of the links between the province and the lost cause of Rhodesia. Too close an identification with the latter could make the Unionist sense of foreboding even greater. Many Unionists could recall that Margaret Thatcher, when Prime Minister of Britain, had described the Zimbabwe Patriotic Front as 'terrorists … just like the IRA', but was later forced to do a deal with its leaders.[97] In June of 1990, the black South African nationalist leader Nelson Mandela, then on a visit to Dublin, caused a diplomatic row with his call to the British government to negotiate with the IRA as it had done in Rhodesia.[98]

'Frankly, neither then nor since has there been a close analogy between Northern Ireland and Rhodesia', the present Duke of Abercorn, a former Unionist MP, assured the writer,[99] notwithstanding the contrary attitudes of many of his fellow Unionists. Part of Ulster loyalist paranoia from the 1960s was due not only to the political crisis within their own state, but also to the withdrawal from Empire which indicated to them an abdication of British power. There was constant fear of United Nations intervention. The collapse of Rhodesia marked for Ulster the end of a familiar world, in which fellow loyalists were willing to fight to the death for an imperial conviction. The British diplomatic triumph in the negotiations which culminated in Zimbabwe's independence under majority rule in 1980 led some Irish politicians south of the border to believe that Britain could follow up with a similar diplomatic coup in Northern Ireland.[100] This was insensitive, because it was precisely such a course which Unionists sought to avoid. Leading Unionists were again offended in 1991 by the suggestion by Northern Ireland Secretary Peter Brooke and Irish Foreign Minister Gerry Collins that the next round of cross-party talks be chaired by Lord Carrington. Carrington was known for his scathing views of Dr Paisley and other prominent Unionists believed that he had 'sold out' Rhodesia in 1980, when, as Foreign Secretary, he had chaired the Lancaster House talks which led to Zimbabwe independence. The Northern Ireland Office was, however, remarkably unaware of the insecurity such an appointment was bound to arouse among Unionists.[101] The strength of British resolve as demonstrated in the Falklands War of 1982, then, provided unionists with only temporary comfort.

Set in an imperial rather than a domestic context the paradoxes of Ulster's loyalist rebellions seem typical rather than strange. Ulster's Britishness was and remains primarily an imperial, not a metropolitan variety of Britishness. Clearly, Irish issues had far wider effects than Scottish and Welsh nationalist issues. As John Hewitt put it: 'for an age we saw ourselves a part / of a world-striding empire's endless prime'.[102] Irish experience informed British responses to imperial crises, while perceptions of Empire came to divide nationalist and Unionist identities, and these perceptions lie at the very heart of the continued alienation of these traditions from each other. Unionist identity and its problems can only be understood and addressed in this context. Moreover, its impact on the colonial Empire was certainly as profound as that of Irish nationalism. Rebellious feelings would doubtless have arisen in Kenya, Rhodesia and Natal in response to local circumstances in any case, as they had elsewhere in the Empire at other times. Ulster, however, set the tone for patriotic direct action in the twentieth century and gave the phenomenon a distinctive style and vocabulary. A faint echo can still be heard in the secessionist sentiments of monarchists in Western Australia and Queensland, currently engaged in a bitter struggle with their Irish-Australian, Catholic federal Prime Minister Paul Keating. *Semper eadem.*[103] Shortly after the Great War, Winston Churchill wrote of the dreary steeples of Fermanagh and Tyrone emerging through the deluge, unaltered by the great crises of Europe, symbolising the integrity, if not the intractability, of the Irish quarrel.[104] By the 1980s, with the demise of the Empire, and Britain's reluctant but inexorable integration in the European Community, the imperialist pride which had been so central to Unionist identity since its inception became even less tenable than in the 1960s and 1970s.[105] With their Rhodesian ally's extinction, those spires seemed shaken, ever more opaque, but still standing, and Ulster was now alone in her struggle.

Notes

1 D. W. Miller, *Queen's Rebels: Ulster Loyalism in Historical Perspective*, Dublin, 1978, p. 91.
2 See D. George Boyce, *Nationalism in Ireland*, London, 1991, Chs 1-4; W. K. Hancock, *Survey of British Commonwealth Affairs, I, Problems of Nationality, 1918-1936*, London, 1937, pp. 221-2; Jack P. Greene, 'Changing identity in the British Caribbean: Barbados as a case study', in Nicholas Canny & Anthony Pagden (eds), *Colonial Identity in the Atlantic World, 1500-1800*, Princeton, 1986, p. 263; J. M. Bumstead, 'Loyalists and nationalists: an essay on the problem of definition', *Canadian Review of Studies in Nationalism*, VI (1979), pp. 218-32; C. Dobbin, 'The Ilbert Bill: a study of Anglo-Indian opinion in India, 1883', *Historical Studies* (Australia and New Zealand), XII (1965), pp. 87-102; P. Way 'Street Politics: Orangemen, Tories and the 1841 election riot in Toronto', *British Journal of Canadian Studies*, VI (1991), pp. 275-303; T. Keegan, 'The making of the Orange Free State, 1846-54: settler sub-imperialism and the imperial response', *Journal of Imperial and Commonwealth History*, XVII (1988), p. 41.

3 G. B. Pyrah, *Imperial Policy and South Africa*, Oxford, 1955, p. 83.

4 See G. R. Searle, 'The "revolt from the right" in Edwardian Britain', in Paul Kennedy & A. J. Nicholls (eds), *Nationalist and Racialist Movements in Britain and Germany before 1914*, Oxford, 1981, p. 36; R. J. Benewick, *The Fascist Movement in Britain*, London, 1972, pp. 24-5, 39-47.

5 See A. M. Gollin, *Proconsul in Politics: A Study of Lord Milner in Opposition and in Power*, London, 1964, Chs 8-9; A. T. Q. Stewart, *The Ulster Crisis: Resistance to Home Rule, 1912-1914*, London, 1969; Alvin Jackson, 'Unionist myths', *Past and Present*, no. 136 (1992), pp. 164-85; Alvin Jackson, 'Larne gun-running, 1914', *History Ireland*, I (1993), pp. 35-8.

6 Rudyard Kipling to H. A. Gwynne, undated (late 1913?), University of Sussex, Kipling Papers, Correspondence 15/15.

7 See Rory Fitzpatrick, *God's Frontiersmen: The Scots-Irish Epic*, London, 1989, p. 261; R. P. Davis, *Irish Issues in New Zealand Politics*, Dunedin, 1974, p. 131.

8 *The Argus* (Melbourne), 13 July 1914.

9 Rudyard Kipling to H. A. Gwynne, 26 November 1913, University of Sussex, Kipling Papers, Correspondence 15/15.

10 Rudyard Kipling to H. A. Gwynne, 2 December 1913, University of Sussex, Kipling Papers, Correspondence 15/15.

11 See Brian Barton, *Brookeborough: the Making of a Prime Minister*, Belfast, 1988, p. 21; 'Lord Brookeborough', *The Times*, 27 August 1973; 'The Brookeborough Memoirs', *Sunday News*, 14 January 1968.

12 See 'The Brookeborough Memoirs', *Sunday News*, 14 January 1968.

13 'Is there to be civil war?' (editorial), *Journal* (Grahamstown), 21 April 1914.

14 *Journal*, 9 April 1914.

15 'Home Rule' (editorial), *Natal Witness*, 27 May 1914.

16 See D. Cole, 'The problem of "nationalism" and "imperialism" in British settlement colonies', *Journal of British Studies*, X (1971), pp. 160-82; T. Cook, 'George R. Parkin and the concept of Britannic idealism', *Journal of Canadian Studies*, X (1975), pp. 15-31; S. F. Wise, 'God's peculiar peoples', in W. L. Morton (ed.), *The Shield of Achilles: Aspects of Victorian Canada in the Victorian Age*, Toronto, 1968, pp. 36-61.

17 See Ian Henderson, 'White populism in Southern Rhodesia', *Comparative Studies in Society and History* XIV (1972), p. 393; H. C. Hummel, 'Sir Charles Coghlan: some reflections on his political attitudes and style', *South African Historical Journal*, IX (1977), pp. 59-79.

18 H. Cullen Gouldsbury, *Rhodesian Rhymes*, Bulawayo, 1923, pp. 244-51.

19 'Ulster 1912', in Rudyard Kipling, *The Years Between*, London, 1921, pp. 9-11.

20 Thomas Jones, *Whitehall Diary* (ed. K. Middlemas), London, 1971, III, p. 190.

21 Editorial, *Morning Post*, 27 January 1921. See also J. H. Grainger, *Patriotisms, Britain 1900-1939*, London, 1986, pp. 251-22.

22 *Gwelo Times*, 22 August 1919.

23 *Livingstone Mail*, 22 August 1919.

24 'The Question for Rhodesia', *The Independent* (Rhodesia), 10 February 1922.

25 'A lover of Rhodesia' to the editor, *The Independent*, 27 January 1922.

26 E. Tawse Jollie, *The Real Rhodesia*, London, 1924, p. 85.

27 Sir Charles Coghlan to Sir Francis Newton, 5 April 1923, National Archives of Zimbabwe, Newton Papers, Correspondence NE1/1/1.

28 See Martin Gilbert, *World in Torment: Winston S. Churchill 1917-1922*, London, 1990, p. 670.

29 St John Ervine, *Craigavon. Ulsterman*, London, 1949, p. 439.

30 Jones, *Whitehall Diary*, III, pp. 74 ff.

31 Ethel Tawse Jollie (1875-1950), born Ethel Maude Cookson, Stafford, England, writer, sometime editor of *United Empire*, journal of the Royal Colonial Institute; member of executive committees of Women's Unionist Association, Imperial Maritime League, National Service League, British Women's Emigration Association and National League for Opposing Women's Suffrage; first married in 1900 to Archibald Ross Colquhoun, explorer, writer and first administrator of Mashonaland, and later in 1915 to John Tawse Jollie, farmer, of Melsetter, South Rhodesia. Founder and principal organiser of Responsible Government Association 1917. Elected to Legislative Council 1920 and to Legislative Assembly, 1923. Lost seat in 1928. See Donal Lowry, '"Amazon of Empire": Ethel Tawse Jollie and the making of white Rhodesia', Institute of Commonwealth Studies, *Collected Seminar Papers, Societies of Southern Africa in the Nineteenth and Twentieth Centuries/Women, Colonialism and Commonwealth*, University of London, forthcoming, 1995; 'Ethel M. Colquhoun (Mrs Tawse Jollie)', *Who Was Who, 1951-1960*, London, 1961, p. 233.

32 Ethel Colquhoun to editor, *The Times*, 9 June 1914.

33 See E. Tawse Jollie, 'A New Constitution', *Independent* (Rhodesia) 27 January 1922. See also the following editorials: 'The Irish Free State', *ibid*, 23 December 1922; 'Dominion Status', *ibid.*, 10 March 1922; 'The Disloyal Union', *ibid.*, 24 March 1922; E. Tawse Jollie, 'Empire or Alliance?', *ibid.*, 25 November 1922; 'The Passing of Empire', *National Review*, LXXVIII (1922), pp. 810-17 'Trust General Smuts', *ibid.*, LXXVIII (1922), pp. 304-11.

34 'Manifesto to the People of Rhodesia and a Statement of Policy', *Independent*, 26 August 1922.

35 E. Tawse Jollie, 'Southern Rhodesia', *South African Quarterly*, III (1921), pp. 10-12.

36 See Ronald Hyam, *The Failure of South African Expansion, 1908-48*, London, 1972; and Martin Chanock, *Unconsummated Union: Britain, Rhodesia and South Africa, 1900-45*, Manchester, 1977.

37 G. C. Lebzelter, 'Henry Hamilton Beamish and the Britons', in K. Lunn & I. Thurlow (eds), *British Fascism: Essays on the Radical Right in Inter-War Britain*, London, 1980, pp. 48-9; B. A. Kosmin, 'Colonial careers for the marginal fascists: a portrait of Hamilton Beamish', *Wiener Library Bulletin*, XXVII (1973-7), pp. 16-23.

38 See Christopher P. Youé, 'The threat of settler rebellion and the imperial predicament: The demise of Indian rights in Kenya', *Canadian Journal of History*, XII (1978), pp. 347-60; C. J. D. Duder, 'The settler response to the Indian crisis of 1923 in Kenya: Brigadier General Philip Wheatley and "Direct Action"', *Journal of Imperial and Commonwealth History*, XVII (1989), pp. 349-73.

39 Elsbeth Huxley, *White Man's Country: Lord Delamere and the Making of Kenya*, 2 vols, III, New York, 1968, p. 135.

40 Brigadier General Philip Wheatley, C.B., C.M.G., D.S.O., born in England in 1871, son of Lieutenant Colonel W. F. Wheatley. Served in the Royal Artillery 1891-1918, chiefly in India, and campaigned in Gallipoli and the Western Front in the Great War. Arrived in Kenya in 1919 via Bombay as member of the Imperial government's 'Soldier-Settler' scheme, under which he received a 4,306 acre farm at Nanyuki in the White Highlands. Elected to the Nanyki 'Vigilance Committee' in 1927. Appointed by 'Central Vigilance Committee' to command settler forces in 1929. Died in Kenya in 1935. See Duder, 'The settler response to the Indian crisis of 1923 in Kenya', pp. 349-373.

41 Youé, 'The threat of settler rebellion and the imperial predicament', p. 354; W. McGregor Ross, *Kenya from Within: A Short Political History*, London, 1927, p. 367.

42 Wheatley to his father, 11 October 1921, 'Letters from and to Philip Wheatley: Correspondence of a Settler in Kenya, 1919-1923', 2 vols, MSS Afr. s799, Rhodes House, Oxford.

43 *Minutes of the Proceedings of the Legislative Council of the Colony of Kenya (1922 Session)*,Nairobi, 1923, p. 112.

44 See Robert M. Maxon, *Struggle for Kenya: The Loss and Reassertion of Imperial Initiative, 1912-1923*, Rutherford, 1993, pp. 161-2.

45 See P. S. Thompson, *Natalians First: Separatism in South Africa 1909-1961*, Johannesburg, 1990. For the British Israelites, see J. Wilson, 'British Israelism', *Sociological Review*, XVI (1968), pp. 41-57.

46 L. S. Amery, *My Political Life*, II, London, 1953, p. 402.

47 20 August 1927, *The Leo Amery Diaries, I: 1896-1929*, (ed. John Barnes and David Nicholson), London 1980, p. 521.

48 Thompson, *Natalians First*, Ch. 7.

[211]

49 Major General Arthur Roland Selby, born in 1893 in Armindale, New South Wales. Educated at Scotch College, Perth, Western Australia and Royal Australian Military College. Served in Australian regular army 1911-30 (severely wounded at Gallipoli) and Royal Ulster Rifles 1930-46 in Northern Ireland, India, Egypt and Eritrea. GOC Iraq and Persia, 1942-44. See *South Africa Who's Who*, Johannesburg, 1960, p. 254, and *Federal News*, III, no. 7, (1957), in Union Federal Party F71, The Campbell Collections MSS, Killie Campbell Library, Durban.

50 See Thompson, *Natalians First*, p. 154; B. L. Reid, 'The Anti-Republican League of the 1950s', *South African Historical Journal*, XIV (1972), pp. 85-94. It would seem that neither of these authors recognised the ancestry of the Natal Covenant.

51 Defenders of the Constitution, *The Case Against the Republic*, Federal Party, Durban, n.d. *c.* 1955.

52 Thompson, *Natalians First*, pp. 153, 156.

53 Ged Martin, 'The Irish Free State and the evolution of the Commonwealth', in Ronald Hyam and Ged Martin (eds), *Reappraisals in British Imperial History*, London, 1978, p. 220.

54 See David M. Cheal, 'Ontario loyalism: a socio-religious ideology in decline', *Canadian Ethnic Studies*, XIII (1981), pp. 40-51.

55 '3rd Duke of Abercorn', *The Times*, 14 September 1953.

56 See H. I. Wetherell, 'N. H. Wilson: populism in Rhodesia', *Rhodesian History*, VI (1975), pp. 53-76, and 'Charles Olley', in *South Africa Who's Who*, Johannesburg, 1960, p. 861.

57 Mr P. Shields (ex-Rhodesian Front MP), Durban, to the author, 14 July 1990.

58 See Paul Moorcraft, A *Short Thousand Years*, Salisbury, 1979, Ch. 1.

59 Miller, *Queen's Rebels*, p. 134.

60 For Rhodesian problems of loyalty see L. J. McFarlane, 'Justifying Rebellion: Black and White Nationalism in Rhodesia', *Journal of Commonwealth Political Studies*, VI (1968), pp. 54-79; R. Hodder Williams, 'White Attitudes to UDI', *Journal of Commonwealth Political Studies*, VIII (1980), pp. 241-64; and B. M. Schultz, 'The theory of fragment and the political development of white settler society in Rhodesia', unpublished Ph.D. thesis, UCLA, 1972, Ch. 5.

61 'A little people', in *The Collected Poems of John Hewitt* (ed. F. Ormsby), Belfast, 1991, p. 540.

62 J. R. T. Wood, *The Welensky Papers*, Durban, 1983, pp. 1017-19.

63 Marjory Perham, 'The Rhodesian Crisis', *International Affairs*, XXXXII (1966), p. 11.

64 P. Joyce, *Anatomy of a Rebel: Smith of Rhodesia*, Salisbury, 1973, p. 336.

65 See Ged Martin, 'The idea of imperial federation', in Hyam and Martin, *Reappraisals in British Imperial History*, pp. 131-8.

66 Mr P. Shields (ex-Rhodesian Front MP) to the author, 14 July 1990.

67 Harold Soref MP, quoted in J. Taylor, 'Memory and desire in *Going Home*', in E. Bertelsen (ed.), *Doris Lessing*, Johannesburg, 1985, p. 90.

68 R. C. Good, *UDI: The International Politics of the Rhodesian Rebellion*, Princeton, 1973, p. 60. According to Paul Moorcroft (a lecturer at the Royal Military College, Sandhurst in 1973-75) British officers exhibited the same qualms of conscience as they had over Ulster and the UVF in 1914. Over a two-year period, 90 per cent of junior officers said they were unwilling to fight Rhodesian 'kith and kin', citing the number of times Rhodesians had won the Sandhurst Sword of Honour and other patriotic links. On the other hand they had no qualms about fighting the IRA. This would seem to reflect British public opinion at large at this time. In an opinion poll conducted at the time of UDI only 27 per cent of Britons supported the use of force in the dispute, while 60 per cent were opposed to it. See Paul Moorcraft, A *Short Thousand Years*, Salisbury, 1979, p. 18. For contrary evidence of officer reliability see M. Loney, *Rhodesia: White Racism and Imperial Response*, Harmondsworth, 1975, p. 141.

69 Denis Healey, *The Time of My Life*, London, 1990, p. 332. In a letter to the author of 19 March 1991, Mr (now Lord) Healey stated that the precedent of the Curragh incident 'had not the slightest effect on the British Government's decision against the

use of force taken solely on military grounds'. However, the argument that a Rhodesian invasion was beyond Britain's capacity seems unconvincing. At the time of UDI, Britain still possessed a powerful strategic capacity, as demonstrated in the Malaysian confrontation with Indonesia in 1964, and, arguably, a Rhodesian operation would have been less difficult than the Falklands landing in 1982, when British forces were more run down than in 1965. Lieutenant General Peter Walls, who commanded the Rhodesian Light Infantry in 1965 (and was later Chief of Rhodesian Combined Operations in the 1970s), told the author in an interview that his orders were to resist any invasion. He believed that it would have been a 'sad duty' to resist 'fellow Britishers', but he was convinced that any scruples of kin would disappear after the first casualties. Interview with the author, Johannesburg, 8 July 1983.

70 Good, *UDI*, p. 60. For allegations about a British Intelligence (MI6) disinformation campaign directed against a British armed intervention in 1965, see Stephen Dorril and Robin Ramsay, *Smear!: Wilson and the Secret State*, London, 1991, pp. 87-93.
71 See Douglas Hurd and Andrew Osmond, *Send Him Victorious*, London, 1969, pp. 19-20, 27.
72 See *All in a Life. Garret FitzGerald: an autobiography*, London, 1991, p. 243.
73 *Parliamentary Debates House of Lords Official Report (Hansard), CCLXX* (1965-66), col. 189.
74 *Irish Times*, 12 November 1965.
75 *The Autobiography of Terence O'Neill, Prime Minister of Northern Ireland*, London, 1972, p. 83.
76 Terence O'Neill, *Ulster at the Crossroads*, London, 1969, p. 143.
77 Terence O'Neill, BBC television broadcast, 9 December 1968, *Ulster at the Crossroads*, London, 1969, p. 143. However, the analogy with Rhodesia could become too close to the bone for O'Neill. In 1968, George Ivan Smith, former personal representative to the UN Secretary General, was on a speaking tour of Northern Ireland. He received a frigid reception from Captain O'Neill at a Stormont luncheon. He discovered the reason at his next meeting. O'Neill had learned that Smith had been an aide to Dag Hammarskjold during the Congo crisis, had spent four years as UN ambassador-at-large in southern Africa during the Rhodesian crisis and was now covering Dublin and London for the UN. O'Neill, then in the midst of violence and calls for UN intervention, was, according to Smith, put off his lunch altogether by the latter's presence. See G. I. Smith, 'Lord O'Neill of the Maine', *Independent*, 25 June 1990.
78 See 'Ulster will be wrong', *New Statesman*, 11 October 1968.
79 Miller, *Queen's Rebels*, p. 119.
80 Robert Kee, *Ireland: a History*, London, 1980, p. 136.
81 See David Boulton, *The UVF,. 1963-73: an Anatomy of Loyalist Rebellion*, Dublin, 1973, Ch. 10.
82 Quoted in Miller, *Queen's Rebels*, p. ix. For useful background to this period, see Boulton, *The UVF, 1963-73*.
83 The Treaty of Rome, which launched the Common Market in 1957, added to Unionist paranoia about a Roman conspiracy against Protestantism, Britishness and what remained of the British Commonwealth.
84 *Protestant Telegraph*, 25 November 1968.
85 *Ibid.*, 11 July 1976.
86 Several Irish missionary priests and sisters were deported from Rhodesia in the second half of the 1970s for contravening the Law and Order Maintenance Act, the most notable of whom was Donal Lamont, Bishop of Umtali. In the Eastern Highlands, at least one Irish priest used Gaelic to make confidential telephone calls to Lamont about the guerilla presence in his area. Anglophobia and anti-imperialism was common among these missionaries. According to Terence Ranger, the leading historian of this period, '[their] Irishness *was* a significant factor [and they were] prominent among the supporters of the guerillas'. One Fr Vernon later recalled, in a telling phrase, advising the British Government's Peirce Commission of enquiry into African opinion in 1971 that the proposed Rhodesian constitution was typical of the

British approach in Northern Ireland: 'They should have solved it a long time ago but they kept on pushing it away'. See Terence Ranger, 'Holy men and rural conflict in Zimbabwe, 1970-1980', in W. J. Sheils (ed.), *The Church and War*, Oxford, 1983, pp. 447, 450, 455.

87 *Protestant Telegraph*, 25 November 1967; 3 November; 7 November 1976.
88 See Donal Lowry, 'The Irish in Rhodesia', in D. P. McCracken (ed.), *Southern African Irish Studies, II, The Irish in Southern Africa, 1795-1910*, Durban, 1992, pp. 242-60.
89 *Protestant Telegraph*, 2 November 1974.
90 *Ibid.*, 28 November 1968.
91 *Ibid.*, Special Issue, July 1976.
92 'Lowering the Flag', *ibid.*, 15 August 1974.
93 *Ibid.*, 25 November 1967.
94 Clifford Smyth, 'The United Kingdom in Crisis', *ibid.*, 20 December 1969. For some of the general background to the influence of British Israelism in Ulster Protestant thought see A. Buckley, '"We're trying to find our history": uses of history among Ulster protestants', in, *History and Ethnicity*, E. Tonkin and M Chapman (eds), London 1989.

   The extension of a pan-Protestant alliance to include Afrikaners was a new and ironic development, marking a complete reversal of Irish relationships with South Africa that had developed earlier in the century. During the Anglo-Boer War of 1899-1902, nationalist Ireland rallied to the side of the Boer republicans, and there was a close relationship between the Irish Free State and the Union of South Africa until after the Second World War. Ulster loyalists, on the other hand, embraced enthusiastically the imperial cause during the Anglo-Boer War, when they regarded the Afrikaners as disloyal republicans rather than fellow Calvinists. Unionist attitudes to Afrikaner nationalists began to change in the 1960s, against the background of the Cold War and the process of decolonisation which brought about an unprecedented alliance of convenience between Afrikaner republicans and erstwhile Rhodesian monarchists, with whose secular allegiances they shared a traditional affinity. In the 1980s, covert links developed between loyalist paramilitaries and elements of the South African secret services. See Donal P. McCracken, *The Irish Pro-Boers*, Johannesburg, 1989; Donal Lowry, 'A "fellowship of disaffection": Irish-South African relations from the Anglo-Boer War to the *pretoriastroika*, 1902-1991', *Etudes Irlandaises*, XII (1991), pp. 105-21; Donal Lowry, 'The "Ulster of South Africa": Ireland, the Irish and the Rhodesian connection', *Southern African-Irish Studies, I, Ireland and South Africa*, Durban, 1991, pp. 122-145; Donal Lowry, 'A "long relationship marked by mutual sympathy"', *Irish Times*, 21 April 1991; 'South African agents plotted assassination with loyalists', *ibid.* 15 July 1992; 'Agents were to probe alleged ANC-IRA links, Pretoria claims', *ibid.*, 16 July 1992; Richard Davis, 'Nelson Mandela's Irish problem: republican and loyalist links with South Africa, 1970-1990', *Eire-Ireland*, XXVII (1992), pp. 47-67.
95 Reverend M. Smyth to the author, 5 June 1990.
96 Rt. Hon. Roy Bradford to the author, 26 June 1990.
97 Quoted in E. McNeill, 'A comparison of the reform movements in Northern Ireland and Southern Rhodesia', unpublished M.S.Sc. thesis, Queen's University, Belfast, 1989, p. 3.
98 *Irish Times*, 4 June 1990.
99 The Duke of Abercorn to the author, 18 June 1990.
100 T. Ryle Dwyer, *Charlie: The Political Biography of Charles J. Haughey*, Dublin, 1987, p. 136; Margaret Thatcher, *The Downing Street Years*, London, 1995, p. 388.
101 See Brendan O'Leary and John McGarry, *The Politics of Northern Ireland*, London, 1993, pp. 314, 325. An analogy between the two territories continues to be drawn. See, for example, R. Weitzer, *Transforming Settler States: Communal Conflict and Internal Security in Northern Ireland and Zimbabwe*, Berkeley, 1991.
102 'A little people', in *The Collected Poems of John Hewitt* (ed. F. Ormsby), Belfast, 1991, p. 540.

103 See Malcolm Turnbull, *The Reluctant Republic*, Melbourne, 1993; Thomas Kenneally, *Memoirs from a Young Republic*, London, 1993; R. Milliken, 'Keating faces the music on nationalism', *Independent*, 14 November 1992; 'Monarchy will be but a memory', *ibid.*, 15 March 1993; Ian Black, 'Canadians follow where the lizard leads', *Guardian*, 28 September 1993.

104 Winston Churchill, *The Aftermath*, London, 1929, pp. 319-20.

105 The contemporary world-view of two sections of Ulster Unionist opinion, the loyalist terrorists and the supporters of Ian Paisley, is examined in Steve Bruce, *The Edge of the Union: The Ulster Loyalist Political Vision*, Oxford, 1994.

INDEX

Gray, Lewis, 184
Greenwood, Sir Hamar and Lady, 158
Gregory, Lady, 45, 47
Gregory, Sir William, 129
Gresham Hotel, Dublin, 13
Grierson, Charles, Dean of Belfast, 156
Griffith, Arthur, 95-6, 152, 196
Grigg, Sir Edward, 7
Gwynn, Gen. Sir Charles, 11

Hale, Alan, 51
Hall, Anna Maria, 30
Halsey, A. H., 162
Hamilton, Marquess of (*later* 3rd Duke of Abercorn), 133
handball, 67
Hanham, H. J., 53, 103
Hankey, Sir Maurice, 13
Hanna, Col. J. C., 34-6
Hanson, Lars, 41-2
Harcourt, Sir William, 191-2
Harington, Gen. Sir Tim, 107
Harkness, David, 5, 181
Harland, Edward, 126
Harris, Richard, 47
Haslett, Sir James, 128
Hastings, Warren, 81
Hawkins, Richard, 10
Healey, Denis, 204
Healy, T. M. (Tim), 5
Hewitt, John, 202-3, 209
Hill, Lord Arthur, 129
Hobson, J. A., 165
hockey, 61, 62-3, 65, 72
Hogan, Michael, 68
Holmes, Rev. Dr Finlay, 165
Holmes, Michael, 73
Holt, Richard, 59, 69, 70, 71
home rule, 78-9; alleged economic cost of, 171-2; for India, 9, 85, 87; for Ireland, 4, 5-6, 14, 108-9, 137-8
Hone, W. P., 62
Hudson, Rock, 52
Hughes, W. M., 110
Hume, A. O., 86
Hurd, Douglas, 204

hurling, 61, 65, 67
Hurst, Brian Desmond, 49-51
Huxley, Elspeth, 198
Hyde, Dr Douglas, 66

Imperial Economic Conference (1923), 176-81
Imperial Economic Conference (1931), *see* Ottawa conference
imperialism, nature of, 2
India, 13, 69, 77-93, 108; Empire Day in, 150; flax production, 182-3; and Irish nationalists, 5, 8-9; trade with, 79, 170
Indian National Congress, 8-9, 79, 86, 88, 91, 92
The Informer, 37, 39-42
Inghinidhe na hEireann, 96
Ireland: economic relations with Great Britain, 16; depiction in film, 39, 45-6, 54; football team, 72-3; leaves Commonwealth, 5; strategic position, 16; *see also*, Irish Free State, Irish Republic
Irish-American community, 37, 95
Irish Convention, 2, 174
Irish Free State, 4-5, 14-15, 90; and recruitment to British army, 101-2; tariff policy, 184
Irish nationality, 3, 4
Irish Republic (Republic of Ireland), 72, 73; and recruitment to British army, 102
Irish Republican Army (IRA), 11, 89; inspiration for anti-colonial struggles, 9, 206; portrayal in film, 33-4, 36, 49-50, 52
Irish soldiers, in British army, 53, 94-122, 130-3; disaffection among, 114-18; qualities of, 31, 103-4
Irish stereotypes, 25-31, 54
Irish Volunteers, 112-13

Jackson, Alvin, 172
Jagger, Mick, 54
James, C. L. R., 59, 70
Jameson, L. S., 133